MEDALS FOR
SOLDIERS AND AIRMEN

MEDALS FOR SOLDIERS AND AIRMEN

Awards and Decorations of the United States Army and Air Force

FRED L. BORCH III

Foreword by MALCOLM J. HOWARD

McFarland & Company, Inc., Publishers

Jefferson, North Carolina, and London

LIBRARY OF CONGRESS CATALOGUING-IN-PUBLICATION DATA

Borch, Fred L., 1954–
Medals for soldiers and airmen : awards and
decorations of the United States Army and Air Force / Fred L.
Borch III ; foreword by Malcolm J. Howard.
p.   cm.
Includes bibliographical references and index.

ISBN 978-0-7864-7412-7
softcover : acid free paper ∞

1. United States. Army — Medals, badges, decorations, etc.
2. United States. Air Force — Medals, badges, decorations, etc.
3. Military decorations — United States.   I. Title.
UB433.B666965 2013   355.1'342 — dc23   2013011174

BRITISH LIBRARY CATALOGUING DATA ARE AVAILABLE

On the cover: medals, soldier silhouette,
aircraft (iStockphoto/Thinkstock)

Manufactured in the United States of America

McFarland & Company, Inc., Publishers
Box 611, Jefferson, North Carolina 28640
www.mcfarlandpub.com

Table of Contents

Foreword 1

Preface 3

1. Decorations for Valor in Combat 5

2. Decorations and Medals for Noncombat Valor 68

3. Dual Purpose Decorations for Performance or Valor 80

4. Awards and Decorations for Outstanding Achievement
   or Meritorious Service 100

Appendices

A. Order of Precedence 171

B. Certificate of Merit 171

C. Oak Leaf Cluster 176

D. "V" Device 178

Notes 180

Bibliography 188

Index 191

Foreword

by Malcolm J. Howard

When I entered the Army as a young West Point cadet in 1958, I knew very little about most of the medals and decorations that a soldier or airman might be awarded. Of course, I was well aware that America's highest military award was the Medal of Honor. I knew that soldiers and airmen wounded in action were awarded the Purple Heart. Only after I began my Army career did I realize that the military has a variety of decorations and medals to recognize not only combat heroism, but also meritorious achievement and service performed by those who serve on the ground and in the air.

In *Medals for Soldiers and Airmen: Awards and Decorations of the United States Army and Air Force,* Fred L. Borch III has not only identified each of the personal decorations that a soldier and airman may be awarded today, but he also has provided the historical background for each award and some illustrative citations. You will learn that the Army has had a Medal of Honor since 1862, while the Air Force version of this famous decoration did not exist until 1965 and that, to date, only fourteen airmen have received it. Similarly, you will read about the Soldier's Medal and the Airman's Medal — the highest decorations that may be awarded to a soldier or an airman for non-combat valor.

The value of *Medals for Soldiers and Airmen,* however, is that it does not focus only on awards for gallantry in combat or other high level decorations. On the contrary, the book covers the full range of personal awards, from the Medal of Honor, Distinguished Service Cross and Air Force Cross to the Purple Heart, Meritorious Service Medal, and Air Force Commendation Medal. This means that the reader will be thrilled to read about the gallantry in action required for a Silver Star. But that same reader also will understand that the level of achievement or meritorious service required for an Army Achievement Medal is significant — and worthy of recognition.

Soldiering has always carried the positive connotation of self-sacrifice for the good of our nation, our Army, and one's fellow soldiers. It is no different in the Air Force, where airmen focus on serving the nation, the Air Force and their fellow airmen — and put their personal interests last. Decorations and medals exist to recognize this selfless service by soldiers and airmen — whether in combat or peacetime — and this book is important because it highlights this truth.

Malcolm J. Howard, senior U.S. district court judge, Eastern District of North Carolina, graduated from the U.S. Military Academy in 1962 and served two tours in Vietnam. His decorations include the Silver Star, two Bronze Star Medals (one with "V" for valor device), the Meritorious Service Medal, two Air Medals and the Purple Heart.

Preface

This book is the first comprehensive historical examination of all the personal awards, decorations and medals that may be awarded to soldiers and airmen.

Chapter 1 is a comprehensive history of Army and Air Force gallantry awards and covers in detail the Army and Air Force versions of the Medal of Honor, the Distinguished Service Cross and Air Force Cross, and Silver Star. Chapter 2 examines the Soldier's Medal and the Airman's Medal — the two decorations for non-combat valor in the Army and Air Force, respectively. Chapter 3 looks at the Distinguished Flying Cross, Bronze Star Medal and Air Medal — decorations intentionally created for both performance and valor. Chapter 4 is a detailed examination of fifteen awards and decorations for outstanding achievement or meritorious service. These range from the Defense Distinguished Service Medal, Legion of Merit and Purple Heart to the Meritorious Service Medal, Aerial Achievement Medal and Air Force Commendation Medal.

Four appendices round out the book, and these include little-known information about the Oak Leaf Cluster, the "V" device, and the obsolete Certificate of Merit. There also is a bibliography listing selected books and articles of interest to historians and collectors.

Since this is a book about personal decorations to soldiers and airmen, I have tried to select photographs that highlight both Army and Air Force awards — and recipients. But I have intentionally avoided too many illustrations of common medals (which are readily available from other sources, especially on the Internet) and instead selected photographs depicting rare or unusual medals, such as Civil War–era Medals of Honor and the very rare reverse enameled Legion of Merit. I have also included some photographs of recipients and their medals because these put a face on what otherwise might be an impersonal study of decorations and medals.

A new medal, announced February 13, 2013, was to be included in this book. The Distinguished Service Medal, said Secretary of Defense Leon D. Panetta, was being established to recognize the extraordinary achievements of military personnel involved in the piloting of unmanned aerial vehicles (drones) and engaged in offensive and defensive information technology (cyber) operations.

Since these technologies have transformed the twenty-first century battlefield, Panetta agreed with those in the Pentagon who argued that a special medal was needed to reward those who were making significant contributions to military operations, even though they were not engaged in actual combat with an enemy.

Veterans groups and others criticized the decision. Some argued that a new medal simply was not needed, as existing military decorations were sufficient to recognize drone operators and cyber warriors. The more vocal critics were upset about the planned order of precedence for the medal, which Panetta had announced would be just behind the Distinguished Flying Cross. Since this meant that the new medal would outrank combat decorations like the Bronze Star Medal and Purple Heart, these critics argued that it was wrong for military personnel located far from the battlefield to receive a medal that outranked decorations for those in actual physical contact with the enemy.

New Secretary of Defense Charles T. "Chuck" Hagel called for a study and on April 15, 2013, announced that, with the concurrence of the Joint Chiefs of Staff and the service secretaries, he was eliminating the medal. The result: the Distinguished Warfare Medal is gone as a new decoration and gone from this book. In its place, according to Hagel, will be a "new distinguishing device that can be affixed to existing medals" and will recognize the achievements of men and women who "directly affect combat operations without being present."

No book of this type is written without the help and encouragement of others, including "Doc" Bahnsen, Philip Conran, Melvin Mueller, Brendan O'Connor, Adam Rohloff, Jon Vastine, Dean Veremakis, James Wise and John Whitehead. Six individuals, however, deserve special recognition: Erich Anderson, Stanley Bozich, Ronald Fischer, Jeffrey Floyd, "Nick" McDowell, and Doug Sterner. Erich Anderson, whose www.veteranstributes.org contains a wealth of information on men and women who have served in uniform, went out of his way to help me find award citations. Stan Bozich, director and curator of Michigan's Own Military & Space Museum in Frankenmuth, Michigan, similarly was enthusiastic in providing me with photographs of Medals of Honor and biographical details of soldiers and airmen highlighted in his museum. Ron Fischer graciously allowed me to photograph medals and decorations in his collection, many of which appear in this book. Jeff Floyd, an expert on Air Force medals and decorations, carefully checked the information on those awards and took the time to read a draft of this work. "Nick" McDowell generously provided me with historical information on many of the medals examined in this book and his earlier monograph, *Military and Naval Decorations of the United States*, has been invaluable in preparing this work. Finally, Doug Sterner, curator of the *Military Times* Hall of Valor (http://projects.militarytimes.com/citations-medals-awards/), helped me identify recipients from his database of more than 350,000 citations.

I have checked and re-checked the facts in this book. Nonetheless, there are sure to be errors, and these are my responsibility alone.

1

Decorations for
Valor in Combat

Five decorations — the Army Medal of Honor, Air Force Medal of Honor, Distinguished Service Cross, Air Force Cross, and Silver Star — may be awarded to soldiers and airmen for valor in combat. Congress authorized the Medal of Honor during the Civil War, and it continues to be the highest-ranking decoration that a soldier or airman may be awarded. During World War I, Congress established the Distinguished Service Cross as a second gallantry decoration to recognize combat heroism that, while extraordinary, did not meet the standard required for a Medal of Honor. The Air Force Medal of Honor and Air Force Cross, authorized in 1965 and 1960, respectively, are simply the airman's version of the older Army awards. A fifth decoration for combat valor — the Silver Star — is the third highest decoration that may be awarded to a soldier or airman.

ARMY MEDAL
OF HONOR

Overview

Establishing Authority and Effective Dates: The Army Medal of Honor was established by an act of Congress on July 12, 1862. Initially, only enlisted personnel were eligible for actions occurring after April 15, 1861. But, on March 3, 1863, Congress authorized officers to receive the new decoration as well.

Criteria: The president may award, and present in the name of the Congress, a Medal of Honor to a soldier who "distinguishes himself conspicuously by gallantry and intrepidity at the risk of his life, above and beyond the call of duty," while (1) engaged in an action against an enemy of the United States; (2) engaged in military operations involving conflict with an opposing foreign force; or (3) serving with friendly foreign forces engaged in an armed conflict against an opposing armed force in which the United States is not a belligerent party.[1]

To justify the award, a soldier must have performed an act "of personal bravery or self-sacrifice so conspicuous as to clearly distinguish the individual above his comrades and must have involved risk of life."[2]

Order of Precedence: The Medal of Honor is the senior decoration in the pyramid of honor and is worn before all other awards.

Nomination and Award Process: The Medal of Honor's status as America's highest award for combat valor has resulted in a unique nomination and award process.

While any person may nominate a soldier for the Medal of Honor, as a practical matter a nomination will occur at the lowest level in the chain of command, i.e., with a company (captain/O-3) or battalion commander (lieutenant colonel/O-5).

As the Army requires "incontestable proof" of the act of heroism, it makes sense for any nomination to occur at the lowest level as this is where soldiers who witnessed the conduct will be located. Those with first-hand knowledge of the act of heroism must provide "eyewitness statements in the form of certificates, affidavits, or sworn statements."[3] Additionally, any Medal of Honor recommendation must contain other details, including: a description of terrain and weather in which the action occurred; enemy conditions (morale, proximity, firepower); the effect of the act on the enemy; the degree to which the act was voluntary; and the overall effects or results of the act. Finally, it makes sense to start the Medal of Honor nomination process at the company or battalion level because those with personal knowledge of the soldier are able to provide a full and fair evaluation of the nomination before it begins to move up the chain of command. But, unlike nominations for other valor awards, all Medal of Honor recommendations *must* be forwarded to the Army's Human Resources Command for action, "regardless of the recommendations by field and intermediate level commanders."[4] This prevents the nomination for the Medal of Honor from being downgraded or otherwise derailed by commanders at the brigade or division level.

Regardless of the rank or position of the person who recommends a soldier for the Medal of Honor, however, as the nomination packet moves forward, the Defense Department requires that the award packet be prepared as follows:

- two copies;
- housed in three-ring binder with an organized table of contents;
- containing supporting documentation (forms, narratives, witness statements, graphs, diagrams, and pictures);
- including a Department of the Army Medal of Honor citation and certificate, in a presentation folder, suitable for presentation by the President of the United States.

Additionally, each award recommendation packet "shall contain," at minimum, the following:

- Recommendation from the Combatant Commander concerned (for example, the Commander, U.S. Central Command or Commander, U.S. Special Operations Command);
- Recommendation from the Chief of Staff of the Army;
- Recommendation from the Secretary of the Army;
- Recommendation from the Chairman, Joint Chiefs of Staff.

After these recommendations are part of a soldier's Medal of Honor nomination packet, it goes to the Secretary of Defense. He then takes the nomination to the President, who approves (or disapproves) the award under his authority as the Commander-in-Chief.[5]

Under Title 10, United States Code, Section 3744, any recommendation for the Army Medal of Honor must be submitted *within two years* of the act and the Medal of Honor itself must be awarded *within three years* after the date of the act justifying the award. There are, however, two exceptions to this general rule. First, if the Secretary of the Army determines that a soldier, in fact, was recommended for the Medal of Honor within the two year period, but that recommendation was "lost" or "through inadvertence ... not acted upon," then the Medal of Honor may be awarded.[6]

Second, under Title 10, United States Code, Section 1130, any Member of Congress may "request" that the Secretary of the Army "review" a nomination of a soldier for a Medal of Honor (or the upgrading of an existing decoration to the Medal of Honor) regardless of the amount of time that has passed since the act of heroism upon which the nomination is based. Section 1130 requires that the Secretary determine "the merits of approving the award" and further requires him to submit to both the House and Senate Committees on Armed

Services "a detailed discussion of the rationale supporting this determination." Assuming that the Secretary informs both the House and Senate committees that the proposed Medal of Honor is meritorious, the next step is for the Congress to enact legislation waiving the time limitations specified in Section 3744 for the specific purpose of giving the President the authority to award the Medal of Honor to the nominated soldier concerned. After that statute is passed, the Medal of Honor may be awarded by the President.

A small number of Medals of Honor have been awarded to soldiers using Section 1130 procedures, including the awards to Roy Benavidez, Alfred V. Rascon, and Theodore Roosevelt.[7]

Designer: Christian Schussel designed the original medal (the same design as the first style Navy Medal of Honor); dies for that medal were made from a model done by Anthony Paquet. In 1904, the Army adopted a new Medal of Honor designed by the Paris (France) firm of Arthur, Bertrand and Berringer; this is the current design.

Description and Symbolism

Obverse (1862–1904)

The obverse is a five-pointed star tipped with point-down trefoils and measuring two inches from point to point. In the center of each arm is a crown of oak and laurel, representing strength and achievement. A circle of thirty-four stars surrounds the center of the star and forms the base of each arm. The stars represent the number of states in the Union at the outbreak of the Civil War. In the center of the medal stands the figure of Minerva, who was the Roman goddess of civic strength and wisdom. She is warding off Discord — described in a May 6, 1862, letter to Secretary of the Navy Gideon Welles as "the foul spirit of secession and rebellion" — who is crouching and holds in his hand serpents striking at Minerva with forked tongues. In her right hand, Minerva holds the shield featured in

Army Medal of Honor (1862–1896), obverse.

the Great Seal of the United States. In her left, she holds a fasces, which represents the lawful authority of the state. The medal is suspended from its ribbon by a trophy composed of crossed cannons resting on eight stacked cannon balls and a sabre (representing the artillery and cavalry). An eagle with extended wings sits atop the trophy. A bar for mounting the bottom of the ribbon is affixed to the reverse of the eagle. At the top of the ribbon is a pin bar consisting of a shield (taken from the Great Seal of the United States) and two cornucopia (symbolizing America as the land of plenty).

Reverse (1862–1904)

The reverse of the Army Medal of Honor is plain to allow for engraving of the words

Army Medal of Honor (1862–1896), reverse, officially engraved to Corporal William Pittinger (misspelled Pettinger), Ohio Volunteers.

"The Congress to" followed by the recipient's name, rank, company, regiment and the date and place of the action being recognized.

Ribbon (1862–1896; 1896–1904)

While the obverse and reverse of the Army Medal of Honor were the same from 1862 until 1904, when a new obverse and reverse were adopted, there were two different ribbons during this period. The first ribbon, used from 1862 to 1896, was identical to that ribbon used by the Navy on its Medal of Honor: a one-inch wide ribbon consisting of a field of dark blue at the top with alternating stripes of red and white. The Secretary of War authorized a new ribbon on November 10, 1896. It was to be made of "silk one inch wide and one inch in length; the center stripe of white one-sixteenth of an inch wide, flanked

on either side by a stripe of blue seven thirty-seconds of an inch wide, bordered by two stripes of red each one quarter of an inch wide."[8] This second ribbon was used until 1904.

Obverse (1904–present)

The shape of the obverse retained Schussel's five-pointed star design with trefoils. The medal is one and 9/16ths of an inch in circumscribing diameter. The bust of Minerva, in profile and facing to the right, is in the center. An annulet surrounding Minerva contains the words UNITED STATES OF AMERICA and at the base of this annulet is a small shield. The five-pointed star is set upon an open wreath of laurel leaves, which connect each arm of the star. The laurel wreath, and the five crowns of oak within each arm of the star, are enameled in green. The star is suspended by a bar containing the word VALOR, and an eagle with its wings extended sits upon the bar; its talons hold arrows and an olive branch.

Reverse (1904–present)

The reverse is plain to allow for engraving of the words "The Congress to" followed by the

Army Medal of Honor (1896–1904), obverse.

recipient's name, rank, company, regiment and the date and place of the action being recognized.

Ribbon (1904–1944; 1944–present)

From 1904 to 1944, the medal was suspended from a short blue silk ribbon with thirteen white stars. While this ribbon had a pinback fastener for attaching it to a uniform, some recipients attached this shorter ribbon to a much longer pale blue ribbon so that they could wear their Medal of Honor around the neck. In 1944, the Army officially authorized a neck ribbon. It is the same shade of light blue as the ribbon used from 1904 to 1944, but contains an eight-sided pad from which the medal is suspended. The pad also is pale blue in color and has thirteen white stars.

Some scholars of the Medal of Honor identify the different versions of the Army Medal of Honor by "types" or "styles" and,

Army Medal of Honor (1904–1944), obverse.

based on the designs explained above, list the following types[9]:

Type I	1862 design; flag ribbon	1862–1896
Type II	1862 design; red-white-blue ribbon	1896–1904
Type III	1904 design; blue ribbon w/13 stars	1904–1913
Type IV	1904 design; ring on brooch; same ribbon	1913–1944
Type V	1904 design; blue neck ribbon w/ pad	1944–present

Those who identify these five types are purists, since the Type IV Army Medal of Honor is different from the Type III "only in that it has a small ring soldered at the back of the brooch allowing the entire medal to be suspended from a cravat."[10]

Historical Background

On December 21, 1861, Congress enacted legislation creating a Navy "medal of honor" for "petty officers, seamen, landsmen, and marines" who distinguished "themselves by their gallantry in action and other seamanlike

Army Medal of Honor (1896–1904), reverse, officially engraved to Captain Wm. E. Miller, Gettysburg, Pennsylvania, July 3, 1863.

Army Medal of Honor Type III (reverse).

soldier-like qualities" were removed, so that the sole criterion for the Army Medal of Honor was heroism in combat.[11]

As Charles P. McDowell explains in *Military and Naval Decorations of the United States*, the Army and Navy Medals of Honor shared the same basic design until 1904. This is because, when Secretary of the Navy Gideon Welles learned that the Army was going to have its own medal of honor, he wrote to Secretary of War Edwin Stanton, and suggested that the Navy's design "might also be appropriate for the Army." Stanton agreed and consequently the first Army Medals of Honor used the Navy's five-pointed star and ribbon. The only difference between the two medals was that the Army used a different device for attaching the star to the ribbon (featuring cannons and an eagle rather than an anchor) and a different brooch for pinning the medal to the uniform.[12]

The first change to the Army Medal of Honor came in 1896, when the Secretary of War (acting in accordance with a Joint Resolution of Congress passed on May 2, 1896), au-

qualities." When President Abraham Lincoln signed the legislation on the same day it had been approved by Congress, Lincoln made history by creating the first U.S. decoration.

Early the following year, on February 17, 1862, Senator Henry Wilson introduced a Senate Resolution proposing a similar medal of honor for enlisted men in the Army. Less than five months later, on July 12, 1862, Congress passed a Joint Resolution authorizing "two thousand medals of honor ... with suitable emblematic devices" for noncommissioned officers and privates who distinguished "themselves by their gallantry in action, and other soldier-like qualities during the present insurrection." Note that the phrase "during the present insurrection" suggests that Congress intended this decoration to be temporary, i.e., it would be awarded only during the Civil War. This Joint Resolution was amended the following year, on March 3, 1863, to make commissioned officers of the Army eligible for the new decoration. At the same time, the words "other

Army Medal of Honor (1944–1964), obverse.

thorized a new ribbon for the decoration. The U.S. flag motif of the original ribbon was replaced with a silk ribbon of one white, two red and two blue vertical stripes of varying widths. The rationale for this change was to differentiate the Army Medal of Honor from the various veterans organizations badges (such as that those issued by the Grand Army of the Republic) that were so similar in design to the Army decoration that that it was difficult to distinguish it from a privately-issued badge.

Despite this 1896 ribbon change, the Army Medal of Honor "continued to be widely copied"[13] and the War Department decided that the resulting confusion would end only with a newly designed medal. In 1903, at the request of Brigadier General Horace Porter, the French jewelry firm of Arthur, Bertrand and Berringer prepared several designs for a new Medal of Honor. The Army's Adjutant General then sent the designs to the Medal of Honor Legion (whose members were Medal of Honor recipients), which was permitted to select a design featuring the goddess Minerva for the new Army Medal of Honor.[14] Congress then passed legislation on April 23, 1904, which authorized the Army to use this new design. But, to ensure that veterans and patriotic organizations would not produce badges similar to the new Army Medal of Honor, General George L. Gillespie obtained a patent (serial number 197,369) for the new design. Gillespie subsequently transferred his ownership in the patent to "W.H. Taft and his successor or successors as Secretary of War of the United States of America."[15]

In adopting a new metal pendant for its Medal of Honor, the Army also decided that a new ribbon was appropriate, and the result was the blue silk ribbon with thirteen white stars familiar to Americans today. From 1904 until 1944, the Medal of Honor was issued with a pin on the reverse of the ribbon, and this was used to attach it to the uniform. While some soldiers attached the shorter ribbon to a longer piece of blue ribbon and wore it around their necks, the Army did not officially adopt the cravat or neck ribbon until 1944.

Today, a number of special entitlements exist for Army Medal of Honor recipients, including: a unique light blue flag bearing 13 white stars (issued to living Medal of Honor recipients or their primary next-of-kin); a special pension of $400 a month from the Department of Veterans Affairs; and a special entitlement to government air transportation. Also, the children of Medal of Honor recipients are not subject to quotas if they are qualified and desire to attend one of the U.S. military academies.[16]

Comparing Medal of Honor Recipients

While it is tempting to "compare" Medal of Honor recipients (usually with a view to determining who is the more highly decorated), this is difficult, if not impossible. First, the earliest recipients of the decoration received it for acts of heroism that today would be recognized with the award of the Silver Star or Bronze Star Medal. The many Medals of Honor awarded to Union soldiers for capturing Confederate battle flags arguably fall into this category, particularly where the official citation for the award provides no evidence of heroism.[17] When one remembers, however, that the Medal of Honor was a new award (lacking the prestige it enjoys today) and that it was *the only decoration* available to recognize outstanding performance on the battlefield, these flag capture awards are understandable.

Not until World War I (with the creation of the Distinguished Service Cross) and World War II (with the availability of the Silver Star and the Bronze Star Medal) did the Medal of Honor begin to increase in prestige in the Army — and consequently in the mind of the American public.

This is because the Army's leadership now had the option to award "lesser" decorations to soldiers for combat gallantry, and save the Medal of Honor for the truly extraordinary feats of heroism under fire.

But even in World War II, when the

Medal of Honor attained the level of respect it still enjoys today, not all awards of the decoration reflected the same level of heroism and, perhaps more importantly, not all acts deserving of the Medal of Honor were recognized with its award.

The best example of the former is the Medal of Honor awarded to General Douglas MacArthur in March 1942. Army Chief of Staff General George C. Marshall decided in early 1942 that awarding the decoration to MacArthur would be a "propaganda counterblow" to claims by the enemy that MacArthur was a "coward" who had fled the Philippines.[18] Using a radio message he had previously received from MacArthur's chief of staff, which lauded MacArthur's "utter contempt of danger under terrific aerial bombardments" and "magnificent leadership and vision,"[19] Marshall personally drafted a Medal of Honor citation. He then took it to the White House for President Roosevelt to sign — and told Roosevelt that he should approve the award "among other things, to offset any propaganda directed by the enemy against [MacArthur's] leaving his command and proceeding to Australia."[20] On March 26, 1942, MacArthur received his Medal of Honor in Australia at a dinner given for him by the Australian prime minister.

The best example of the latter is the failure of the Army to award a Medal of Honor to Master Sergeant Llewellyn M. Chilson — because his nomination packet lacked "incontestable proof" of extraordinary heroism.

The gist of Chilson's exploits under fire is that, between March and April 1945, Chilson saved countless American lives in a series of bold attacks in which he single-handedly killed at least 58 enemy soldiers; on April 25 alone, Chilson killed 40 Germans. In any event, in August 1945, months after fighting in Europe had ended, Chilson's regimental commander recommended that Chilson be awarded the Medal of Honor. In May 1946, that recommendation, after an unexplained 10-month delay, finally made it to the desk of Gen. Joseph T. McNarney, commander of all U.S. Forces

in Europe. McNarney agreed "after careful consideration" that Chilson should be awarded the nation's highest combat decoration "for the period 26–31 March 1945."[21]

In May and June 1946, the Army Adjutant General, acknowledging that "action on this case has already been long delayed," requested additional "eyewitness" information from Captain Raymond E. Wantz, Chilson's ex-company commander, and other former officers who had served with Chilson. Wantz provided an additional four typewritten pages to the War Department Decorations Board. Others former officers did as well. But it was not sufficient: on August 28, 1946, a majority of the Board disapproved the award of Medal of Honor. "The recommendation," wrote the Board, "reveals a highly commendable performance as a platoon leader, but does *not clearly establish incontestable proof* of conspicuous gallantry and intrepidity at the risk of life above and beyond the call of duty" (emphasis added).[22]

As a result of the Board's August 1946 decision, McNarney's recommendation for a Medal of Honor was returned to his successor in command, who then awarded Chilson an unprecedented three Distinguished Service Crosses, two Silver Stars, one Legion of Merit, and one Bronze Star Medal. When Chilson received these decorations from President Harry S. Truman at the White House on December 6, 1946, no American had ever received so many high-ranking awards at one time. Said Truman at the ceremony, "This is the most remarkable set of citations I have ever seen.... For any one of these, this young man is entitled to all the country has to offer.... This ought to be worth a Medal of Honor."[23]

Compare Chilson's heroism to that of 2nd Lt. Audie Murphy. On January 16, 1945, when a force of 250 German infantry and tanks overran Murphy's unit, he ordered his men to fall back. Then, after climbing atop an abandoned tank, Murphy single-handedly fought the Germans with a .50 caliber machine gun, *killing or wounding* about 50 enemy soldiers and, although wounded in the leg, nonetheless later led a counterattack that drove off the surviving Germans.[24]

First Recipient

The first recipient of the Army Medal of Honor was Private Jacob Parrott, Company K, 33rd Ohio Infantry, who was the youngest of six soldiers to receive the new decoration from Secretary of War Stanton on March 25, 1863. Parrott had participated in a daring Union Army raid behind Confederate lines in April 1862. While this Andrews Raid (named after civilian spy James J. Andrews, who led the operation) was a military failure, it involved an exciting train locomotive chase and the Union soldiers who took part were hailed as heroes in the North.[25]

Selected Recipients

Civil War

THOMAS W. CUSTER: APRIL 2, 1865, AND APRIL 6, 1865

Thomas Ward Custer is the *only* soldier to have been awarded two Medals of Honor during the Civil War; he is one of only 19 double Medal of Honor recipients. "Tom" Custer was the younger brother of Brigadier General George A. Custer; Tom Custer was serving under his brother when both were killed at Little Big Horn.

Custer's first Medal of Honor was awarded to him for capturing a flag at Namozine Church, Virginia, on April 2, 1865. His second Medal of Honor was awarded for his combat gallantry at Sailors Creek, Virginia, when Custer "leaped his horse over the enemy's works and captured two stands of colors." His horse was "shot under him" and Custer received "a severe wound." At the time of these two acts of heroism, Custer was serving as a second lieutenant, Company B, 6th Michigan Cavalry.[26]

WILLIAM H. CARNEY: JULY 18, 1863

In July of 1863, former slave William Harvey Carney became the first African American to earn the Medal of Honor. He was serving as a sergeant in Company C, 54th Massachusetts Volunteer Infantry (an all-black unit) at Fort Wagner, S.C. Carney's citation reads:

> When the color sergeant was shot down, this soldier grasped the flag, led the way to the parapet, and planted the colors thereon. When the troops fell back he brought off the flag, under a fierce fire in which he was twice severely wounded.[27]

Indian Wars

LEONARD WOOD: SUMMER 1886

Then Assistant Surgeon Leonard Wood was awarded the Medal of Honor for his actions during the Apache campaign in the summer of 1886. His citation states that he

> voluntarily carried dispatches through a region infested with hostile Indians, making a journey of 70 miles in one night and walking 30 miles the next day. Also for several weeks, while in close pursuit of Geronimo's band and constantly expecting an encounter, [he] commanded a detachment of Infantry, which was then without an officer, and to the command of which he was assigned at his own request.[28]

Born in New Hampshire in October 1860, Leonard Wood graduated from Harvard's medical school in 1884 and worked briefly in Boston before joining the Army in 1886 as a contract surgeon with the rank of first lieutenant. Although he achieved a measure of fame during the 1886 expedition against Geronimo, Wood's career did not take off until the Spanish-American War, when he was given command of the 1st Volunteer Cavalry, the "Rough Riders." Ten years later, in 1910, Wood was a major general and Army Chief of Staff. Although mostly forgotten today, Wood's institutional reforms transformed the Army into a modern fighting force.[29]

Philippine Insurrection

FREDERICK FUNSTON: APRIL 27, 1899

Frederick Funston was awarded the Medal of Honor his heroism at Rio Grande de la Pampanga, Luzon, Philippine Islands. On

April 27, 1899, then Col. Funston, "crossed the river on a raft and by his skill and daring enabled the general commanding to carry the enemy's entrenched position on the north bank of the river and to drive him at great loss from the important strategic position of Calumpit."[30]

Born in Springfield, Ohio in November 1865, Funston grew up in Iola, Kansas. He wanted to attend the U.S. Military Academy, but he was small in stature at 5'4" and his grades were only average. But they were good enough for the University of Kansas: Funston attended classes, although he did not graduate. He subsequently worked as a newspaperman in Kansas and Arkansas and as a U.S. Department of Agriculture botanist in Montana, the Dakotas and Alaska.[31]

He began his military career in Cuba when, inspired after hearing a speech praising the Cuban insurgency against Spain, Funston joined the guerrillas. Beginning as a volunteer captain, he participated in twenty-two engagements and rose to the rank of lieutenant colonel before returning to the United States.

In 1898, Funston was in Kansas when the United States declared war against Spain. He received authorization to raise the 20th Kansas Volunteers, and subsequently served with them in the Philippines. He was promoted to colonel of volunteers and awarded the Medal of Honor for his gallantry at Calumpit, where he not only crossed the river but also led forty-five soldiers in a successful attack against 2,500 enemy insurgents. Shortly hereafter, Funston received a promotion to brigadier general of volunteers.

Recognizing that his days as a soldier were over unless he could obtain a Regular Army commission, Funston persuaded his superiors to support him with the War Department. Since his daring capture of Emilio Aguinaldo had brought the fighting on Luzon to an end, Funston was rewarded with a commission as a Regular Army brigadier general.

After returning to the United States, Funston was promoted to major general and given command of the Department of California. After the devastating San Francisco earthquake of 1906, Funston received national attention — and praise — for organizing relief work and maintaining law and order.

In February 1915, Funston was given command of the Southern Department and consequently was in overall command of the Mexican border during Brigadier General John J. Pershing's Punitive Expedition of 1916. He was held in such high regard that many believed Funston would command the American Expeditionary Force in Europe. But this was not to be: while in San Antonio, Funston died suddenly of heart attack on February 19, 1917.

China / Boxer Rebellion

CALVIN P. TITUS: AUGUST 14, 1900

Musician Calvin Pearl Titus was awarded the Medal of Honor "for gallant and daring conduct in the presence of his colonel and other officers and enlisted men of his regiment ... while serving with Company E, 14th Infantry, at Peking China. Musician Titus was the first to scale the wall of the city."[32]

Born in Iowa in 1879, Titus enlisted in the Iowa National Guard in 1898 and transferred to the Regular Army's 14th Infantry Regiment after the Spanish American War. He sailed to the Philippines with his regiment to fight against guerrillas in the on-going insurrection but, when the regiment was sent to China to fight the Boxers in the summer of 1900, then-Corporal Titus went with it.

On August 14, 1900, during the heavy fighting in Peking, Titus overheard his commander say that the thirty-foot high Tartar Wall needed to be scaled. He answered with the now-famous reply: "I'll try, Sir."

The Americans had no ropes or ladders, but Titus, by holding on to exposed bricks and crevices in the ancient wall, managed to climb to the top. Other soldiers then followed his courageous example, and soon two companies of 14th Infantry were in control of the wall.

Their covering fire subsequently allowed British Army troops to reach the Boxer's stronghold.

In 1901, Titus received an appointment to the U.S. Military Academy. He had been recommended for the Medal of Honor and, when it was presented to him at West Point, Titus became the only cadet in history to receive America's highest combat decoration while attending classes at the Academy. Titus graduated in 1905 and retired as a lieutenant colonel in 1930.

World War I

ALVIN C. YORK: OCTOBER 8, 1918

Corporal Alvin Cullum York received the Medal of Honor for his heroism near Chatel-Chehery, France. On October 8, 1918, "after his platoon had suffered heavy casualties and three other noncommissioned officers had become casualties, Corporal York assumed command. Fearlessly leading seven men, he charged with great daring, a machine-gun nest which was pouring deadly and incessant fire upon his platoon. In this heroic feat, the machine-gun nest was taken, together with four officers and 128 men and several guns."[33]

From the beginning, York's superiors were suspicious of reports of his exploits near Chatel-Chehery. How could one man kill more than 20 Germans and capture another 132? But York's heroism has survived repeated scrutiny and there is no basis to doubt that York did what he is credited with having done. While leading a small party whose mission was to envelop a German position, York and his men were themselves taken under fire by another enemy unit. As his fellow soldiers took cover, York coolly shot one German soldier after another until their commander attempted to rush York's position. After six enemy soldiers in a nearby trench charged York with fixed bayonets, he killed all six with his pistol. Shortly thereafter, the German battalion commander, believing that it was no longer possible to stop York, offered to surrender. York accepted, and then used the battalion commander to order

his remaining machine gunners to surrender. By the time it was all over, York had not only killed and captured an unbelievable number of Germans, but had silenced 32 enemy machine guns.[34]

After the war, York's modesty quickly won the admiration of the American public. He was uninterested in either money or fame and retired instead to his mountain home in Tennessee. York did not agree to allow a film to be made about his life until shortly before World War II, when he decided that this would be the best way to earn money to support his local church and a Bible school. The resulting Hollywood movie, *Sergeant York*, starring Gary Cooper, won two Oscars and was the top-moneymaking film in 1941. York died in 1964 at the age of 76.

World War II

HENRY E. ERWIN, SR.: APRIL 12, 1945

In the closing months of World War II, Henry E. "Red" Erwin, Sr. picked up a burning phosphorous smoke bomb that was in danger of exploding inside his aircraft and threw it out a window, thereby saving both the plane and his fellow crewmembers. It was a remarkable act of unselfishness.

Born in May 1921 in Adamsville, Ala., Erwin was known to his family as "Gene" but, after enlisting in the Army Air Force in World War II, picked up the nickname "Red" from his fellow airmen. According to the official Medal of Honor website, Erwin was "a country boy, quiet, unassuming, and religiously devout."[35] He also was a first class radioman.

On April 12, 1945, then Staff Sgt. Erwin demonstrated the extraordinary heroism that was later recognized with the award of a Medal of Honor. At the time, he was aboard the "City of Los Angeles," a B-29 Superfortress which was part of the Guam-based 52nd Bombardment Squadron, 29th Bombardment Group, 20th Air Force.

Erwin's B-29 was leading a formation in an attack on a gasoline production plant at

Koriyama, located 120 miles from Tokyo. He was the radio operator but he had the additional duty of dropping phosphorous smoke bombs through a launch chute in the aircraft floor. These smoke bombs were jettisoned before any high explosive ordnance was dropped and were used to aid in assembling the bombers when their launching point was reached.

As Erwin pulled the pin on one bomb and dropped it into the chute, the bomb's fuse malfunctioned and the device exploded prematurely, igniting the phosphorous. Erwin was knocked down and engulfed in flames from the burning chemical. At the same time, smoke began to fill the B-29 and its pilot and co-pilot were unable to see their instrument panel, much less control the aircraft.

As for Erwin, he was horribly burned. Although he had been blinded by the blast, he realized that his aircraft and its crew were at grave risk because the phosphorous bomb would burn through the B-29's floor and ignite the ordnance in the bomb bay.

Using his bare hands, Erwin felt along the floor, located the burning bomb, and picked it up. His face and arms were covered with burning phosphorous, but he was not deterred. With incredible courage and amazing willpower, he managed to carry the bomb up to the flight deck, where he threw the bomb out the co-pilot's window.

With the bomb and smoke gone, the B-29's pilot pulled the plane out of a dive at 300 feet and headed for Iwo Jima so that Erwin could get medical help—although no one thought he would survive his horrific injuries. But he did, and he also received the Medal of Honor.

In October 1947, after a long hospitalization that included 41 operations, Erwin was discharged from the Army Air Force as a master sergeant. He subsequently spent 37 years as a counselor at a Veterans Administration hospital in Birmingham, Ala.

The Air Force has not forgotten Erwin's dedication and presents an annual outstanding enlisted aircrew member award in his name. Erwin died in January 2002, aged 80.

LEONARD A. FUNK, JR.: JANUARY 29, 1945

Leonard Funk, a paratrooper in Company C, 508th Parachute Infantry, 82d Airborne Division, was awarded the Medal of Honor, Distinguished Service Cross, Silver Star, Bronze Star Medal and three Purple Hearts for his combat gallantry in 1944 and 1945. Funk may have been the most highly decorated noncommissioned officer in World War II.

Born in Pennsylvania in 1916, Funk enlisted in the Army before the U.S. entered World War II. Although he stood only 5 feet, 5 inches tall, the 24-year-old wanted physical challenges and volunteered for paratrooper training. After completing jump school at Fort Benning, Georgia, Funk was assigned to the 508th Parachute Infantry and, when that unit sailed to England to join the 82d Airborne Division, Funk was with it.

On June 6, 1944, Funk and the division parachuted into France. He survived brutal fighting in the hedgerows and jumped into combat a second time when the 508th went into the Netherlands on September 17, 1944. During this operation, called Market Garden, Funk received the Distinguished Service Cross for leading an attack on an enemy stronghold.

On January 29, 1945, during the Battle of the Bulge, then 1st Sergeant Funk earned the Medal of Honor. At the time, Funk's unit had advanced "15 miles in a blinding snowstorm" near Holzheim, Belgium, and was getting ready to attack 15 German-held houses through "waist-deep drifts" of snow. After the company executive officer was wounded, however, Funk took command and formed the headquarters company soldiers — mostly clerks — into a platoon. The Americans then attacked and cleared all 15 German houses, and took 30 prisoners without suffering a single casualty. Funk then left four American GIs to guard the Germans while the rest of his platoon-sized unit mopped the remaining resistance.[36]

As the citation for Funk's Medal of Honor explains, when Funk and another soldier returned later to check on the prisoners, Funk was met "by a German officer who pushed a machine pistol into this stomach" and ordered him to surrender; in Funk's absence, an enemy patrol had come upon their German comrades, overpowered the American guards, and freed the prisoners. "Although overwhelmingly outnumbered and facing almost certain death, First Sergeant Funk, pretending to comply with the order, began slowly to unsling his machine gun from his shoulder and then, with lightning motion, brought the muzzle into line and riddled the German officer."[37]

Funk not only killed the German but, after reloading his submachine gun, opened fire on the other Germans, shouting to the Americans to seize the enemy's weapons. In the firefight that followed, 21 enemy soldiers were killed, many more were wounded and the rest were taken captive. Funk's "bold action and heroic disregard for his own safety were directly responsible for the recapture of a vastly superior enemy force, which, if allowed to remain free, could have taken the widespread units of Company C by surprise and endangered the entire attack plan."[38]

For his bravery that day, Funk received the Medal of Honor from President Harry S. Truman in a White House ceremony in September 1945. After being honorably discharged from the Army, Funk returned home. In 1947, he joined the Veterans Administration. Funk was a Division Chief in the VA's Pittsburgh Regional Office when he retired in 1972. Funk died of cancer in 1992; he was 76 years old. He was the last surviving World War II Medal of Honor recipient from the 82d Airborne.

JOHN R. McKINNEY: MAY 11, 1945

Private First Class McKinney's Medal of Honor is unusual for two reasons: it was awarded for heroism during the closing days of World War II (after the fighting in Europe had ended) and was in recognition of a "one-man stand against the Japanese" in the Philippines. His citation reads, in part:

He fought with extreme gallantry to defend the outpost which had been established near Dingalan Bay. Just before daybreak approximately 100 Japanese stealthily attacked the perimeter defense, concentrating on a light machinegun position manned by three Americans. Having completed a long tour of duty at this gun, Pfc. McKinney was resting a few paces away when an enemy soldier dealt him a glancing blow on the head with a saber. Although dazed by the stroke, he seized his rifle, bludgeoned his attacker, and then shot another assailant who was charging him. Meanwhile, one of his comrades at the machinegun had been wounded and his other companion withdrew carrying the injured man to safety. Alone, Pfc. McKinney was confronted by 10 infantrymen who had captured the machinegun with the evident intent of reversing it to fire into the perimeter. Leaping into the emplacement, he shot seven of them at pointblank range and killed three more with his rifle butt. In the melee, the machinegun was rendered inoperative, leaving him only his rifle with which to meet the advancing Japanese, who hurled grenades and directed knee mortar shells into the perimeter. He warily changed position, secured more ammunition, and reloading repeatedly, cut down waves of the fanatical enemy with devastating fire or clubbed them to death in hand-to-hand combat. When assistance arrived, he had thwarted the assault and was in complete control of the area. Thirty-eight dead Japanese around the machinegun and two more at the side of a mortar 45 yards distant was the amazing toll he had exacted single-handedly. By his indomitable spirit, extraordinary fighting ability, and unwavering courage in the face of tremendous odds, Pfc. McKinley saved his company from possible annihilation and set an example of unsurpassed intrepidity.

The son of a poor sharecropper, John Randolph "J.R." McKinney was born near Woodcliff, Georgia in February 1921. He completed only the third grade before dropping out of school to help support his family. After being drafted into the Army in 1942,

Army Medal of Honor (1944–1964), reverse, engraved to Sgt. Donald R. Moyer, 25th Infantry Division.

McKinney joined the 123rd Infantry Regiment, 33rd Infantry Division, and deployed with it to the Pacific in 1943. His fellow soldiers remembered him as a good marksman with an M-1 and as a "skinny, polite, easy-to-like fellow with powerful arms and hands."[39]

On the morning of May 11, 1945, McKinney was located at the tip of a sandbar peninsula in a tiny outpost at the mouth of the Umiray River, on the island of Luzon. The Japanese attacked his position about 5:30 a.m. and the entire battle — described in McKinney's Medal of Honor citation — lasted about 35 minutes.

For his unbelievable heroism that day, McKinney was recommended for the Medal of Honor a few days later. From the beginning, however, "a problem existed regarding the exact number of 'kills' credited to McKinney." The number "was way over 100, maybe as high as 140." But, believing that those processing the award recommendation through the chain of command would be suspicious of such a high number, only the thirty-eight to forty-

two enemy soldiers killed by McKinney in or near his foxhole were credited to him.[40]

Regardless of how many Japanese soldiers McKinney actually had killed, however, it was sufficient for the Army: then Sergeant McKinney received the Medal of Honor from President Truman in a White House ceremony in January 1946. After the war, McKinney returned to civilian life and worked as a farmhand. He died in April 1997 and is buried in Sylvania, Georgia.

ROBERT B. NETT: DECEMBER 14, 1944

Then First Lieutenant Robert B. Nett was awarded the Medal of Honor for his heroism in combat against the Japanese in World War II. He later served in Korea and Vietnam before retiring after 33 years of soldiering.

Born in New Haven, Connecticut, in June 1922, Nett decided to enlist in the Connecticut National Guard in 1940, when he was 17 years old. Since the minimum age to enlist was eighteen, Nett had a problem. But, as Nett once told a television reporter in an interview, he took his birth certificate and "folded it real hard on '1922'" so that the last digit was unclear. While the recruiting sergeant was unable to see Nett's birth year clearly, he assumed that the young man in front of him was old enough to enlist. The result was that Nett began what was to be an outstanding career as an infantryman.[41]

Nett was on active duty prior to the Japanese attack on Pearl Harbor in December 1941 and, in the rapid expansion of the Army that followed, then Private Nett volunteered for Officer Candidate School at Fort Benning, Georgia. After graduating in 1942, he received a commission as an infantry second lieutenant.

On December 14, 1944, then First Lieutenant Nett was in the Philippines at Cognon, Leyte and was commanding Company E, 305th Infantry Regiment. According to the citation for his Medal of Honor, Nett led his company in an attack against a reinforced enemy battalion which had held up the American advance for two days. Advancing "against heavy enemy machine gun and other automatic weapons fire," Nett spearheaded the assault against the Japanese. During "the fierce hand-to-hand" combat that followed, he personally killed seven Japanese soldiers with his rifle and bayonet. Nett was seriously wounded during this fighting, but he refused to quit and pressed ahead with his company. He was then wounded a second time, but "gallantly continued to lead his men forward, refusing to relinquish his command."

In the final assault on the Japanese strongpoint, Nett was wounded a third time. With great presence of mind, he "calmly made all arrangements" for the resumption of the attack, turned over command to another officer, and then "walked unaided to the rear for medical treatment for his three wounds."[42]

After recovering from his wounds, Nett returned to his unit and fought on Okinawa in the spring of 1945. But his heroism in the Philippines was not forgotten: Nett's sheer determination and inspiring leadership resulted in the award of the Medal of Honor in a February 1946 ceremony.

Nett liked soldiering, and remained in the Army after World War II. He helped train South Korean soldiers during the Korean War and, as the Inspector General for the Southwestern Area Command, also was "responsible for conducting classified missions for General MacArthur's Far East Headquarters."

During the Vietnam War, then Colonel Nett served as an advisor to South Vietnam's 2d Infantry Division. His last assignment was as the Chief of Reserve Affairs for Europe, the Middle East, and North Africa. Nett retired as a colonel in 1973 with 33 years of active duty and then began a second 17-year long career as a school teacher. Nett died in Columbus, Georgia in 2008. He was 86 years old.

Korea

LEWIS L. MILLET: FEBRUARY 7, 1951

Captain Lewis Lee "Red" Millet was awarded the Medal of Honor for his heroism while leading his company in a bayonet attack against strongly-held Chinese positions in the vicinity of Soam-Ni, Korea. His citation reads, in part:

> While personally leading his company in an attack against a strongly held position, he noted that the 1st Platoon was pinned down by small-arms, automatic, and antitank fire. Capt. Millett ordered the 3d Platoon forward, placed himself at the head of the two platoons and, with fixed bayonet, led the assault up the fire-swept hill. In the fierce charge Capt. Millett bayoneted two enemy soldiers and boldly continued on, throwing grenades, clubbing and bayoneting the enemy, while urging his men forward by shouting encouragement. Despite vicious opposing fire, the whirlwind hand-to-hand assault carried to the crest of the hill. His dauntless leadership and personal courage so inspired his men that they stormed into the hostile position and used their bayonets with such lethal effect that the enemy fled in wild disorder. During this fierce onslaught Capt. Millett was wounded by grenade fragments but refused evacuation until the objective was taken and firmly secured.

Born in December 1920 in Mechanic Falls, Maine, Millet joined the Massachusetts National Guard at age seventeen. In 1940, he enlisted in the Army Air Corps, where he was trained as a machine gunner. But, after hearing President Roosevelt say in October 1941 that no Americans would fight on foreign soil, twenty-one-year-old Miller deserted the Army. There was a war on in Europe, and Miller wanted to be a part of it, so he hitchhiked north to Canada and joined the Canadian Army.

By the time Millet sailed for England, America had declared war on Germany, so Millet went to the U.S. Embassy in London and asked to be transferred back to the U.S. Army. Miller subsequently saw combat against the Germans in North Africa and in Italy.

After World War II, Millet joined the Maine National Guard before returning to active duty in 1949. He was assigned to the 27th Infantry Regiment "Wolfhounds" and was in Korea when the North Koreans launched their

June 25, 1950 attack. Millet initially served as an artillery observer on the ground and in the air. Six months later, then Captain Millet took command of Company E, 27th Infantry Regiment. While in command of that unit on February 7, 1951, Millet led it in the bayonet charge that earned him the Medal of Honor. Historian S.L.A. Marshall later wrote that Millet's attack "was the most complete bayonet charge by American troops since Cold Harbor" in the Civil War.[43]

Millet remained in the Army after the Korean War. He attended Ranger School at Fort Benning and, while with the 101st Airborne Division, founded the Army Recondo School, a combat-realistic, small-unit training program for reconnaissance commandos. Miller later served in Vietnam, where he helped establish ranger and commando programs for the South Vietnamese Army. Millet retired as a colonel in 1973 and settled in California. He died in November 2009.

Vietnam

FRANKLIN MILLER: JANUARY 5, 1970

Then Staff Sergeant Miller was awarded the Medal of Honor for his heroism while leading a seven-man team of Vietnamese Montagnard tribesmen and Americans on a patrol deep in enemy-controlled territory.

Born in Elizabeth City, North Carolina, in 1945, Franklin Douglas Miller grew up in New Mexico and joined the Army after finishing high school. He first arrived in Vietnam in March 1966 as a 20-year-old private first class. Assigned to a reconnaissance platoon in the 1st Cavalry Division, he did so well — and enjoyed life in Vietnam so much — that he extended for a second year.

In the fall of 1967, then Specialist Four Miller was still with the 1st Cavalry and had received his first Silver Star, for gallantry in action, while covering the withdrawal of his unit during a firefight in the Central Highlands.

After two years of airborne infantry reconnaissance work, Miller decided to join Spe-

The reverse of the machine-engraved Medal of Honor to Sergeant Gordon R. Roberts, awarded for extraordinary heroism in Vietnam.

cial Forces. As he put it: "I'd seen what the regular Army had to offer and I decided I'd like to test my abilities in some faster waters."[44] Of the 500,000 plus U.S. military personnel in Vietnam at the time, about 4,000 were in Special Forces. Miller, however, joined an even smaller elite, the Military Assistance Command's Studies and Observation Group. For the next four years, until he left Vietnam in November 1972, Miller took part in many secret operations, including raids across the borders of Cambodia and Laos.

On January 5, 1970, Miller was in South Vietnam's Kontum Province — and deep in enemy-controlled territory — with a seven-man team of Montangard tribesmen and Americans. One of the men set off a booby trap that wounded four soldiers. Miller knew the explosion would alert the enemy and, after administering first aid to the wounded, moved his team to a more secure position.

Miller was correct — within minutes the North Vietnamese launched a furious attack and soon every man in the platoon except Miller was out of action. Miller had been wounded as well, as he had been shot in the chest. Although he thought that the resulting loss of blood might cause him to go into shock at any moment, Miller continued to fight alone against more than 30 enemy troops.

As the citation for his Medal of Honor explains, Miller "moved the patrol to a more protected position." He then moved forward to again "single-handedly meet the hostile attackers and gallantly repelled two attacks by the enemy before a friendly relief force reached the patrol location."[45]

President Nixon presented the Medal of Honor to Miller in a White House ceremony in June 1971. Afterward, Nixon asked Miller what he wanted to do now. Replied Miller: "I want to go back to my unit in Vietnam." And he did, until November 1972, when the Army reassigned him to a Special Forces unit at Fort Bragg, North Carolina.

Miller retired as a command sergeant major in 1992. He died of pancreatic cancer in Florida in June 2000, at age 55.

Afghanistan

SALVATORE A. GIUNTA: OCTOBER 25, 2007

Then Specialist Salvatore A. Giunta received his Medal of Honor for combat heroism in the Korengal Valley, Afghanistan in October 2007. When President Barack Obama presented the decoration to him in a White House ceremony in November 2010, Giunta became the first living recipient of the Medal of Honor since the Vietnam War.[46] The citation reads, in part:

> While conducting a patrol as team leader with Company B, 2d Battalion (Airborne), 503d Infantry Regiment, Specialist Giunta and his team were navigating through harsh terrain when they were ambushed by a well-armed and well-coordinated insurgent force. While under heavy enemy fire, Specialist Giunta immediately sprinted towards cover and engaged the enemy. Seeing that his squad leader had fallen and believing that he had been injured, Specialist Giunta exposed himself to withering enemy fire and raced towards his squad leader, helped him to cover, and administered medical aid. While administering first aid, enemy fire struck Specialist Giunta's body armor and his secondary weapon. Without regard to the ongoing fire, Spe-

Army Staff Sergeant Salvatore A. Giunta is the first living recipient of the Medal of Honor since the Vietnam War (U.S. Army).

cialist Giunta engaged the enemy before prepping and throwing grenades, using the explosions for cover in order to conceal his position. Attempting to reach additional wounded fellow soldiers who were separated from the squad, Specialist Giunta and his team encountered a barrage of enemy fire that forced them to the ground. The team continued forward and upon reaching the wounded soldiers, Specialist Giunta realized that another soldier was still separated from the element. Specialist Giunta then advanced forward on his own initiative. As he crested the top of a hill, he observed two insurgents carrying away an American soldier. He immediately engaged the enemy, killing one and wounding the other. Upon reaching the wounded soldier, he began to provide medical aid, as his squad caught up and provided security. Specialist Giunta's unwavering courage, selflessness, and decisive leadership while under extreme enemy fire were integral to his platoon's ability to defeat an enemy ambush and recover a fellow American soldier from the enemy.[47]

Salvatore A. Giunta's uniform reflects the award of the following personal awards: Army Medal of Honor Type V, Bronze Star Medal, Purple Heart, Army Commendation Medal with oak leaf cluster and Army Achievement Medal (U.S. Army).

Born in Clinton, Iowa on January 21, 1985, Salvatore Augustine Giunta enlisted in the Army in November 2003. Giunta deployed to Afghanistan from March 2005 to March 2006 and from May 2007 to May 2008. He is the third soldier to receive the Medal of Honor for heroism in Afghanistan: the next-of-kin of Sergeant First Class Jared C. Monti and Staff Sergeant Robert James Miller were presented posthumously awarded Medals of Honor in September 2009 and October 2010, respectively.

AIR FORCE MEDAL OF HONOR

Overview

Establishing Authority and Effective Dates: The Air Force Medal of Honor is authorized by Title 10, United States Code, Section 8741, effective November 1, 1965. In fact, Section 8741 simply permits the Air Force to have its own design for the Medal of Honor; this means that the Civil War-era Army Medal of Honor statute is the legal basis for the Air Force decoration.

Criteria: The Air Force Medal of Honor is awarded to any person who, while serving with the Air Force, distinguishes himself conspicuously by gallantry and intrepidity at the risk of his life above and beyond the call of duty (1) while engaged in an action against an enemy of the US, or (2) while engaged in military operations involving conflict with an opposing foreign force, or (3) while serving with friendly foreign forces engaged in an armed conflict against an opposing force in which the U.S. is not a belligerent party.[48]

Nomination and Award Process: The award process for the Air Force Medal of Honor generally follows the same procedure outlined for the Army, discussed above. Additionally, under Air Force Instruction 36–2803, any recommendation of an airman for the Medal of Honor must "clearly state" how "the act characterizes courage, intrepidity, or gallantry." Additionally, as the Air Force Medal of Honor may only be awarded when the act of gallantry involves voluntary risk of life, the recommendation must "clearly show that the individual would not have been censured had he or she not voluntarily accomplished the act."[49]

Time limits set out in Title 10, United States Code, Section 8744 (which are identical to those applicable to the Army Medal of Honor) control the award of the Air Force Medal of Honor: the recommendation for an Air Force medal must be made within two years of the act justifying the decoration and the Medal of Honor must itself be awarded within three years "after the date of the act justifying the award." However, as with the Army Medal of Honor, these time limits do not apply to a recommendation for the Air Force Medal of Honor that was "lost" or not acted upon "through advertence."

Finally, Section 1130, Title 10, United States Code, gives authority to a Member of Congress to "request" that the Secretary of the Air Force "review" a nomination of an airman for a Medal of Honor (or the upgrading of an existing decoration to the Medal of Honor) regardless of the amount of time that has passed since the act of heroism upon which the nomination is based. This provision was the basis for the Air-Force-Cross-to-Medal-of-Honor awards to Airman 1st Class William H. Pitsenbarger in 2000 and Chief Master Sergeant Richard L. Etchberger in 2010.

Finally, a few words on the award process for the Air Force Medal of Honor, with a focus on the political and other intangible factors that have influenced its award. Given the short life of the Air Force Medal of Honor (and the relatively few recipients), the impact of politics and other intangibles so evident in the Army Medal of Honor award

process is less pronounced. However, national security concerns did deny one airman — Chief Master Sergeant Richard L. Etchberger — the Medal of Honor for more than 40 years. The circumstances of that award are detailed in the "Selected Recipients" category below.

Designer: Lewis J. King, Jr., a civilian employee at the Army's Institute of Heraldry, designed the Air Force Medal of Honor.

Description and Symbolism

Obverse (1965–present)

The decoration is two inches high, and two and one-sixteenth inches in width. The obverse is a wreath of laurel in green enamel, within which is a gold-finished, five-pointed star, one point down. Each point of the star is tipped with trefoils and each point contains a crown of laurel and oak on a green enamel background. Centered upon the star is an annulet of thirty-four star (representing the number of states in the Union at the outbreak of

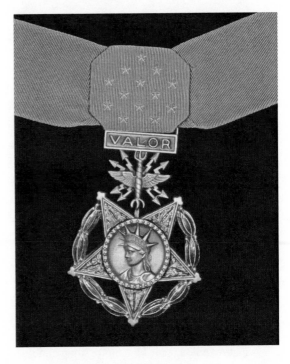

Air Force Medal of Honor (obverse).

the Civil War in 1861) which surround the profile of the head of the goddess of Liberty.

The star is suspended by a connecting bar and pinned hinge from a trophy that consists of an outstretched wing and eight thunderbolts; at the top of the trophy is a bar with the word VALOR.

Lewis' design echoes the Army and Navy Medals of Honor, in that a five-pointed star is the central feature of the decoration. The profile of Liberty symbolizes American ideals and the wing and thunderbolts indicate that this is an Air Force decoration.

Reverse (1965–present)

The reverse is plain so that the recipient's rank, name, and organization may be engraved.

Air Force Medal of Honor (reverse).

Ribbon (1965–present)

The VALOR bar is suspended from a slightly oblong pale blue moiré silk pad, folded at the corners. There are thirteen stars (each

$^{7}\!/_{64}$ inches in diameter) embroidered on the pad. The stars represent the original thirteen colonies and are arranged in the form of a triple chevron. The pad is attached to a pale blue neck cravat (ribbon) of the same blue material, measuring twenty-four inches in length and having a width of $1^{3}\!/_{16}$ inches. Three nickel-plated metal snaps are used to fasten the ribbon around the recipient's neck.

Historical Background

While the Air Force separated from the Army and became an independent service in 1947, it continued to use Army decorations and medals. For example, all airmen decorated for the highest levels of heroism during the Korean War received the Army version of the Medal of Honor or the Army's Distinguished Service Cross.

In the late 1950s, however, as the Air Force developed its own identity, it began looking at replacing these Army awards with medals of its own design. On February 9, 1961, Col. John E. Horne of the Air Force's Personnel Services Division wrote to Lt. Col. J. T. French, the Army Quartermaster General's Heraldic Officer. In that letter, Horne stated that the Air Force Chief of Staff had approved "the establishment of a distinctive [Air Force] pendant for the Medal of Honor," but "with no change to the present ribbon design."[50] With this in mind, Horne now requested that the Heraldic Officer develop "suitable designs" for a new Air Force medal. While Horne was imposing "no restrictive guidelines ... on the development of designs," he nevertheless told French that any Air Force Medal of Honor design produced by the Institute of Heraldry should consider the following:

a. The pendant design should possess sculptural effect, and must be of outstanding quality and symbolic of the dynamic role of the Air Force in the national defense structure.

b. The shape of the medal must be unique and should follow the idea of individualism expressed by current decorations of the services. (Round-shaped designs are not acceptable).

   c. Do not use an eagle as the main element of the design.

   d. Designs of the medal pendants should specify gold substance.[51]

For the next year and a half, the Army Institute of Heraldry worked closely with the Air Force to develop a design for a new Medal of Honor. Arriving at a final product, however, was not an easy process, and appears to have been acrimonious at times. The Institute submitted at least five basic designs, with a number of variations, to the Air Force, before that service finally accepted a design for the new medal. But even this Medal of Honor design changed again, as the Commission of Fine Arts required more modifications to the design before it would approve the decoration familiar to airmen today.

The process began in mid-1961, when the Army Institute of Heraldry submitted four different designs to Air Force headquarters. Unfortunately, as a September 14, 1961 letter from Col. Horne indicates, none of these designs were acceptable. There were two basic objections: the Institute, following the Army Medal of Honor format, proposed a five-pointed star with one point *facing down*. As Air Force insignia use a five-pointed star with one point *facing up*, Air Force headquarters wanted any Medal of Honor to likewise have any "star design placed in an upright position." The second objection to the four designs was that the all proposed using either Mercury or Minerva as the center-piece of a five-pointed star design. While the Air Force liked the star design, it did not want to use the god Mercury because he was on the newly created Airman's Medal. Similarly, the Air Force did not want to use Minerva because that goddess was on the Army Medal of Honor — and the Air Force wanted to break with its Army past. Consequently, Horne suggested in his September 1961 letter that the Institute submit

a fifth design using "the head of the Goddess of Liberty."[52]

The Army's Institute did not think much of either objection — or the suggestion that Liberty be considered for the Air Force Medal of Honor. As Lt. Col. French wrote to the Air Force on November 28, 1961:

> Placing one point of the star in an upright position is not considered the most suitable positioning for this medal. The arrangement with two points upward, as used by the Army and Navy Medals of Honor, is *unique* for this highest award [and] *in contradistinction to the Silver Star, the Bronze Star Medal* and other military and civilian usage [emphasis supplied].[53]

As French also explained, having one point of the star upright presented "an awkward appearance" and gave rise to "mechanical difficulties" when attaching a suspension. On the other hand, "suspension of the star with two points upward" looked better and made it easier to attach the suspension that would link the five-pointed star to the ribbon.[54]

As for the Air Force suggestion that Liberty be the centerpiece of the new Medal of Honor, French wrote:

> The head of the Goddess of Liberty, even with the additions of neckline and shoulders, looks too much like the U.S. ten-cent coin and may tend to degrade the value of the medal. While the head of Minerva is used on the Army Medal of Honor (except for facing in the opposite direction), its use on the Air Force Medal of Honor would perpetuate the prestige attached to this award. However, the head of Mars, God of War … may be considered equally appropriate as an alternate choice.[55]

To say that the Air Force was unreceptive to the Institute's November 1961 letter is an understatement: the service rejected the suggestions about the placement of the star, and using Minerva or Mars. On the contrary, in a January 15, 1962, letter to the Army, Col. Russell G. Pankey, Chief of the Air Force's Personnel Services Division, insisted not only that the Institute should incorporate her likeness into its design proposals, but wrote that the Air

Force "would like to see the face of the Goddess *from our Statute of Liberty* used as the central figure" in future drawings. (emphasis supplied) Pankey's letter also reveals that Air Force leaders still very much undecided about even a basic design for the new Air Force Medal of Honor: Pankey also asked the Institute to provide "at least three [new] different designs" and requested that Institute "artists come up with two additional ideas which do not use the star design or ancient Greek figures as the principal theme."

On May 4, 1962, Air Force representatives met at the Institute's offices to "review new design sketches" for the Medal of Honor. In accordance with Air Force desires, the Institute had produced "several versions of two basic design concepts ... using elements of the Statue of Liberty as the central device."[56] Army artists also had acquiesced on the placement of the star, as "all of the designs had the star with one point up as requested by the Air Force." Both designs also incorporated a laurel wreath around the star, similar to that used on the Army's Medal of Honor, except that the wreath on the Air Force design was open at the top to differentiate it from the Army version. Finally, the Institute also had designed two "suspension devices" from which to hang the star and attach the ribbon.[57]

The Air Force, now satisfied with the Institute's product, selected a design that featured a three-quarter view of the face of the Statute of Liberty, with her arm visible at the lower left. The selected design apparently also had a five-pointed star with one point up but there is a mystery here: the design forwarded to the U.S. Commission of Fine Arts for approval had the star pointed down. Similarly, there is a mystery about the suspension device selected for the new Medal of Honor: while Air Force representatives selected a suspension device consisting of "an Air Force eagle with open cloud," the suspension device ultimately approved by the Commission was a thunderbolts-and-wing device taken directly from the Air Force Coat-of-Arms, attached to a bar with

the word VALOR. It seems that the Institute and Air Force changed the placement of the star and substituted the thunderbolt-and-wing suspension device sometime between May and September, when the Institute forwarded the final design to the Commission of Fine Arts.

In any event, on September 25, 1962, Mr. David E. Finley, the Commission's chairman, wrote to the Institute. In that letter, he stated that the proposed Medal of Honor design was "approved in general" except that the Commission wanted a "smaller profile of the head from the Statue of Liberty, without the arm." This was because the design selected by the Air Force was too "crowded" and a smaller profile would "enhance the sculptural quality of the medal."[58]

On October 5, 1962, the Institute notified the Air Force that it was revising its design to comply with the Commission's comments and, on November 13, 1962, asked the Air Force if it wanted to comment on the modified design before the Institute sent it to the Commission for final approval. On November 20, the Air Force informed the Institute that it was "pleased with the design as revised" and requested that it be submitted to the Commission "for final review." The Commission approved the final design on December 19, 1962.

On March 25, 1963, the Air Force Chief of Staff approved the new design for the Medal of Honor and, on May 1, 1963, Brigadier General Godfrey T. McHugh, Air Force aide to the president, showed the new design to John F. Kennedy. Since Kennedy "liked" the design, the Air Force had its new decoration.[59] Since the approved design was chiefly the work of Lewis J. King, Jr., a civilian employee at the Institute of Heraldry, he is credited being the designer of the medal. A final note on the design process: when the *Army–Navy–Air Force Journal* announced on November 9, 1963 that the Air Force had a new Medal of Honor, it claimed that the medal's design "offers one example of inter–Service harmony, cooperation, and economy."[60]

First Recipient

Major Bernard Francis Fisher received the first Air Force Medal of Honor in a White House ceremony on January 19, 1967. His medal was awarded for conspicuous gallantry on March 10, 1966 when, despite "withering ground fire," Fisher landed his airplane on a "battle-torn airstrip" to rescue a downed pilot.[61]

Selected Recipients

There have been a total of fourteen awards of the Air Force Medal of Honor.[62] The recipients are: Lieutenant Colonel Steven L. Bennett, Colonel George E. Day, Major Merlyn Dethlefsen, Chief Master Sergeant Richard D. Etchberger, Major Bernard F. Fisher, 1st Lieutenant James P. Fleming, Lieutenant Colonel Joe M. Jackson, Colonel William A. Jones III, Airman 1st Class John L. Levitow, Airman 1st Class William H. Pitsenbarger, Captain Lance P. Sijan, Lieutenant Colonel Leo K. Thorsness, Captain Hilliard A. Wilbanks, and Captain Gerald O. Young.

Only Air Force personnel who performed acts of conspicuous gallantry in Southeast Asia have been awarded the Air Force Medal of Honor; there have been no awards of the decoration since the Vietnam War.

RICHARD L. ETCHBERGER: MARCH 11, 1968

Then Chief Master Sergeant Etchberger was awarded a posthumous Air Force Cross for his extraordinary heroism in Laos on March 11, 1968. Some forty years after the enemy attack that cost Etchberger his life, his Air Force Cross was upgraded to a Medal of Honor.

Born in March 1933 in Hamburg, Pennsylvania, Richard Loy "Dick" Etchberger graduated from high school in 1951 and enlisted in the Air Force a few months later. He liked being an airman and decided to make the Air Force a career. Etchberger excelled as a radio and radar maintainer, and his expertise was re-warded: he was promoted to the highest enlisted rank, chief master sergeant (E-9) in April 1967.

In March 1968, Etchberger and 15 airmen — along with two CIA officers and a forward air controller — were living at Lima Site 85 in Laos. This was a highly secret radar facility needed by the Air Force to direct strike missions in Laos and North Vietnam. Since targets located deep inside North Vietnam were impossible to bomb during darkness and during bad weather, the Air Force had built a radar site atop Phou Pha Thi, a 5,600-foot mountain in northeastern Laos. Located fifteen miles from the North Vietnamese border, the station was critical to the success of Operation ROLLING THUNDER, the on-going bombing campaign begun by the Air Force in March 1965.

The radar site's existence inside Laos was highly classified. The operation also was illegal, because the United States had signed an international treaty in which it agreed that it would not station any military personnel in Laos. In fact, Etchberger and his fellow airmen at Lima Site 85 were technically not in the military because the Pentagon had "honorably discharged" them so that they could be hired as "civilians" by Lockheed Aircraft Services. This explains why Etchberger was wearing civilian clothes and had no rank insignia — like everyone else on the mountaintop base.

In the months that followed Etchberger's arrival at the secret radar station in Laos, he and his fellow airmen used their talents with radar to direct more than 500 bombing missions in Laos and North Vietnam. But the North Vietnamese soon realized that if Air Force bombers were able to strike despite heavy cloud cover and poor visibility, it was because the Americans were operating a radar base near the border — and they soon moved to destroy it.

On the night of March 10–11, 1968, hundreds of North Vietnamese soldiers encircled the site and blocked any ground escape routes. In the meantime, 33 enemy sappers, who had spent two days climbing the mountain, launched an attack against the Americans with machine guns and rocket propelled grenades.

The Americans operating the radar site were killed almost immediately. Etchberger's team, which was resting nearby, managed to escape and take cover on a ledge. But the North Vietnamese soon discovered Etchberger and the six Americans who were still alive out of the initial 19, and opened fire. Two airmen were shot and killed; two more were badly wounded. Soon, everybody was dead or wounded except for Etchberger. Despite withering fire, he fought back with an M-16 rifle as he and the others kicked away the enemy grenades being thrown at them before they could explode.

Using a radio, Etchberger managed to call in American A-1E Skyraiders to bomb the site and the North Vietnamese attackers. As the morning sun rose, a CIA-operated UH-1H helicopter managed to reach the stranded Americans. Ignoring the hail of bullets pinging all around him, Etchberger helped two of his fellow airmen to get into the helicopter. Etchberger then saved another American by embracing him in a bearhug as both were lifted into the helicopter.

As the CIA chopper began to fly away, the North Vietnamese let loose a hail of gunfire and at least one round struck Etchberger as he was being raised into the helicopter or just after he had been pulled inside. He bled to death before he could reach medical care in Thailand.

Etchberger's extraordinary heroism was recognized at the time as deserving of the Medal of Honor. His chain of command recommended him for the award and he was posthumously restored to active duty so that he would be eligible to receive it. When the award recommendation reached the Pentagon, however, General Bruce K. Holloway, the Air Force vice chief of staff, advised against approving it. Giving Etchberger the nation's highest military award would reveal the existence of the top-secret radar facility in Laos,

and highlight the fact that the Americans had been operating in violation of international law.

The result was that President Johnson declined to award the Medal of Honor, and the Air Force instead presented Etchberger's widow with the Air Force Cross in a private ceremony in the Pentagon. She knew that her husband had been on a secret mission — and she did not reveal this secret even to her three children. Not until 1986 was the truth about Etchberger's death revealed, when the Air Force declassified the Lima Site 85 mission.

Some years later, a group of Air Force veterans requested that Etchberger's Air Force Cross be upgraded to the Medal of Honor for which he had originally been recommended. Congressman Earl Pomeroy of North Dakota submitted the original Medal of Honor upgrade package to the Air Force in 2006 and, after Congress enacted special legislation waiving the two-year time limitation ordinarily applicable to a Medal of Honor recommendation, Etchberger's Air Force Cross was upgraded to the nation's highest military award.[63]

On September 21, 2010, President Barack Obama presented the medal to Etchberger's three sons in a White House ceremony.

JOHN L. LEVITOW: FEBRUARY 24, 1969

On February 24, 1969, Airman 1st Class Levitow threw himself on a flare that was about to explode inside an AC-47 gunship. For saving the lives of the crew, he was awarded the Medal of Honor by President Nixon in a White House ceremony on January 14, 1970. Levitow's award is unique: he is the lowest ranking airman man to receive the decoration.

Levitow was the loadmaster of an AC-47 "Dragon Ship" on February 24, 1969, and routinely flew on a combat air patrols over South Vietnam. Levitow's gunship was patrolling in the vicinity of Tan Son Nhut, when the nearby Army base at Long Binh came under a Viet Cong mortar attack.

Diverted to help in the defense of soldiers at Long Binh, the gunship launched flares to help locate enemy positions and, firing its miniguns, knocked out two enemy mortar positions. Then, as the AC-47 flew toward other enemy targets, an enemy mortar shell struck the plane's right wing. The result was a huge explosion that put a two-foot hole in that wing, shook the aircraft violently, and riddled the fuselage with 3,500 pieces of white-hot shrapnel.

At the time the mortar struck their aircraft, Levitow and another crewman were standing near the open cargo door, dropping parachute illumination flares. The explosion knocked both airmen to the floor of the aircraft, and a flare that they were handling fell inside the cargo compartment. Spewing toxic smoke, this magnesium flare was soon going to separate explosively from its canister and ignite — with disastrous consequences.

Levitow had suffered a concussion and had some 40 wounds on his back and legs. Despite his wounds — Levitow was stunned and bleeding profusely — he moved forward in the

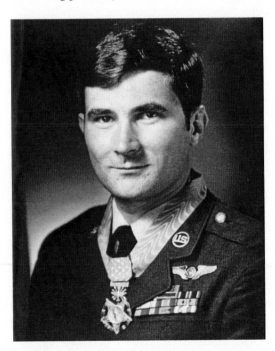

Airman 1st Class John A. Levitow is the lowest ranking recipient of the Air Force Medal of Honor (U.S. Air Force).

compartment and flung himself on the flare to keep it from rolling. Levitow then dragged himself and the flare back toward the cargo door and tossed it out. The flare ignited just as it cleared the aircraft. As the citation for his Medal of Honor puts it, "Sergeant Levitow, by his selfless and heroic actions, saved the aircraft and its entire crew from certain death and destruction."

Levitow subsequently spent two and one half months in a hospital recovering from his injuries. He then returned to Vietnam where he completed twenty more missions as a loadmaster. Levitow retired from active duty in 1974 and died from cancer in 2000. He was 55 years old.[64]

LANCE P. SIJAN: NOVEMBER 9, 1967

Lance Peter Sijan was the first U.S. Air Force Academy graduate to be awarded the Medal of Honor.

Then 25-year-old First Lieutenant Sijan was flying over Laos in an F-4C Phantom when defective fuses on the bombs carried by the aircraft detonated prematurely, crippling the fighter-bomber. After successfully ejecting, Sijan evaded capture for more than six weeks, despite being seriously injured (he had a compound fracture of his left leg) and suffering from shock and extreme weight loss due to lack of food.

After being captured by North Vietnamese soldiers, Sijan tried to escape by overpowering a guard and crawling into the jungle. When the enemy recaptured him several hours, he was brutally beaten and then transferred to another prison camp where he was kept in solitary confinement.

The North Vietnamese repeatedly tortured Sijan in an attempt to obtain useful information, often by twisting his badly damaged right hand. But he did not divulge any information to his captors. Unfortunately, Sijan's physical health deteriorated rapidly and he was placed in the care of another prisoner. During intermittent periods of consciousness until his death, he never complained of his physical condition and, on several occasions, spoke of future escape attempts. Sijan died on January 22, 1968.[65]

Born in Milwaukee, Wisconsin in April 1942, Lance Sijan graduated from the Air Force Academy in 1965. On March 4, 1976, President Gerald Ford presented the Medal of Honor posthumously to Sijan's parents.[66]

DISTINGUISHED SERVICE CROSS

Overview

Establishing Authority and Effective Dates: The Distinguished Service Cross was first authorized by President Woodrow Wilson on January 9, 1918, and the new decoration was announced on January 12, 1918, in War Department General Orders No. 6. Congress later superseded Wilson's presidential authorization when it created the Distinguished Service Cross by an act of Congress (Public Law 193, 65th Congress) on July 9, 1918; this original legislation was amended on July 25, 1963.

The July 1918 statute provided that the Distinguished Service Cross could be awarded for acts occurring "since the 6th day of April 1917," the day the United States entered World War I. But two exceptions to this qualifying date were permitted. First, Congress passed a statute allowing the War Department to award the Distinguished Service Cross to a small number of officers who had been nominated for brevet promotions for extraordinary heroism prior to World War I, but whose nominations had not been acted upon; most of these awards were announced in War Department General Orders between 1919 and 1925.

Second, Congress enacted legislation in 1934 permitting the award of the Distinguished Service Cross to recipients of the Certificate of Merit. Since the last Certificate of Merit was awarded in 1918, it follows that some awards of the Distinguished Service Cross in lieu of the Certificate of Merit were for acts occurring prior to April 6, 1917.[67] See Appendix B

for a history of the Certificate of Merit and its relationship to the Distinguished Service Cross.

Criteria: The Distinguished Service Cross is awarded to any person who, while serving in any capacity with the U.S. Army, distinguishes himself or herself by extraordinary heroism not justifying the award of a Medal of Honor: (1) while engaged in an action against an enemy of the United States; (2) while engaged in military operations involving conflict with an opposing or foreign force; or (3) while serving with friendly foreign forces engaged in an armed conflict against an opposing Armed Force in which the United States is not a belligerent party.

The act or acts of heroism must have been so notable and have involved risk of life so extraordinary as to set the individual apart from his or her comrades.[68]

Order of Precedence: The Distinguished Service Cross is worn after the Medal of Honor and before the Distinguished Service Medal.

Devices: Additional awards of the Distinguished Service Cross are denoted by oak leaf clusters.

Designers: The first style Distinguished Service Cross was designed by Captain Aymar E. Embury "with the assistance of Lieutenant Andre Smith."[69] The plaster model for the first style cross was sculpted by Gaetano Cecere; he would later design the Soldier's Medal.

The second style — and current — Distinguished Service Cross is a re-worked version of the first style; the modifications were done by Embury. The plaster model for the second style cross was done by John R. Sinnock, an employee of the U.S. Mint in Philadelphia; Sinnock would later design the Purple Heart.[70]

Description and Symbolism

Obverse: First Style

The first style Distinguished Service Cross was a bronze cross, measuring approximately 1⅞ inches high and 1⅝ inches wide. An American eagle with its wings spread, facing to the left, is in the center of the cross, and is superimposed over a four-pointed diamond. One point of each diamond is centered in each arm of the cross, and a five-pointed star is affixed to the end of each point of the diamond. The arms of the cross are decorated with oak leaves. Below the eagle and the cross is a scroll with the words "E Pluribus Unum." The cross was suspended from a ball through which the suspension ring passes.

Reverse: First Style

Centered on the reverse of the first style cross is a rectangular plaque containing the words "For Valor." This plaque sits on a wreath of laurel leaves; in the center of the wreath is a decorative staff.

Obverse: Second (Current) Style

The second style Distinguished Service Cross is a modified version of the first style, and measures two inches in height and 1¹³⁄₁₆ inches in width. A slightly larger eagle with displayed wings is centered on the cross and, instead of that eagle being superimposed on a diamond, the eagle on the second style Distinguished Service Cross is imposed on a circular wreath of laurel leaves. Below the eagle and cross is a scroll bearing the inscription "For Valor" (rather than "E Pluribus Unum"). The

Top: **Army Distinguished Service Cross, First style (obverse).** *Above:* **Army DSC First style (reverse).**

Army DSC (current) obverse.

Army DSC (current) reverse.

chief difference between the two styles, however, is not the scroll. Rather, the four arms of the second style cross are plain; they lack the heavily decorated oak leaves of the first style version.[71]

Reverse: Second (Current) Style

Unlike the first style, there are no words on the reverse of the second style. Rather, the center of the cross is circled by a wreath with a rectangular space for engraving the name of the recipient.

Ribbon

The ribbon is the same for both styles of the Distinguished Service Cross. It has a one-inch wide stripe of blue in the middle, which is edged on both sides by a narrow stripe of white, and a larger stripe of red next to the white. From left to right, the colors are red-white-blue-white-red. Captain Andre Smith designed the ribbon, and he chose the colors of the U.S. flag.

Historical Background

When the United States entered World War I in April 1917, the Army did not have any decoration or medal for recognizing combat heroism of a lesser degree than that required for a Medal of Honor. There also was no award for distinguished non-combat service, and no decoration that could be awarded to deserving foreign military personnel. As soon as General John J. Pershing arrived with the American Expeditionary Force in France, he saw that the lack of such awards was depriving him — and other commanders in the field — of the ability to quickly reward combat gallantry. As American military medal expert Charles P. McDowell noted, "this last point was important, as many heroes were so badly wounded that they either died of their wounds or had to be evacuated quickly."[72]

Pershing wanted decorations similar to the British Military Cross and Military Medal, which had been created in 1914 and 1916, respectively, and the French Croix de Guerre, which had been instituted in 1915. Pershing relayed his views to Secretary of War Newton D. Baker and, on December 28, 1917, Baker formally recommended to President Woodrow Wilson that a "Distinguished Service Cross" and "Distinguished Service Medal" be established. On January 9, 1918, Wilson (using his authority as Commander-in-Chief) authorized the two new decorations for the Army. The legal basis for the two new decorations, however, was superseded by 65th Congress when, on July 9, 1918, it authorized "the President ... to present ... a distinguished service cross ... to any person who, while serving in any capacity with the Army of the United States since the 6th day of April 1917, has distinguished or who shall hereafter distinguish himself in connection with military operations against an armed enemy."[73]

After President Wilson authorized the Distinguished Service Cross, the Army asked for designs for the new decoration. Captain Aymar E. Embury, with the assistance of First Lieutenant Andre Smith, submitted a design that was accepted by the War Department. Embury, a well-known New York City architect, was serving alongside Smith in Company

B, 40th Engineers (Camouflage Section), in Washington, D.C.

The medal designed by Embury and Smith was approved by the Army and struck by the U.S. Mint in Philadelphia in February. Since General Pershing decorated three soldiers with the Distinguished Service Cross on March 18, 1918, it follows that the new decoration had been shipped to him earlier that month. But, even as Pershing was distributing the new heroism medal to deserving soldiers (medals numbered 1 to 100 had been shipped to France from Philadelphia), not everyone was pleased with the artistic quality of the new Distinguished Service Cross. On the contrary, Paul W. Bartlett, the president of the National Sculpture Society, "sent a formal protest to Secretary of War Baker on June 14, 1918, in which he alleged that the medal was of inferior artistic design."[74]

Baker sent Bartlett's letter to President Wilson, who replied on June 17, 1918, that he wondered if it might be advisable to have the new decoration "reconsidered" by the Commission of Fine Arts. Baker's reply: "To my mind, this Cross is good ... I frankly do not think it will be possible to get any medal which will satisfy the artists of this country and my disposition would be to let the matter rest where it is."[75]

While Wilson agreed with Baker that Embury and Smith's Distinguished Service Cross should remain unchanged, this was not to be. On the contrary, unbeknownst to either Baker or Wilson, the War Department already had decided—on its own initiative in April 1918—to modify the decoration by making "certain minor changes that would add to the beauty and attractiveness of the same." Consequently, while Baker and Wilson were agreeing in June 1918 that the Distinguished Service Cross designed by Embury and Smith was acceptable, the Army had already decided to make changes to the decoration.

The modifications were done by Embury, and the result was a second style Distinguished Service Cross. Struck at the U.S. Mint

in Philadelphia, the new style Distinguished Service Cross was also sent to Pershing in France.

Most of the first style Crosses were presented—and the Army kept track of which numbered medal went to a particular recipient. However, as the second style Distinguished Service Cross arrived in France, some soldiers exchanged their first style awards for the new second style Cross. They were not, however, *required* to exchange them and photographs taken in early 1919 show six individuals still wearing first style Crosses.[76] In any event, these early Distinguished Service Crosses are extremely rare. A roster also exists of individuals awarded the second style Distinguished Service Cross—matching recipients with numbered Crosses—but medals numbered above 8000 cannot be traced.

The last historical development in the evolution of the Distinguished Service Cross occurred in 1963, when Congress enlarged the award criteria governing the decoration. Since there was no declaration of war against North Vietnam (or their Viet Cong allies), it was not legally possible for American soldiers fighting in Southeast Asia to be "engaged in action *against an enemy of the United States.*" (emphasis supplied) Consequently, Congress added two new categories to the award criteria for the Distinguished Service Cross so that it could be awarded for extraordinary heroism "while engaged in military operations involving conflict with an opposing foreign force, or while serving with friendly foreign forces engaged in an armed conflict against an opposing armed force in which the United States is not a belligerent party."[77] This 1963 amendment continues to be important as the United States is unlikely to declare war in the future.

First Recipients

The first soldiers to be awarded the Distinguished Service Cross were Second Lieutenant John N. Greene, Sergeant William

N. Norton, and Private Patrick Walsh. All were members of the 1st Division and were presented their decorations by General John J. Pershing on March 18, 1918.

Selected Recipients (Chronological)

World War I

WILLIAM MITCHELL: MARCH 26, 1918

William "Billy" Mitchell was awarded the Distinguished Service Cross for "displaying bravery far beyond that required by his position as Chief of Air Service, 1st Army, American Expeditionary Force."[78]

Born in 1879, Mitchell enlisted in a Wisconsin Volunteer Army regiment as a 19-year-old private in 1898. A month later, he had obtained a commission and was the youngest second lieutenant in the Army's Signal Corps. Mitchell subsequently served in Alaska, Cuba and the Philippines. In 1915, now Captain Mitchell was assigned to the aerial section of the Signal Corps and, after learning to fly in 1916, was send to France as an observer.

When America entered World War I in April 1917, Mitchell was promoted to lieutenant colonel and appointed as the "air officer" of the American Expeditionary Force. In May 1918, now Colonel Mitchell became the first U.S. officer to fly over German lines. In September, he led a raid of 1,476 American, French, British and Italian aircraft against the St. Mihiel salient, and subsequently led other air raids on German rear areas during the Meuse-Argonne campaign.

At the end of World War I, Mitchell became an outspoken advocate of airpower, and angered many in the Army with his call for the creation of a separate air force. After the crash of the dirigible USS *Shenandoah* in September 1925, Mitchell loudly proclaimed that the War and Navy Departments were guilty of "incompetency, criminal negligence and almost treasonable administration of the national defense."[79] This outburst led to his high-profile court-martial for insubordination. After his conviction (his punishment was to be suspended from rank, command, and duty for five years), Mitchell resigned from the Army on February 1, 1926.[80] But he continued trumpet loudly the superiority of airpower until he died in 1936.

EDWARD V. RICKENBACKER: APRIL 29, 1918, MAY 17, 22, 28 AND 30, 1918, SEPTEMBER 14, 15 AND 25, 1918

Fighter pilot "Eddie" Rickenbacker was the top ace of World War I and earned an unprecedented eight Distinguished Service Crosses — one of which was later cancelled so that it could be upgraded to the Medal of Honor.

Born in 1890 in Ohio, Rickenbacker worked building railroad cars at age 14. He had a knack for mechanics and became interested in automobiles and internal combustion engines. By the time he was sixteen years old, Rickenbacker was racing cars professionally. He made many appearances at the Indianapolis 500 and, in 1917, Rickenbacker set a land speed record of 134 miles per hour at Daytona Beach, Florida.

With America's entry into World War I, Rickenbacker tried to join the Army in early May 1917. Initially, he was rejected because of his lack of formal education, but Rickenbacker was persistent. He enlisted in the Signal Enlisted Reserve Corps on May 25 and, after Rickenbacker arrived in France, his reputation as a mechanic and driver led Gen. John J. Pershing to assign Rickenbacker to his motor pool.

Sergeant Rickenbacker soon decided that wanted to fly. His job with Pershing brought him into contact with Colonel William "Billy" Mitchell who, impressed with Rickenbacker, arranged his transfer to the Air Service. Rickenbacker then attended pilot training in Tours, France, and pinned on pilot wings in October 1917. Given his unusual knowledge of gasoline engines, Rickenbacker was made the engineer officer at the U.S. flying school at Issoudun.

But he wanted to be a fighter pilot and lobbied successfully for a transfer to the 94th Aero Pursuit Squadron, the famous "Hat in the Ring" squadron, in March 1918.

Rickenbacker shot down his first German plane in April 1918 and became an ace in May with his fifth aerial victory. One on occasion, a lone Rickenbacker attacked seven German fighters and shot down two, for which he later received the Medal of Honor. By the end of World War I, then Major Rickenbacker had shot down 26 planes and was the top U.S. ace. The citations for his eight Distinguished Service Crosses follow:

on April 29, 1918, he attacked an enemy Albatross monoplane, and after a vigorous fight, in which he followed his foe into German territory, he succeeded in shooting it down near Vigneulles-les-Hatton Chatel....

on May 17, 1918, he attacked three Albatross enemy planes, shooting one down in the vicinity of Richecourt, France, and forcing the others to retreat over their own lines....

on May 22, 1918, he attacked three Albatross monoplanes 4,000 meters over St. Mihiel, France. He drove them back into German territory, separated one from the group, and shot it down near Flirey....

on May 28, 1918, he sighted a group of two battle planes and four monoplanes, German planes, which he at once attacked vigorously, shooting down one and dispersing the others....

on May 30, 1918, 4,000 meters over Jaulny, France, he attacked a group of five enemy planes. After a violent battle, he shot down one plane and drove the others away....

on September 14, 1918, in the region of Villecy, he attacked four Fokker enemy planes at an altitude of 3,000 meters. After a sharp and hot action, he succeeded in shooting one down in flames and dispersing the other three....

on September 15, 1918, in the region of Bois-de-Wavrille, he encountered six enemy planes, who were attacking four Spads, which were below them. Undeterred by their superior numbers, he unhesitatingly attacked them and succeeded in shooting one down in flames and completely breaking the formation of the others....

on September 25, 1918, near Billy, France, while on voluntary patrol over the lines he attacked seven enemy planes (five type Fokker, protecting two type Halberstadt). Disregarding the odds against him, he dived on them and shot down one of the Fokkers out of control. He then attacked one of the Halberstadts and sent it down also.[81]

This last award of the Distinguished Service Cross was cancelled after Rickenbacker was awarded the Medal of Honor for the same action. President Herbert Hoover presented the nation's highest decoration to Rickenbacker on November 6, 1930.

After leaving active duty in January 1919, Rickenbacker started an automobile company in Detroit and developed a reputation as an innovator. In 1926, he purchased the Indianapolis Speedway and joined General Motors as an engineer. Ten years later, in 1935, General Motors put Rickenbacker in charge of its money-losing subsidiary, Eastern Airlines. Rickenbacker's people skills and business savvy soon returned Eastern to profitability.

During World War II, the Army asked Rickenbacker to visit the Pacific theater. In 1942, he was feared dead after the B-17 Flying Fortress in which he was a passenger crashed into the ocean 600 miles from land. But Rickenbacker's luck held and he and seven other men were rescued from a life raft three weeks later. In the highly acclaimed *Rickenbacker, An Autobiography*,[82] Rickenbacker remembered that he and his companions survived on rainwater and fish and by capturing and eating a bird that had the ill-luck to land on their raft.

Rickenbacker returned to Eastern Airlines and ran it successfully until retiring in 1963. He died in Switzerland in 1973.[83]

JANE JEFFREY: JULY 15, 1918

Civilian Nurse Jane Jeffrey was one of four women to be awarded the Distinguished Service Cross in World War I. Jeffrey was a nurse with American Red Cross Hospital No. 107, located at Jouy-sur-Morin (Seine-et-Marne), France. Her citation reads, in part:

While she was on duty ... Miss Jeffrey was severely wounded by an exploding bomb during an air raid. She showed utter disregard for her own safety by refusing to leave her post, though suffering great pain from her wounds. Her courageous attitude and devotion to the task of helping others was inspiring to all her associates.

Born in England in 1881, Jane Jeffrey was a British citizen and registered nurse. She was living in Dorchester, Massachusetts and caring for a sick relative when she volunteered to serve in France as a Red Cross nurse in October 1917. Jeffrey was sent to Bordeaux, France, where she served before being transferred to Red Cross Hospital No. 107 at Jouy-sur-Morin.

While in France, Jeffrey found difficult conditions. Tents housed the hospital wards and there was no plumbing. The large number of wounded soldiers strained the ability of doctors and nurses to treat them.[84]

After the war, Jeffrey married Alvan Bolster Ricker of Poland Spring, Maine. Jeffrey died in 1960.

ARTHUR S. CHAMPENY: SEPTEMBER 12, 1918, MAY 11–14, 1944, AND SEPTEMBER 5, 1950

Arthur Seymour Champeny is the only man in history to be awarded the Distinguished Service Cross in three wars. Then Captain Champeny received his first award for gallantry in action near St. Mihiel, France in September 1918, and his second Distinguished Service Cross for heroism while serving as an infantry colonel near Infante Santa Maria, Italy in May 1944. Champeny was awarded his third Distinguished Service Cross for extraordinary heroism near Haman, Korea, in September 1950. His three citations follow:

for extraordinary heroism ... September 12, 1918. Assisting the battalion commander, who had been severely wounded in the early fighting, he maintained the liaison personally, making many journeys himself through heavy shelling. When the battalion commander had been evacuated, he assumed command, and moved the battalion to its new position....[85]

for extraordinary heroism ... while serving with the 351st Infantry Regiment, 88th Infantry Division ...from 11 to 14 May 1944. Colonel Cham-

peny's outstanding leadership, personal bravery, and zealous devotion to duty exemplify the highest traditions of the military forces of the United States...."[86]

for extraordinary heroism ... while serving as commanding officer, 24th Infantry Regiment, 25th Infantry Division ... on 5 September 1950. Colonel Champeny came under direct attack by a numerically superior enemy force which had broken through the Regimental Sector. Confusion developed throughout the area and in the burning village where the Regimental Command Post was located. Small enemy groups infiltrated the village. Colonel Champeny directed and supervised the withdrawal of the depleted Regiment and the Regimental Command Post. When the new Regimental Command Post had been established, Colonel Champeny returned to reorganize battered elements of the Regiment. He came under fire and was wounded twice. Although severely wounded, he gave instructions for organizing the new defensive positions and transmitted the plans to Division Headquarters. His military poise and battle courage inspired the regiment to withstand the assault.[87]

Although described as an officer "of amazing energy and courage," Champeny also was controversial; his command of the all-black 24th Infantry Regiment in Korea was not without problems.[88] Promoted to brigadier general in 1951, Champeny returned to Korea as an adviser to the South Korean armed forces. When he retired in 1953, Champeny also had been awarded — in addition to three awards of the Distinguished Service Cross — the Silver Star and five Purple Hearts. Champeny died in 1979. He was 85 years old.

GEORGE C. KENNEY: OCTOBER 9, 1918, AND JULY 23, 1942–JANUARY 8, 1943

First Lieutenant Kenney was a pilot in the 91st Aero Squadron when he received his first Distinguished Service Cross. He subsequently had a distinguished career as an airman and retired as a four-star Air Force general in 1951. His citation reads, in part:

for extraordinary heroism near Jamets, France. This officer gave proof of his bravery and devotion to duty when he was attacked by a superior number of aircraft. He accepted combat, destroyed one plane, and drove the others off. Notwithstanding that the enemy returned and attacked again in strong numbers, he continued his mission and enabled his observer to secure information of great value.[89]

Born in Canada in 1889, George Churchill Kenney grew up in Massachusetts and enlisted in the Army as a flying cadet in June 1917. During World War I, he flew 75 combat missions in France and is credited with shooting down two German airplanes while with the 91st Aero Squadron.

In the 1930s, then-Lt. Colonel Kenney was assigned to the Air Corps Tactical School, where he focused his attention on improving low-altitude bombing. When World War II began, Kenney quickly established himself as one of American's top airman. After being promoted to major general, Kenny assumed command of General Douglas MacArthur's air forces in Southwest Asia in July 1942. He was wearing three stars — and was Commander, Allied Air Forces, Southwest Pacific Area — when he was awarded an oak leaf cluster to his Distinguished Service Cross (for extraordinary heroism in the New Guinea campaign between July 23, 1942 and January 8, 1943).[90] Kenney finished the war as a four-star general and retired from active duty in 1951. He died in Florida in 1977.[91]

LEONARD C. ST. JAMES: OCTOBER 9–11, 1918

Private First Class St. James received his Distinguished Service Cross (No. 3421) for "extraordinary heroism in action near Romagne, France" when he "repeatedly crossed an open area 500 meters wide under intense machine gun fire." St. James was a runner "carrying messages to battalion headquarters" across an open space "which afforded absolutely no protection from German machine gunners." On one of his trips "across this fire swept area" (called "Death Valley" by the soldiers of the 32d Division), St. James "came upon a wounded man to whom he cooly ad-

ministered first aid. He then picked up the wounded soldier and cooly carried him to the first aid station in spite of the most intense machine gun fire from the flanks."[92]

Leonard Clifford St. James was born in Whittmore, Michigan and enlisted in the National Guard on July 19, 1917. He was nineteen years old when he sailed for France in February 1918. In addition to the Distinguished Service Cross, St. James was also awarded the French Croix de Guerre with gilt star for being "an admirably courageous soldier."[93]

AULBERT D. COX: MARCH 3, 1919

Sergeant Aulbert D. Cox was awarded the Distinguished Service Cross for extraordinary heroism at Vistofka, North Russia in March 1919. He was serving with Company D, 339th Infantry, 85th Division when, "upon learning that two companies of the enemy had worked their way to the rear of the allied lines, Sergeant Cox, a patient in a hospital, voluntarily left his bed, secured a Lewis gun, and successfully held off the enemy until assistance came."[94]

World War II

VIRGINIA HALL: MARCH–SEPTEMBER 1944

Virginia "Dindy" Hall was the sole civilian female recipient of the Distinguished Service Cross in World War II; no woman has received the decoration since then. She was a civilian intelligence officer in the Special Operations Branch, Office of Strategic Services. Her citation reads, in part:

> Miss Virginia Hall ... voluntarily and served in enemy-occupied France from March to September 1944. Despite the fact that she was well known to the Gestapo because of previous activities, Miss Hall established and maintained radio communications with London headquarters, supplying valuable operational and intelligence information. With the help of a Jedburgh team, she organized, armed, and trained three battalions of French resistance forces in the Department of the Haute Loire. Working in a region infested with enemy troops and continually at the risk of

capture, torture, and death, she directed the resistance forces with extraordinary success in acts of sabotage and guerrilla warfare against enemy troops, installations, and communications. Miss Hall displayed rare courage, perseverance, and ingenuity. Her efforts contributed materially to the successful operations of the resistance forces in support of the Allied Expeditionary Forces in the liberation of France.[95]

Born in Baltimore, Maryland, in April 1906, Hall attended Radcliffe and Barnard College and studied in Austria, France and Germany. Fluent in French, Italian and German, Hall hoped for a career with the Foreign Service, and managed to obtain a job as a Consular Service clerk at the U.S. Embassy in Warsaw in 1931. But, while stationed in Turkey in 1932, Hall accidentally shot herself in the left leg while snipe hunting. The injury required her leg to be amputated just below the knee and required her to wear an artificial leg for the rest of her life. The injury also dashed any hopes she may have had for a career as a diplomat, and she resigned from the Department of State in 1939.

General Curtis E. LeMay was awarded the Distinguished Service Cross for his extraordinary heroism on August 17, 1943 (U.S. Air Force).

When World War II began in Europe in September 1939, Hall was in Paris. She joined the Ambulance Service before the fall of France and, after the German victory in 1940, traveled to London where she joined the British Special Operations Executive. Returning to France in August 1941, Hall spent the next fifteen months working with the French Resistance in Vichy-controlled territory and in German-occupied France. Luckily, Hall managed to escape to Spain in November 1942, after the Germans suddenly seized all of France.

She worked for a short time in Madrid before returning to London, where she was decorated with the Order of the British Empire. In March 1944, Hall left her British employers to join the newly formed U.S. Office of Strategic Services Special Operations Branch. She immediately asked to return to France to aid the French in their struggle against the Germans. Her request was granted and Hall was taken by boat to Brittany (she could not parachute into France because of her wooden leg). Hall soon linked up with the French Resistance in central France and, affectionately known to her French colleagues as the "Limping Lady," she mapped drop zones for supplies and commandos, found safe houses, and linked up with Jedburgh personnel after the Allies landed in Normandy in June 1944."[96]

Brigadier General William J. "Wild Bill" Donovan, head of the OSS and a recipient of the Medal of Honor in World War I, personally awarded Hall the Distinguished Service Cross on September 27, 1945. Hall married a fellow OSS agent, Paul Gaston Goillot, in 1950. The next year, she joined the Central Intelligence Agency, for whom she worked until retiring in 1966. Virginia Hall Goillot died in Rockville, Maryland, in July 1982. She was 76 years old.

Vietnam

JOHN L. BAHNSEN: JANUARY 23, 1969

Major "Doc" Bahnsen received his decoration for heroism in Vietnam while in com-

Brigadier General John L. "Doc" Bahnsen was awarded the Distinguished Service Cross for extraordinary heroism in Vietnam (U.S. Army).

mand of Air Cavalry Troop, 11th Cavalry Regiment.

On January 23, 1969, Bahnsen landed his helicopter in an area containing a large hostile force, and then "reconnoitered and marked a landing zone for a rifle platoon." As he left the area, Bahnsen "saw fifteen communists and engaged them with his rifle, firing from the window of his helicopter. He killed two of the enemy and remained at a low altitude to direct additional fire upon them until his crew chief was seriously wounded by the hostile barrage which struck their ship." As his citation explains, "Major Bahnsen evacuated the crew chief, refueled and rearmed, and sped back to the battle. Again taking the communists under fire and forcing them to a confined area, he marked their position and directed five air strikes against them, while at the same time controlling four separate rifle platoons." After "intense enemy fire crippled his ship," Bahnsen was forced to return to base and "acquire another aircraft." After he landed

his helicopter "to guide in the lift ships carrying an additional infantry unit," Bahnsen then remained on the ground, and "led a rifle platoon through dense terrain to personally capture two enemy who were attempting to escape. While the captives were evacuated by helicopter," Bahnsen "remained on the ground and led the squad two kilometers back to friendly positions."[97]

Born in Albany, Georgia, on November 8, 1934, "Doc" (the nickname comes from his grandfather, who was a veterinarian) Bahnsen graduated from the U.S. Military Academy in 1956. He subsequently completed the infantry officer basic course, and fixed-wing and rotary-wing training.

After completing the Army's Command and General Staff College at Fort Leavenworth, then Captain Bahnsen deployed to Vietnam in October 1965, where he flew helicopter gunships out of Bien Hoa Air Base as part of the 118th Aviation Company. He also served with the 12th Combat Aviation Group before returning to the United States in late 1966.

After a tour in the Pentagon, Major Bahnsen returned to Vietnam in October 1968. He joined the famous 11th Armored Cavalry Regiment ("Blackhorse") as the commander of the unit's Air Cavalry Troop. This unit consisted of UH-1H utility aircraft, OH-6 scout helicopters, AH-1 attack gunships and a platoon of infantry, plus an administrative and support element. Soldiers in Bahnsen's unit saw almost daily combat over the next 13 months and Bahnsen himself fought in the air (from his UH-1H helicopter) and on the ground; he often led his soldiers in infantry operations against the enemy. Bahnsen's reputation as a combat leader (he encouraged his soldiers, "Fight fiercely") resulted in his being given command of 1st Armored Squadron — and made him the only major to command a squadron in the 11th Armored Cavalry Regiment during the Vietnam war.

After departing from Vietnam in September 1969 (with a Distinguished Service Cross and a Legion of Merit in addition to his four

Silver Stars), Bahnsen served in a variety of assignments and locations. He commanded an armor battalion in Germany and an aviation brigade at Fort Rucker. After being promoted to one-star rank, Bahnsen served as the assistant division commander, 2nd Armored Division, Fort Hood, Texas, and chief of staff, Combined Field Army ROK/U.S. in Korea. His final assignment was as the chief of staff, III Armored Corps, Fort Hood, Texas. "Doc" Bahnsen retired from active duty in 1986. In 2007, he published *American Warrior*, a memoir of his combat experiences in Vietnam; Gen. H. Norman Schwarzkopf lauded it as "among the best books on the Vietnam War."[98]

See below for details on Bahnsen's Silvers Stars and Chapter 3 for information on his Distinguished Flying Crosses and Bronze Star Medals.

John Paul Vann: April 23–24, 1972

John Paul Vann is the only civilian recipient of the Distinguished Service Cross for combat heroism in Vietnam. He was a civilian employee of the Agency for International Development, Department of State, and made history in Vietnam as the first civilian to command U.S. Army troops in combat. Vann's Distinguished Service Cross was posthumously awarded because he was killed in action on June 9, 1972. The citation reads, in part:

> During an intense enemy attack by mortar, artillery and guided missiles on the 22d Army of the Republic of Vietnam Division forward command post at Tan Canh, Mr. Vann chose to have his light helicopter land in order to assist the Command Group. After landing, he ordered his helicopter to begin evacuating civilian employees and the more than fifty wounded soldiers while he remained on the ground to assist in evacuating the wounded and provide direction to the demoralized troops. With total disregard for his own safety, Mr. Vann continuously exposed himself to enemy artillery and mortar fire. By personally assisting the wounded and giving them encouragement, he assured a calm and orderly evacuation. As the enemy fire increased in accuracy and tempo, he set the example by continuing

> to assist in carrying the wounded to the exposed helipad. His skillful command and control of the medical evacuation ships during the extremely intense enemy artillery fire enabled the maximum number of soldiers and civilians to be safely evacuated. On the following day the enemy launched a combined infantry tank team attack at the 22nd Division Headquarters compound. Shortly thereafter, the Army of the Republic of Vietnam (ARVN) defense collapsed, enemy tanks penetrated the compound, and the enemy forces organized .51 caliber anti-aircraft positions in and around the compound area. To evade the enemy, the United States advisors moved under heavy automatic weapons fire to an area approximately 500 meters away from the compound. Completely disregarding the intense small arms and .51 caliber anti-aircraft fire and the enemy tanks, Mr. Vann directed his helicopter toward the general location of the U.S. personnel, who were forced to remain in a concealed position. In searching for the advisors' location, Vann's helicopter had to maintain an altitude and speed which made it extremely vulnerable to all forms of enemy fire. Undaunted, he continued his search until he located the advisors' position. Making an approach under minimal conditions, he landed and quickly pulled three United States advisors into the aircraft. As the aircraft began to ascend, five ARVN soldiers were clinging to the skids. Although the total weight far exceeded the maximum allowable for the light helicopter, Mr. Vann chose to save the ARVN personnel holding on to the skids by having the helicopter maneuver without sharp evasive action. Consequently, the aircraft sustained numerous hits. In order to return to Tan Canh as soon as possible to save the remaining advisors and to save the soldiers clinging to the skids, Mr. Vann detoured his aircraft from Kontum to a nearby airfield. Throughout this time Mr. Vann was directing air strikes on enemy tanks and anti-aircraft positions. While en route back to Tam Canh, Mr. Vann's helicopter was struck by heavy anti-aircraft fire, which forced it to land. Throughout the day Mr. Vann assisted in extracting other advisors and soldiers in the Dak To area. On one such occasion another group of ARVN soldiers attempted to cling to one side of his helicopter, causing it to crash. Undaunted by these occurrences, Mr. Vann continued directing air strikes and maneuvering friendly troops to safe areas. Because of his fearless and tireless efforts, Mr. Vann was di-

rectly responsible for saving hundreds of personnel from the enemy onslaught.

Born in Norfolk, Virginia, in July 1924, John Paul Vann served more than 20 years as a soldier before retiring as a lieutenant colonel. While he did serve as a military advisor to the South Vietnamese Army from 1962 to 1963, Vann is best known for his time in Vietnam as a civilian official in the Agency for International Development. Neil Sheehan's Pulitzer Prize–winning *A Bright and Shining Lie: John Paul Vann and America in Vietnam* examines Vann's remarkable career as a soldier and civilian.

As a civilian, Vann was ineligible for the Medal of Honor and this explains, at least in part, why he was awarded the Distinguished Service Cross. But President Richard M. Nixon did honor Vann by posthumously awarding him America's highest civilian award, the Presidential Medal of Freedom, on June 18, 1972.[99]

Afghanistan

Brendan W. O'Connor: June 24, 2006

Then Sergeant First Class O'Connor was decorated for his heroism under fire in Panjawal District, Kandahar Province, Afghanistan. While serving as the senior medical sergeant in a Special Forces operational team, O'Connor "was instrumental in keeping his team alive during an intense battle with more than 250 Taliban fighters."

On June 23, 2006, while making a temporary stop during a patrol in Khandahar Province, O'Connor's 16-man team and the 46 Afghan National Army soldiers accompanying them "were attacked from all sides with small-arms fire, heavy machine guns, rocket propelled grenades, recoilless rifles, and mortars." In the 17½ hours of combat that followed, O'Connor and his fellow soldiers "fought off wave and wave of Taliban attackers" and the enemy was so near that the Americans could hear "cursing and taunting" from them.

After learning that two soldiers had been wounded at another location, O'Connor took

Master Sergeant Brendan W. O'Connor was awarded the Distinguished Service Cross for his heroism during an intense battle with more than 250 Taliban fighters on June 24, 2006 (courtesy Brendan O'Connor).

off his body armor and, despite heavy enemy machine-gun fire, low-crawled to treat the wounded men. When he later stood up and carried one of the wounded men to a safer area, the automatic weapons fire was so intense that another soldier later remarked that it "mowed the grass" around O'Connor.[100] O'Connor's citation reads:

> For extraordinary heroism in combat as the Senior Medical Sergeant for Special Forces Operational Detachment Alpha 765, Company A, 2d Battalion, 7th Special Forces Group (Airborne) ... on 24 June 2006, during Operation Kaiki, Sergeant O'Connor led a quick-reaction force to reinforce a surrounded patrol and rescue two wounded comrades. He maneuvered his force through Taliban positions and crawled alone and unprotected, under enemy machine-gun fire to reach the wounded soldiers. He provided medical care while exposed to heavy vol-

umes of Taliban fire, then carried one of the wounded 150 meters across open ground to an area of temporary cover. He climbed over a wall three times, in plain view of the enemy, to assist the wounded soldiers in seeking cover while bullets pounded the structure around them. Sergeant O'Connor assumed duties as the detachment operations sergeant and led the consolidation of three friendly elements, each surrounded, isolated, and receiving fire from all directions.

Born in June 1960 in West Point, New York, Brendan Wright O'Conner grew up in Moorestown, New Jersey. After graduating from high school in 1978, O'Connor enlisted in the Army Reserve's 11th Special Forces Group in September 1979. He was commissioned the following year and subsequently served in a variety of infantry and special forces assignments in the Army Reserve until 1994, when he resigned his commission and enlisted in the active Army as a special forces medic.

In 1996, O'Connor was assigned to 7th Special Forces Group, where he served as a medical sergeant in Operational Detachment-Alpha Team 765. After a tour at the John F. Kennedy Special Warfare Center and School, O'Connor returned to Alpha 765 where he served as both medical sergeant and operations sergeant until November 2007.

In December 2007, now Master Sergeant O'Connor was assigned as the command surgeon's senior enlisted medical advisor in the 7th Special Forces Group. Two years later, O'-Connor was assigned to U.S. Army Cadet Command as Reserve Officer Training Corps senior military science instructor.

O'Connor was the second soldier to be awarded the Distinguished Service Cross in Operation ENDURING FREEDOM.

AIR FORCE CROSS

Overview

Establishing Authority and Effective Dates: The Air Force Cross was authorized by Congress on July 9, 1960 (Public Law 86–593).

This law did not, however, create a new decoration. Rather, it permitted the Air Force to have its own design for the Army Distinguished Service Cross created by Congress in July 1918. Consequently, the Air Force Cross is, in fact, the Air Force version of the Distinguished Service Cross.

Criteria: The Air Force Cross may be awarded to any person who, while serving in any capacity with the U.S. Air Force, distinguishes himself by extraordinary heroism (1) in action against an enemy of the United States; (2) while engaged in military operations involving conflict with an opposing foreign force; or (3) while serving with friendly foreign forces engaged in an armed conflict against an opposing armed force in which the United States is not a belligerent party.

While the Air Force Cross is second only to the Medal of Honor as an award for combat heroism, the Air Force interprets the phrase "while engaged in military operations involving conflict" to permit the Air Force Cross to be awarded *for non-combat valor*, provided the act of heroism occurred in a combat theater. This is very different from the Army's interpretation of the identical language governing the award of the Distinguished Service Cross, as the Army's view is that the act of extraordinary heroism must occur in *direct combat*. As a practical matter, however, all but two Air Force Crosses have been awarded for heroism in direct combat. However, as two awards have been made for non-combat heroism, this means that the award criteria for the Air Force Cross and the Airman's Medal "overlap," since the latter is the top Air Force award for non-combat valor.[101]

Order of Precedence: The Air Force Cross is worn after the Air Force Medal of Honor and before all other decorations and medals.

Devices: Additional awards of the Air Force Cross are reflected by bronze (and silver) oak leaf clusters.

Designer: Eleanor Cox, an Air Force civilian employee, designed the decoration.

Top: Air Force Cross (obverse). *Above:* Air Force Cross (reverse).

Thomas Hudson Jones, a civilian employee at the Army's Heraldic Branch (today's Institute of Heraldry), took Cox's sketch and sculpted the new award in plaster. Jones (1892–1969),

an accomplished artist, designed a number of U.S. decorations and medals during his career, including the Airman's Medal, Army of Occupation of Germany service medal, Korean Service Medal, and National Defense Service Medal.

Description and Symbolism
Obverse

A bronze cross and on it an American eagle with its wings displayed, superimposed on a cloud formation; both are finished with a gold patina. The eagle and cloud are encircled by a laurel wreath finished in green patina with the leaves edged in gold. The design intentionally follows the shape of the Army Distinguished Service Cross, so as to preserve a link between the two decorations; the eagle and cloud formation are taken from the Air Force Coat of Arms.

Reverse

The reverse is plain, except for a rectangular box for engraving the recipient's name.

Ribbon

The Air Force Cross ribbon measures 1⅜ inches in width and consists of a ⅛ inch red stripe, a ¹⁄₁₆ inch white stripe, a one-inch Brittany blue stripe, a ¹⁄₁₆ inch white stripe, and a ⅛ inch red stripe. This makes it very similar to the ribbon of the Army Distinguished Service Cross, except that the Brittany blue is a lighter shade.

Historical Background

Although the Air Force continued using Army awards after becoming an independent service in 1947, Air Force leaders wanted their own distinctive awards by the late 1950s. While it took some years for this to occur, the final result was an Air Force version of the Medal of Honor and Distinguished Service Medal, an Airman's Medal — and an Air Force Cross.

In early 1958, Ms. Eleanor Cox, an Air

Force civilian employee, began working on a design for the pendant for the Air Force version of the Army Distinguished Service Cross. Recognizing that the new award was closely linked to the older Army decoration, Cox intentionally modeled her first suggested design after the Distinguished Service Cross. One of her proposed designs was simply the Army cross with the Air Force Coat of Arms substituted for the older award's eagle motif. Another design was a much plainer and simpler looking cross with the Air Force Coat of Arms centered on it.

When Cox's drawings were presented to the Army's Heraldic Branch for comment, however, that organization severely criticized her work. The chief problem, said the Army's heraldic experts, was that the relatively new Air

James "Jimmy" Jabara stands on his F-86 Sabre in April 1953. Jabara was the first American jet ace and was awarded the Distinguished Service Cross during the Korean War (U.S. Air Force).

Force Coat of Arms had been used on so many flags, badges and insignia that it was now "preferable" to avoid using it once again for the new Air Force Cross.

While the actual impact of the Army's criticism on Cox and her Air Force superiors is not known, they certainly had some influence since, in late 1959, Cox had radically reworked her proposed design. For the obverse, she retained the bronze cross. But she took only the eagle and cloud from the Air Force Coat of Arms — which she placed in the center of the cross. For the remainder of the obverse, Cox encircled the eagle and cloud with a green wreath of laurel leaves, the traditional decoration of heroes in antiquity. For the reverse of the decoration, she proposed that it be left plain, except for a rectangular block for engraving the recipient's name.

The Air Force approved Eleanor Cox's work and submitted it to the Commission of Fine Arts for its consideration. That organization, concluding that Cox's sketch had "merit," approved the design on January 20, 1960. Thomas H. "Tom" Jones, a civilian employee and sculptor at the Heraldic Branch, used Cox's drawings to produce the plaster casts of the Air Force Cross and then hand carried them to Medallic Art Company of New York. Jones' plaster images — four times the size of the actual metal pendant — were used by Medallic Art to produce the first Air Force Crosses in mid–1961. After some additional modifications to the design, the Air Force formally accepted Medallic's work in late September 1962 and official production of the Air Force Cross began. In December, President Kennedy presented the first cross — a posthumous award — to the widow of Major Rudolf Anderson, who had been killed during the Cuban Missile Crisis.[102]

A final comment about the effective award date of the Air Force Cross. While the decoration is awarded for extraordinary heroism occurring after July 6, 1960 (the date Congress established the new decoration), an award based on an earlier act of gallantry may be made if the recommendation for it was never acted upon or was lost. In fact, two awards of the Air Force Cross for heroism during World War II have been made; in both cases, the original recommendations for the Army Distinguished Service Cross were lost or misplaced and, when the Air Force finally acted upon the recommendations in 1968 and 1983, respectively, it determined that it was more appropriate to award the newer decoration to the two World War II recipients.[103]

First Recipient

The first Air Force Cross was posthumously awarded to Major Rudolf Anderson. He was a U-2 pilot who was killed when his airplane was shot down by a Cuban surface-to-air missile on October 27, 1962 — during the Cuban Missile Crisis. President John F. Kennedy presented the award to Anderson's widow in December 1962.[104]

The first living recipient of the Air Force Cross was then Lt. Col. Robinson Risner, who received the decoration for extraordinary heroism on April 3–4, 1965.

Selected Recipients

Vietnam

ROBINSON RISNER: APRIL 3–4, 1965 AND OCTOBER 31–DECEMBER 15, 1965

Lieutenant Colonel Risner was awarded two Air Force Crosses during the Vietnam War. The first was for his heroism in the air; the second was for his valor as a prisoner of war in North Vietnam. His citations read, in part:

> for extraordinary heroism ... as mission commander and air coordinator for air strikes in North Vietnam on 3 and 4 April 1965. On each of these two days, he directed 90 aircraft against the railway and highway bridge at Thanh Hoa, North Vietnam. On the April 3rd mission, Colonel Risner's aircraft was severely damaged by heavy ground fire, but with this cockpit filled with smoke, he managed to return to a friendly airfield where he landed safely.

> for extraordinary heroism ... while a Prisoner of War in North Vietnam from 31 October to 15 December 1965.

Even before Lt. Col. "Robbie" Risner received his first Air Force Cross — and became the first living recipient of the decoration — he was a "larger than life" personality in the Air Force. A Korean War ace (eight victories), a test pilot, and an aviation record holder (he had set a transatlantic speed record while flying the Lindbergh Anniversary Flight in 1957), Risner received his first Air Force Cross after being shot down over North Vietnam and rescued at sea. He was the subject of a *Time* cover story that "extolled his achievements and portrayed him as an exemplar of the dedicated and skilled American fighting man in Vietnam."[105] Consequently, when Risner was shot down on September 16, 1965 — only a month after returning to his unit in Thailand — the North Vietnamese had already heard about him when they captured him and brought him to the "Hanoi Hilton." As the *Time* magazine article had revealed that Risner had led several air missions that had destroyed key bridges and killed many enemy soldiers, the North Vietnamese were anxious to extract as much information from Robbie Risner as they could. He was interrogated for 10 days but refused to answer questions, even when told that he would be burned at the stake if he did not cooperate.

While the North Vietnamese initially gave up on Risner, they redoubled their efforts between October 31st and December 15th. Between those dates — the period during which his extraordinary heroism brought him a second Air Force Cross — Risner was brutally tortured. According to the definitive book on the U.S. prisoner of war experience during the Vietnam War, Robbie Risner "absorbed as much or more punishment between November 1965 and the summer of 1966 as many of the men would face during their entire PW [Prisoner of War] term."[106] The North Vietnamese used every tactic and "correctional device" to break him. For 32 consecutive days, he was in leg stocks and received only one piece of bread and a sip of water as his daily ration. The enemy made him lie down in his own filth when he lost control of his bowels. After being released from the leg stocks, the torture sessions continued. At one point, the North Vietnamese asked Risner to read a prepared statement on the camp's radio. When he refused, the enemy forced Risner on his knees for two days without food or water. Determined to prevent the North Vietnamese from breaking him, Risner contemplated killing himself or cutting his hand so that he could not write a confession. But, understanding that "it was my voice they wanted most," he tried to damage his vocal chords. When striking his larynx did not work, Risner obtained a small amount of lye and gargled with it, hoping the acid would destroy his voice. Over the next few years, the enemy repeatedly brutalized Robbie Risner; by 1968, "unremitting threats and torture had forced him finally to produce incriminating propaganda tapes and statements."[107] But, as fellow prisoner of war Jerry Coffee later wrote, "Robbie lost battles — as we all would — but he never lost the war." Risner was released from captivity on February 12, 1973 and, within a year, had published a memoir about his seven years of captivity in Hanoi.[108] Risner retired from the Air Force as a brigadier general — one of a handful of prisoners of war to achieve flag rank.

Besides his two awards of the Air Force Cross, Risner's decorations also include the Air Force Distinguished Service Medal, two Silver Stars, three Distinguished Flying Crosses, two Bronze Star Medals (for valor), three Air Medals and three Purple Hearts.

DELBERT W. FLEENER: DECEMBER 17, 1965

Then Captain Fleener was an early Vietnam War recipient of the Air Force Cross. He also is the only recipient of the decoration to be court-martialed for criminal conduct. His citation reads, in part:

Near the District of Binh Duong, Republic of Vietnam ... Captain Fleener was diverted from his original target to search for a pilot who had been shot down over hostile territory. With complete disregard for his personal safety, and though exposed to an intensive barrage of small arms, automatic weapons and antiaircraft fire, Captain Fleener continuously flew his aircraft at extremely low altitude over hostile positions in an effort to locate the downed pilot. The wreckage was sighted and almost entirely hidden by hostile forces attempting to camouflage the plane. With only four rockets, Captain Fleener made repeatedly low passes over the wreckage, firing one rocket on each pass. This daring and aggressive attack by Captain Fleener caused the hostile forces to disperse and temporarily denied them access to secret material and valuable radio equipment. After expending his ordnance, he landed his badly damaged aircraft on a nearby airstrip to refuel and rearm his aircraft. After returning to the area, he provided air cover for a helicopter crew which was attempting to discover the fate of the downed pilot. Although wounded in the right leg and in great plain, Captain Fleener continuously provided protection for the helicopter for over 30 minutes before being ordered to leave the area. While fighting off the loss of consciousness, Captain Fleener successfully flew his crippled aircraft into a remote airstrip and landed without further incident.

In addition to the Air Force Cross, Fleener also was awarded the Silver Star, two Distinguished Flying Crosses, 23 Air Medals, the Air Force Commendation Medal, and Purple Heart.

After being promoted, Major Fleener served as a pilot for U.S. Ambassador to Vietnam Ellsworth Bunker and was assigned to the 6250th Support Squadron based at Tan Son Nhut airfield near Saigon. In February 1970, cardboard boxes containing about 500 pounds of processed opium and 350 pounds of unprocessed opium were discovered in Fleener's living quarters in Saigon. An investigation revealed that Fleener was smuggling opium from Bangkok, Thailand to Saigon for later shipment to Hong Kong.

At his trial by general court-martial, Fleener insisted that "he was unaware that the boxes contained opium." Despite this claim, Major Fleener was convicted of seven offenses, including possession of opium and wrongful introduction of opium into a military installation. Fleener, who had served 18 years in the Air Force, was sentenced to 16 years confinement at hard labor, total forfeiture of all pay and allowances, and a dismissal — the officer equivalent of the dishonorable discharge. On appeal, Fleener argued that his "outstanding combat record" — and his Air Force Cross — entitled him to a reduction in his sentence. The appeals court agreed, and reduced Fleener's imprisonment to 12 years.[109]

JAMES H. KASLER: JUNE 22, 1966, AUGUST 6, 1966 AND AUGUST 1966–MARCH 1973

James H. Kasler received an unprecedented three awards of the Air Force Cross. His first two were for heroism while piloting an F-105. His last award was for his valor while a prisoner of war in North Vietnam. His three citations read, in part:

> extraordinary heroism as a pilot of an F-105 on 29 June 1966. On that date, Major Kasler was the mission commander of the second and largest wave of fighter-bombers to strike the heavily defended Hanoi petroleum products storage complex. Despite a seemingly impenetrable canopy of bursting projectiles thrown up by hostile defenses of this key facility, Major Kasler determinedly and precisely led his striking force to the exact release point where he and his followers placed their ordnance directly on target, causing it to erupt in a huge fireball of burning petroleum. Performing armed reconnaissance during his withdrawal, Major Kasler, with total disregard for his personal safety, personally destroyed five trucks before low fuel reserves forced him to terminate his attack....
>
> extraordinary heroism while piloting an F-105 ... on 6 August 1966. On that date, Major Kasler led a flight of fighter-bombers against a heavily defended target in evaluating a low level ordnance delivery tactic. While carrying out this hazardous mission, a wingman was forced to eject over unfriendly territory. Major Kasler located the downed airman and flew cover until perilous-

ly low fuel compelled him to leave. Refueling aerially, Major Kasler returned to relocate the downed pilot so he could direct rescue operations. At great risk to his own life, he explored the gun-infested countryside at tree-top level, valiantly searching, but was unable to locate his fellow American. Major Kasler's Thunderchief was hit by destructive ground fire during this valorous search, and he too ejected into unfriendly hands....

> extraordinary heroism while a prisoner of war in North Vietnam. Colonel Kasler accomplished an amazing feat of resistance against the North Vietnamese when they attempted to force him to meet a visiting delegation and appear before television and news cameras. Through personal fortitude and absolute heroism, he completely withstood the most brutal of Vietnamese tortures and caused his captors extreme embarrassment in their failure to gain useful propaganda statements.

Born on May 2, 1926, in South Bend, Indiana, "Jim" Kasler enlisted in 1943 and served as a tail gunner in a B-29 Superfortress during World War II. Although honorably discharged in 1946, Kasler immediately joined the Army Air Force Reserve and, in 1950, entered pilot training. He received his wings and commission as an Air Force second lieutenant in March 1951. Posted to South Korea in November 1951, Kasler flew more than 100 missions as an F-86 Sabre pilot until returning to the United States in June 1952. During this combat tour, he was credited with destroying six Russian MiG-15 fighters flown by North Korean pilots, making him an "ace."

Following the Korean War, Kasler completed a number of assignments, both in the U.S. and overseas. He also finished the college work he had started after World War II by finishing a B.S. at the University of Nebraska. Then Major Kasler deployed to Southeast Asia in February 1966 and, while flying his 91st mission, he was shot down over North Vietnam and taken prisoner on August 6, 1966. He spent the next 2,401 days in captivity. After being released from Hanoi on March 4, 1973, now Colonel Kasler resumed his Air Force career. His final assignment was as an F-

111 Aardvark pilot at Mountain Home Air Force Base, Idaho. Kasler retired from active duty in 1975.

Prior to being captured by the North Vietnamese in 1966, Kasler had received one Air Force Cross, one Silver Star, and one Bronze Star Medal for valor. In the 1973 ceremony in which Kasler was awarded his second and third Air Force Crosses, he also was presented with a second Silver Star, the Legion of Merit, and a second Bronze Star Medal for valor. In addition to these decorations, Kasler also holds nine Distinguished Flying Crosses, eleven Air Medals, and two Purple Hearts.[110]

DUANE D. HACKNEY: FEBRUARY 6, 1967

Airman 2d Class Hackney was the first living enlisted man to be awarded the Air Force Cross. He also is the most highly decorated airman of the Vietnam War. His citation reads:

> for extraordinary heroism ... as a paramedic on an unarmed HH-3E rescue helicopter near Mu Gia Pass, North Vietnam. Airman Hackney flew two sorties in a rescue effort of an American pilot downed in a heavily defended hostile area. On the first sortie, despite the presence of armed forces known to be hostile entrenched in the vicinity, Airman Hackney volunteered to be lowered into the jungle to search for the survivor. He searched until the controlling Search and Rescue agency ordered an evacuation of the rescue forces. On the second sortie, Airman Hackney located the downed pilot, who was hoisted into the helicopter. As the rescue force departed the area, intense and accurate 37-mm flak tore into the helicopter amidship, causing extensive damage and a raging fire aboard the craft. With complete disregard for his own safety, Airman Hackney fitted his parachute to the rescued man. In this moment of impending disaster, Airman Hackney chose to place his responsibility to the survivor above his own life. The courageous paramedic located another parachute for himself and had just slipped his arms through the harness when a second 37-mm round struck the crippled aircraft, sending it out of control. The force of the explosion blew Airman Hackney through the

open cargo door and, though stunned, he managed to deploy the unbuckled parachute and make a successful landing. He was later recovered by a companion helicopter."[111]

Born in Flint, Michigan, on June 5, 1947, Hackney enlisted in the Air Force after graduating from high school in June 1965. After completing basic training at Lackland Air Force Base, Texas, he completed airborne, medical technician, and scuba training to qualify as a Pararescueman.

In September 1966, Hackney joined Detachment 7, 38th Aerospace Rescue and Recovery Squadron, which was located at the airport in Da Nang, Vietnam. While assigned to this unit, then Airman 2d Class Hackney performed the act of heroism that would result in the award of the Air Force Cross. In March 1967, then Airman 2d Class Hackney transferred to the 37th Aerospace Rescue and Recovery Squadron and served with this unit in Thailand. By the time he left Southeast Asia, he had flown more than 200 rescue missions and participated in the recovery of over 40 U.S. pilots.

In addition to the Air Force Cross, Hackney also was awarded the Silver Star, four Distinguished Flying Crosses, the Airman's Medal, seventeen Air Medals, three Air Force Commendation Medals, the Purple Heart "and more than 20 other U.S. and foreign decorations, including the Vietnamese Cross of Gallantry."[112]

Chief Master Sergeant Hackney died on September 3, 1993. He was 46 years old.

ROBIN OLDS: AUGUST 11, 1967

Colonel Olds received his Air Force Cross for heroism while leading a strike on the Paul Doumer Bridge crossing the Red River in Hanoi, North Vietnam. His citation reads, in part:

> On 11 August 1967 ... Colonel Olds led his strike force of eight F-4C aircraft against a key railroad and highway bridge in North Vietnam. Despite intense, accurately directed fire, multiple surface-

Brigadier General Robin Olds was awarded the Air Force Cross, four Silver Stars, the Legion of Merit, five Distinguished Flying Crosses and 38 Air Medals (U.S. Air Force).

to-air missile attacks on his force, and continuous harassment by MiG fighters defending the target, Colonel Olds, with undaunted determination, indomitable courage, and professional skill, led his force through to help destroy this significant bridge. As a result, the flow of war materials into this area was appreciably reduced.[113]

After graduating from the U.S. Military Academy in June 1943, Olds completed flight training and then deployed to Europe. Between May 1944 and April 1945, then 22-year-old Olds shot down thirteen Luftwaffe aircraft and destroyed another 11½ on the ground. In twelve short months, he achieved "double ace" status, went from went from second lieutenant to major, and commanded a P-51 Mustang squadron.

After World War II, Olds made history as a wingman on the first jet demonstration team, as a racer in the Thompson Trophy race, and as the only U.S. exchange officer to command a Royal Air Force squadron.

More than twenty years later, in Septem-

ber 1966, now Colonel Olds took command of the 8th Tactical Fighter Wing at Ubon Royal Thai Air Force Base, Thailand. On January 2, 1967, he made Air Force history when he led the wing of F-4 Phantoms that destroyed seven MiGs "in the biggest air battle of the Vietnam War." Olds accomplished this feat by creating an aerial trap for the enemy. He used radar jammers to fool the North Vietnamese into thinking that they were facing F-105 Thunderchiefs instead of F-4 Phantoms. The ruse worked, and Olds and his fellow Phantom pilots shot down seven MiGs. Since Olds himself destroyed one enemy aircraft, he now became "the only American fighter ace with scores in both World War II and Vietnam. As he shot down three more MiGs before his tour ended a few months later — bringing his World War II and Vietnam total to 17 — Olds also was a "triple ace."[114]

After returning from Vietnam, Olds was forced to shave his distinctive and well-known waxed handlebar moustache. He subsequently served as the commandant of cadets at the U.S. Air Force Academy and was promoted to brigadier general while in this assignment. Olds' last tour was as an Air Force inspector general and he retired in 1973. Robin Olds died in June 2007 in Steamboat Springs, Colorado.[115]

RALPH S. PARR: MARCH 16, 1968

Colonel Parr is unique in military history: the only recipient of both the Distinguished Service Cross (for extraordinary heroism in Korea) and the Air Force Cross (for extraordinary heroism in Vietnam). His citation for the Air Force Cross reads, in part:

> As an F-4C Aircraft Commander near Khe Sanh ... on 16 March 1968 ... Colonel Parr participated in a flight providing cover for cargo aircraft. Upon arrival over the target, the forward air controller advised the flight that the airfield was under heavy attack by hostile mortar positions, which were located a few feet below a ridge line. Although the target area was covered with dense smoke and haze, Colonel Parr successfully

destroyed one mortar position on his first pass, as six well-camouflaged heavy automatic weapons positions opened fire on him. Although sustaining severe damage to his aircraft, he pressed his second attack and destroyed another mortar position. Again, completely disregarding his personal safety and the withering hostile gun fire, Colonel Parr succeeded in destroying a heavy caliber automatic weapons position. In between his own passes, his accurate and timely directions to his wingman effectively insured the accuracy of ordnance delivery in close proximity to friendly forces. Only after delivering all his ordnance at point-blank range in eight consecutive passes did Colonel Parr terminate his attack. By destroying these strategically placed weapons, he not only impaired the hostile force's capability to impede the resupply of Khe Sanh, but also reduced further losses to friendly cargo aircraft and crews.

Ralph Parr, who flew more than 500 combat missions in Southeast Asia, was a double jet ace in the Korean War, getting his tenth victory less than 10 hours before the armistice took effect. In addition to the Distinguished Service Cross and Air Force Cross, Parr also was awarded the Silver Star, three Legions of Merit, nine Distinguished Flying Crosses, the Bronze Star Medal, and 39 Air Medals.[116]

DENNIS M. RICHARDSON: MARCH 14, 1968

Retired Chief Master Sergeant Richardson received his Air Force Cross in April 2008 — more than forty years after the act of heroism upon which the award was based. His citation says that he showed

extraordinary heroism ... as Flight Engineer of an HH-3E Jolly Green rescue helicopter in Southeast Asia on 14 March 1968 ... Sergeant Richardson flew two sorties in an effort to rescue United States Air Force pilots who were surrounded by enemy troops along the Ho Chi Minh Trail. During the initial rescue attempt another helicopter had been driven off and Sergeant Richardson's helicopter had itself sustained significant battle damage. Despite their situation, and with complete disregard for their own safety, Sergeant Richardson and his crew elected to return and make a second rescue attempt. Coming

to a hover 10 feet above the survivor's position, Sergeant Richardson stood fully exposed in the helicopter door and began lowering the jungle penetrator with one hand while gripping his M-60 machine gun with the other. Unknown to anyone, the enemy had occupied the area but held their fire, waiting to ambush the helicopter. Suddenly intense enemy fire erupted from all quadrants, resulting in additional damage to "Jolly Green 22" and wounding Sergeant Richardson. In an extraordinary display of courage and valor, Sergeant Richardson, despite his wounds, leaned far outside the door and neutralized charging enemy combatants who appeared intent on boarding the helicopter. Sergeant Richardson continued to lay down an effective blanket of defensive fire which enabled the pilot to maneuver safely out of the area. The selfless actions of Sergeant Richardson undoubtedly saved his helicopter and crew from certain disaster.

Richardson was the flight engineer on a HH-3 "Jolly Green" that was one of two helicopters attempting to rescue two Marine pilots who had ejected from their F-4 Phantom over North Vietnam. After one pilot had been successfully picked up, heavy machine gun fire forced both aircraft to return to their base in South Vietnam. Before Richardson's helicopter could take off a second time to try to save the second Marine aviator, he and the aircraft pilot "huddled on the runway around their shot up Jolly Green." The two airmen had to decide if their helicopter "could continue to fly after taking a .50 caliber round through its power turbine engine exhaust system minutes earlier."

Deciding that the risk was worth taking to attempt to save Marine 1st Lt. Edward Hamm, "who was desperately trying to radio in his position," Richardson's helicopter took off and returned to Hamm's last reported position. The crew saw the red panel that Hamm had used to mark his location. But what the Americans did not know, however, was that Hamm was already dead. He had been killed by the enemy, which now used the panel to set a trap for Richardson and the rescue party.

As the Jolly Green Giant hovered over the red panel, the North Vietnamese "unleashed a torrent of fire, including rounds from Russian anti-aircraft guns." One enemy soldier then jumped up and, from 25 feet away, began firing rounds from his AK-47 into the helicopter. Richardson, holding his M-60 machine gun in one hand and the hoist in another as he waited for Lt. Hamm to appear, fired five rounds into the chest of the North Vietnamese soldier. One crewmember later insisted that "if Richardson had not exposed himself by leaning out the door to fire his M-60, the entire crew would have been killed."

Despite the relentless enemy fire, the airmen waited as long as they could but, with no sign of Hamm, the Americans returned to base. When they returned, an inspection of the aircraft revealed 68 rounds in the fuselage, including a shot-out windshield. There also were holes in the rotor blades.

According to news accounts, Richardson had been nominated for the Air Force Cross in 1968 and the decoration had, in fact, been awarded to him — only to be mysteriously rescinded by the Air Force or "lost in paperwork" some time later. The Air Force Board for the Correction of Military Records decided in December 2007, however, that "the Air Force made a mistake" and that Richardson's official military records should be corrected to reflect that he "did, in fact, earn the Air Force Cross." Richardson's Air Force Cross was presented to him at New York's Francis S. Gabreski Airport on April 5, 2008.[117]

TILFORD W. HARP: APRIL 4, 1975
DENNIS W. TRAYNOR III: APRIL 4, 1975

Then Captains Harp and Traynor received the Air Force Cross under highly unusual circumstances, as their awards were for *non-combat* aerial heroism. Their citations differed only in that Traynor's identified him as the aircraft commander while Harp's identified him as the co-pilot. Traynor's citation mentions his

> extraordinary heroism and airmanship while engaged in a humanitarian mission as Aircraft

Commander of an Air Force C-5 aircraft at Saigon, Vietnam, on 4 April 1975. On that date, the aircraft, carrying 330 passengers and crew, experienced a serious inflight emergency which could have resulted in loss of life for all aboard. With no aircraft controls except one aileron and the engines, he guided the crippled aircraft to a crash landing in a rice paddy, thereby saving the lives of 176 of the people on board.

On April 4, 1975, Captains Traynor and Tilford W. Harp were flying the first mission in Operation BABYLIFT, a U.S. government plan to evacuate South Vietnamese orphans out of their war-torn country. While some 3,300 children would eventually be transported out of South Vietnam before that country fell on April 30, 1975, this first flight out of Saigon was a disaster: it crashed several minutes after takeoff, killing 138 people, mostly children. The extraordinary heroism of Captains Traynor and Harp, however, ensured that hundreds of lives were saved. In addition to their Air Force Crosses, both men also were awarded the Airman's Medal for the same event since, after successfully landing the C-5, both Harp and Traynor risked their lives to help passengers and crew in the aftermath of the crash.[118]

Somalia
TIMOTHY A. WILKINSON: OCTOBER 3–4, 1993

Then Master Sergeant Wilkinson received the first Air Force Cross awarded since the Vietnam War. He also was the only recipient of the decoration for Somalia. His citation reads, in part:

> for extraordinary heroism ... as a 24th Special Tactics Squadron Pararescueman in the vicinity of the Olympic Hotel, Mogadishu, Somalia, from 3 October to 4 October 1993. During that period, in response to an incident in which a U.S. helicopter had been shot down by a rocket propelled grenade, Sergeant Wilkinson conducted a fast rope insertion into the crash site and came under extremely heavy enemy fire from three directions. In the initial rescue effort, he repeatedly exposed himself to intense small arms fire

Staff Sergeant Zachary Rhyner received his Air Force Cross from Secretary of the Air Force Michael B. Donley on March 10, 2011 (U.S. Air Force).

and grenades to clear debris, provide emergency medical treatment to the survivors, and extract dead and wounded members of the crew from the wreckage. On his own initiative, Sergeant Wilkinson broke cover on three separate occasions to locate and provide emergency medical treatment to three Ranger casualties. In doing so, he ignored all concern for his personal safety to cross a 45-meter wide open area blanketed with intense fire from small arms and rocket propelled grenades. Sergeant Wilkinson's medical skills and uncommon valor saved the lives of multiple gravely wounded American soldiers in the longest sustained fire fight involving U.S. combat forces in over 20 years.[119]

Afghanistan

JOHN A. CHAPMAN: MARCH 4, 2002
JASON D. CUNNINGHAM: MARCH 4, 2002

Technical Sergeant Chapman and Senior Airman Cunningham were posthumously awarded the Air Force Cross for their ground combat heroism in the vicinity of Gardez in the eastern highlands of Afghanistan. Both men were part of an effort to rescue a missing Navy SEAL, Petty Officer 1st Class Neil Roberts, who had inadvertently been left behind in the area on an earlier military operation — and who then had been captured by enemy guerrillas.

Chapman, a Combat Controller, had killed two al Qaeda fighters and was attacking a "dug-in enemy machine gun next" when he came "under effective enemy fire from three directions." Despite the lack of personal cover, Chapman continued to exchange fire with the enemy until he "succumbed to multiple wounds." Cunningham, a Pararescueman, used his medical skills to save the lives of his comrades; wounded by an enemy bullet, he died before he could be medically evacuated.[120]

THE SILVER STAR

Overview

Establishing Authority and Effective Dates: The Silver Star was originally established as a "citation star" for soldiers in War Department General Orders No. 6 on January 12, 1919. It was modified slightly and affirmed as an Army decoration by an act of Congress (Public Law 193, 65th Congress) on July 9, 1918. While the Silver Star "medal" was created by an Army regulation in 1932, legislative authority to award the decoration to soldiers and airmen did not exist until December 15, 1942, when Congress passed an act authorizing the Silver Star as an award for gallantry in action.

Criteria: The Silver Star may be awarded to any person who, while serving in any capacity with the Armed Forces of the United States, is cited for gallantry in action (1) against an enemy of the United States, (2) while engaged in military operations involving conflict with an opposing foreign force, or (3) while serving with friendly foreign forces engaged in armed conflict against an opposing armed force in which the United States is not a belligerent party. The required gallantry, while of a lesser degree than that required for the award of a

Distinguished Service Cross or Air Force Cross, must nevertheless have been performed with marked distinction.[121]

Order of Precedence: The Silver Star is worn after the service Distinguished Service Medal and before the Defense Superior Service Medal.

Devices: Additional awards of the Silver Star are denoted by oak leaf clusters.

Designer: The Silver Star medal was designed by Rudolf Freund (1878–1960) of Bailey, Banks and Biddle.

Description and Symbolism

Obverse

The overall design of the medal is a point-up five-pointed star that is 1¾ inches in circumscribing diameter and finished in gilt-bronze. In the center of the medal is a smaller, point-up five-pointed star that is ³⁄₁₆ of an inch in diameter. The inner star, which is the "silver [citation] star" created by the 1919 legislation, is centered within a wreath of laurel tied at its base by a bow. The center lines and rays of both stars coincide. The top of the medal has a rectangular metal loop that is 0.35

Silver Star (obverse).

Silver Star (reverse).Officially hand-engraved Army Silver Star to Lt. John T. Hains, Jr., for gallantry in action in Germany on March 12, 1945.

inch in length and 0.45 inch in width (outside finished dimensions) with rounded corners. This loop is struck as part of the pendant. The laurel wreath alludes to achievement, and the larger gilt-bronze star is symbolic of military service.

Reverse

The reverse is plain except for the inscription in raised letters at the top of the medal reading "For Gallantry in Action." The space below is for engraving the recipient's name.

Ribbon

The ribbon has a center stripe of red flanked on either side by a stripe of white of equal width. The white stripes are flanked by equal blue bands having borders of white with blue edging. These are the colors of the U.S. flag.

Historical Background
Origins as an Army Award

The Silver Star grew out of the practice of citing a soldier in the dispatches of the day, which meant that an individual was publicly recognized for some noteworthy action performed during the heat of battle. The Army began publishing citations for gallantry or "specially meritorious acts or conduct" in 1891, but there was no special insignia, medal, or emblem to reflect those awards.

During World War I, Gen. John J. Pershing, who was then commanding the American Expeditionary Forces, requested the establishment of a Distinguished Service Cross and Distinguished Service Medal. On January 12, 1918. the War Department issued General Orders No. 6, which, among other things, established those two decorations. The order also provided that

> no individual will be entitled to more than one distinguished-service cross or one distinguished-service medal, but each additional citation in War Department orders for conduct or service that would warrant the award of either of these decorations will entitle the person so cited to wear upon the ribband of the decoration and upon the corresponding ribbon a bronze oak leaf of approved design, and the right to wear such oak leaf will be announced as part of the citation. *Other citations for gallantry in action published in orders issued from the headquarters of a force commanded by a general officer will be indicated in each case by a silver star three-sixteenths of an inch in diameter worn upon the ribband of the distinguished-service cross and upon the corresponding ribbon* [emphasis added].[122]

When Congress passed the law formalizing the Distinguished Service Cross and the Distinguished Service Medal in July 1918, it retained the citation star but provided that it was to be worn on the ribbon of the appropriate campaign medal by any officer or enlisted man who had been cited in orders for gallantry in action under conditions not warranting the award of the Medal of Honor or Distinguished Service Cross. Thousands of citation stars were affixed by World War I veterans on the ribbon of their Victory Medals, and more than 1,000 stars were authorized for wear on campaign medal ribbons for service in previous conflicts, including the Civil War, Spanish-American War, and Philippine Insurrection.

Development of the Silver Star Medal

Although the silver citation star was widely used during and after World War I, it was not a popular award. As one contemporary source notes, it was "insignificant in size and constitutes very little tangible evidence of gallantry, is not an article which can be handed down to posterity and, therefore, serve as an evidence of a grateful nation and people with attendant stimulation to patriotism."[123]

So what was to be done? The Army had avoided legislative action on the new Purple Heart by claiming that it was simply "reviving" the Badge of Military Merit that George Washington created for troops during the American Revolution. It took a similar approach with the citation star, with General MacArthur playing a key role. In early 1932 MacArthur "authorized" Arthur E. DuBois, chief of the Army Quartermaster General's Heraldic Section, to "hang" the 3/16-inch silver star on a bronze pendant. MacArthur further directed DuBois to omit the word "citation" in describing the new award, which resulted in its designation as the "Silver Star."[124] At DuBois' request, Rudolf Freund designed the actual medal, and that design was approved by the Army Adjutant General.

As the original congressional legislation had never specified a name for the citation star device, much less how it was to be worn, MacArthur's directive that it be placed in the center of a metal pendant rather than on a campaign ribbon satisfied the letter of the law. When, on July 16, 1932, Secretary of War Patrick Jay Hurley approved this redesigned "Silver Star," a new gallantry decoration was born and MacArthur had found an ingenious solution to what had been a vexing problem.

On August 9, 1932, the Army announced that "those who are now authorized to wear citation stars may, at their option, continue to do so, or they may make application for the Silver Star and such oak leaf clusters to which they may be entitled." The Army also began accepting applications for the new award from sailors and Marines who had either been cited for gallantry in orders or received a certificate of gallantry while serving as part of the American Expeditionary Force. As a result, a small number of Army Silver Stars were awarded to a handful of sailors and Marines who had fought alongside soldiers in France in World War I.[125]

The Silver Star Becomes an Air Force Award

On July 15, 1942, Congress enacted legislation authorizing the War Department to award the Silver Star for gallantry in action to soldiers and airmen; this statute superseded the regulatory basis for the medal that had been the basis for its award since 1932. When the Air Force was created as an independent branch of the Armed Forces by the National Security Act of 1947, Congress also amended the laws governing military awards so that the new Department of the Air Force retained the statutory authority for awarding the Silver Star to Air Force personnel.

First Recipient

The first Silver Star medal (No. 1) was awarded to Gen. Douglas MacArthur in August 1932.

Selected Recipients

The record for the most Silver Stars to one recipient belongs to Colonel David Hackworth, who was awarded an unprecedented 10 Silver Stars during his controversial career as an infantry officer.

Cuba

JOHN L. HINES: JULY 1, 1898

Major General (retired) Hines was issued the Silver Star medal in 1934 on the basis of the Silver Star Citation awarded to him "for gallantry in action against Spanish forces at Santiago, Cuba, July 1, 1898."

John Leonard Hines soldiered from 1891 until 1932, and served in China, Cuba, France, Mexico, and the Philippines before achieving the top Army job as chief of staff. Few soldiers have equaled his achievements as a warrior and staff officer — or his longevity, as Hines celebrated his 100th birthday.

Born in May 1868 in White Sulfur Springs, West Virginia, Hines graduated from the U.S. Military Academy in 1891 and was commissioned an infantry second lieutenant. He served the next seven years with the 2nd Infantry Regiment in Nebraska and Montana.

After the United States declared war on Spain in 1898, then 1st Lt. Hines deployed to Cuba with the Quartermaster Corps, where he saw hard fighting. After returning to the United States for a brief time, Hines sailed to the Philippines where, from 1900 to 1901, he participated in combat operations against the insurgent forces led by Emilio Aguinaldo. Hines would later serve in the Philippines as a captain from 1903 to 1905.

After returning to the U.S. from his second tour in the Philippines, Hines served in a variety of adjutant and quartermaster positions until 1916, when he was selected to be Gen. John J. Pershing's adjutant for the Punitive Expedition into Mexico.

The next year, when Pershing's American Expeditionary Force sailed to France, Hines was promoted to colonel and appointed assistant adjutant general. In November, he was given command of the 16th Infantry Regiment but, after being given his first star in April 1918, he left that unit to assume command of the 1st Brigade, 1st Division. For his heroism while leading this brigade in action at Berzy-le-Sec, France, on July 21, 1918, Hines later received the Distinguished Service Cross. According to the citation for his award, he "personally went through terrific artillery fire to the front lines" and linked up two regiments that had become separated in the chaos of battle, "thereby enabling the operations to be pushed forward successfully."

Hines received his second star in August 1918 and then commanded the 4th Division in the St. Mihiel and Meuse-Argonne offensives. Shortly before World War I ended, Hines was given command of III Corps, which he led until 1919. This last job put Hines into the history books, as he was the only Army officer in World War I to command a regiment, brigade, division and corps in combat.

After World War I, Hines had a series of important jobs, including command of the 5th Division and VII Corps area. In 1923, he became Deputy Chief of Staff of the Army and, in September 1924, reached the pinnacle of his remarkable career as Army Chief of Staff. After leaving this position in 1926, however, Hines did not retire. On the contrary, he remained on active duty, with his last assignment being commander of the Department of the Philippines.

Hines retired as a major general in 1932 but was advanced to four star rank in 1940. He died five months after celebrating his 100th birthday, and was buried in Arlington National Cemetery.

Hines has not been forgotten: in 2000, the U.S. Postal Service issued a postage stamp honoring him.[126]

Philippines

ABNER PICKERING: MAY 3, 1905

Major Pickering received the Silver Star for his gallantry in combat at the capture of Peruka Utig's Cotta on the island of Mindanao on May 3, 1905. The medal was issued to Pickering in 1932 on the basis of a citation for gallantry published in General Orders No. 43, Department of Mindanao (Philippines), dated December 31, 1905.

World War II

CREIGHTON W. ABRAMS: DECEMBER 26–27, 1944

Lieutenant Colonel Abrams was awarded one of two Silver Stars for his heroism in relieving the 101st Airborne Division in Bastogne, Belgium, during the Battle of the Bulge. At the time, he was commanding the 37th Tank Battalion (part of the 4th Armored Division) and had previously led the advance by Gen. George S. Patton's 3rd Army across France.[127]

Born in 1914 in Springfield, Massachusetts, Abrams graduated from the U.S. Military Academy in 1936. During World War II, his fearless, aggressive leadership style earned him high praise from Patton who said: "I'm supposed to be the best tank commander in the Army, but I have one peer, Abe Abrams. He's the world's champion."[128]

When the fighting in Europe ended in May 1945, Abrams had commanded a battalion and a combat command. He also had been awarded two Distinguished Service Crosses, two Silver Stars, a Bronze Star Medal for valor, and the Legion of Merit. He also had received a battlefield promotion to colonel.

Abrams remained in the Army after World War II and continue to advance in rank. As a two-star general, he served as commander of the 3rd Armored Division and had his picture on the cover of Time magazine in 1961. Abrams became a full general and vice chief of staff of the Army in 1964. In this job, he had an early role in formulating Army policy in Vietnam, and succeeded General William C. Westmoreland as the top U.S. officer in the war zone in 1968.

After Richard Nixon took office, Abrams implemented a new program, known as "Vietnamization." The idea was that there would be a gradual end to U.S. involvement in Vietnam as the South Vietnamese took over responsibility for the war effort against the North Vietnamese and their Viet Cong ally.

Abrams left Vietnam in 1972 to become Army Chief of Staff. Two years later, while still serving as the Army's top officer, he died of cancer at age 59. The Army, however, has not forgotten Abrams: its M1 Abrams main battle tank is named after him.

JOHN T. CORLEY: NOVEMBER 10, 1942; JULY 22, 1943; JUNE 9, 1944; OCTOBER 18, 1944; NOVEMBER 27, 1944

John Thomas Corley was a superb soldier by any measure, and his heroism under fire in North Africa and Europe was recognized with five Silver Stars. His citations follow:

> for gallantry ... in the vicinity of Ferme Combier, Algeria, November 10, 1942. Although subjected to direct small-arms fire, Major Corley, on his own initiative, made extensive reconnaissance to locate observation points for our artillery observers. His keen tactical judgment and fearlessness materially assisted in the defeat of the enemy....[129]
>
> for gallantry ... in the vicinity of Bompietro, Sicily, July 22, 1943. Given the mission of supporting a tank attack upon an important objective, Colonel Corley skillfully coordinated his battalion elements and, although fierce enemy resistance compelled other attacking units to withdraw, moved into the offensive at the designated hour. Remaining in the vanguard of the assault force and repeatedly risking his life to more effectively maneuver troops and weapons, select targets, and adjust fire, he inspired his men to supreme heights of courage and determination and drove relentlessly forward until the objective was taken....[130]
>
> for gallantry ... in the vicinity of Ste. Anne, Normandy, France, June 9, 1944. When a flank element of his battalion was overrun by German infantry and armor, Colonel Corley fearlessly proceeded to the vulnerable area and, by his personal bravery and determination, encouraged the troops to resist further penetration of our lines. After checking the enemy onslaught, Colonel Corley seized the offensive and, repeatedly risking his life to more advantageously maneuver personnel and weapons, assaulted and routed the hostile forces....[131]
>
> for gallantry ... in the vicinity of Aachen, Germany, October 18, 1944. Given the important mission of neutralizing several enemy strong points, Colonel Corley personally reconnoitered

the designated structures, guided self-propelled artillery and tanks to strategic locations and, from a position vulnerable to intense fire, directed systematic and complete destruction of the objectives....[132]

for gallantry ... in the vicinity of Jungersdorf, Germany, November 27, 1944. Repeatedly moving to the head of his attacking forces during a fierce engagement with the enemy, Colonel Corley, despite intense machine-gun and small-arms fire, aggressively led his battalion against a numerically superior and strongly entrenched foe and compelled the Germans to abandon a strategically important objective.[133]

Born in Brooklyn, New York, in August 1914, John T. Corley graduated from the U.S. Military Academy in 1938 and was commissioned in the infantry. In addition to the five Silver Stars he received in World War II, Corley also was awarded the Distinguished Service Cross, Legion of Merit, Soldier's Medal, four Bronze Star Medals, and the Purple Heart.

While serving as a battalion commander in the 24th Infantry Regiment during the Korean War, Corley received a battlefield to promotion to colonel and was decorated with a second Distinguished Service Cross, three more Silver Stars (see below) and second Legion of Merit.

After the Korean War, Corley served in a number of increasingly important assignments, including: Director of the Ranger Department at the Infantry School at Fort Benning, Georgia (1958–1960); assistant division commander, 2d Infantry Division (1962–64); chief of staff, First U.S. Army (1964–66); and deputy commanding general, Fort Jackson, South Carolina (1966). He retired as a brigadier general in 1966 and died in 1977. His son, John T. Corley, Jr., was killed in action in Vietnam in September 1968 and was posthumously awarded the Silver Star.

GORDON M. GRAHAM: OCTOBER 1944–APRIL 1945

Then Colonel Graham was awarded the Silver Star "for gallantry in action as com-

mander of a fighter squadron." His citation reads, in part:

To better equip himself for the responsibilities attendant to leading Fighter units in combat, Colonel Graham flew practically every position in the squadron formation. His willingness to share in the same risks and dangers as the other pilots quickly earned for him the respect and admiration of the entire unit. As proof of his combat skill, enthusiasm, and zealous fighting spirit, Colonel Graham can look with pride on his outstanding record of nine (9) enemy planes destroyed between 8 April 1945 and 16 April 1945.

Born in 1918 in Colorado, Gordon Graham grew up in California and began his flying career as an aviation cadet in 1940. After serving as a gunnery instructor and instructor pilot at various locations, Graham joined the 355th Fighter Group, Eighth Air Force in Europe in August 1944. He subsequently commanded the 354th Fighter Squadron. Then, after transferring to the 361st Fighter Group, Graham commanded the 374th Fighter Squadron. By the end of World War II, Graham had flown 73 combat missions in the P-51 Mustang and was a triple ace with 16½ kills to his credit.

After a brief stint as a civilian in 1946, Graham returned to active duty and served in a variety of increasingly important assignments. During the Vietnam War, he was vice commander of the Seventh Air Force and flew 146 combat missions in F-4 and RF-4 aircraft. Graham retired as a lieutenant general in 1973 and died in March 2008. He was 90 years old.[134]

GRIGORI FEDOROVICH LEONTIEV: MARCH 5–APRIL 17, 1944

During World War II, the War Department authorized the U.S. Military Mission to Moscow to award Silver Stars to Soviet soldiers in recognition of their "gallantry in action against our common enemy." Guard Private Leontiev received his decoration for his combat heroism "during the operations against the

Warsaw-Odessa rail communications and the Uman offensive." During "an engagement for the capture of a bridgehead on the right bank of the Dnepr," Leontiev made "a brave advance and, in hand-to-hand fighting, killed 5 Germans. Then, crawling up to an enemy machine-gun nest, he destroyed crew and gun with hand grenades."[135]

AUBREY S. NEWMAN: OCTOBER 21–29, 1944

Then Colonel Newman was awarded the Silver Star for his gallantry in action on Leyte in the Philippines. His citation reads:

> During this period, Col. Newman, after capturing hills dominating Red Beach, drove his regiment up the broad Leyte Valley, across the Mainit River, and secured a foothold in Jaro in advance of enemy reinforcements. His regiment advanced straight at the enemy, often at extreme range of radio communication, sometimes beyond the limit of artillery supporting fire, without regard for his line of communications and well beyond the ready help of other troops. Col. Newman without regard for his personal safety, was constantly with forward elements encouraging them to still greater efforts. On one occasion he was with the lead squad of one of his companies which was successfully attacking up narrow trails, through high cogon grass, a position from which the company had been driven the preceding day. On another occasion he accompanied the leading company in a daring river crossing which flanked the enemy position and secured the Mainit River.[136]

Born in South Carolina in January 1903, Aubrey Strode Newman graduated from the U.S. Military Academy in 1926 and was commissioned as an infantry officer. He served in a variety of command and staff assignments in the late 1920s and 1930s and, after the United States entered World War II, saw extensive combat in the Pacific.

On October 20, 1944, then Colonel Newman was in command of the 34th Infantry Regiment when that unit made an amphibious assault on Leyte island in the Philippines. When the attack by his troops stalled, however,

and his men were pinned down on the beach, Newman stood up and shouted "Get up and get moving! Follow me!" He then walked forward and his men followed — securing the beachhead. Newman's extraordinary heroism that day resulted in the award of the Distinguished Service Cross and, after the war, the Army produced a recruiting poster memorializing the event.

Newman fought with the 34th Infantry for the next 77 days, until he was wounded in the stomach and medically evacuated. He never saw combat again, but served in a number of important positions that included commanding airborne soldiers at Fort Bragg, North Carolina. Newman retired as a major general in 1960.

In retirement, Newman wrote *The Forward Edge*, a monthly column in *Army* magazine that focused on what he called techniques of leadership. These columns were later collected and republished in a series of bestselling books.[137] Newman died in Sarasota, Florida in 1994.[138] For more on Newman's role in the history of medals and decorations, see Chapter 4, The Purple Heart.

ADOLPH H. SCHULTZ: APRIL 9, 1945

Then Technician Four (later Staff Sergeant) Schultz was serving in Company G, 15th Infantry Regiment, 3rd Infantry Division, when he was awarded the Silver Star. His citation commends his

> gallantry in action. At 0500 hours, on April 9, 1945, near Neustadt, Germany, when machine gun and sniper fire temporarily halted his platoon, Sgt. Schultz advanced, alone, over 300 yards of open terrain to a point overlooking enemy positions. When a hostile five-man squad appeared thirty yards from him, Sgt. Schultz stood erect and opened fire with his sub-machine gun, killing three and wounding two enemy soldiers. He then deployed his squad and directed their fire against the attacking enemy.[139]

Korea

THOMAS W. BATES: JULY 30, 1951

Sergeant Bates was posthumously awarded the Silver Star for his gallantry in the vicinity of Taeusan, Korea, on July 30, 1951. His citation reads:

> While the company was in the attack to secure dominating positions held by the enemy, Sergeant (then Corporal) Bates, with complete disregard for his own safety, led his squad in a daring assault on the enemy's position which had stalled the attack of the platoon. Under intense enemy small arms and grenade fire, he advanced towards the crest of the hill using marching fire and grenades, while the remainder of the platoon moved forward. He continually exposed himself to enemy fire to keep the attack moving forward until such time as he was fatally wounded by enemy sniper fire.[140]

JOHN T. CORLEY: AUGUST, 11, 1950, SEPTEMBER 16, 1950, NOVEMBER 30, 1950

Then Colonel Corley received three Silver Stars during the Korean War. As he had been awarded five Silver Stars in World War II (see above), he received a total of eight during his career as an infantry officer. His citations follow:

> for gallantry ... on August 11, 1950 near Wonson, Korea. Colonel Corley was leading his battalion in an attack when the advance elements were subjected to devastating small arms and mortar fire. Despite exposure to the deadly barrage, he calmly deployed his men to maximum advantage and directed the forward observer to a favorable position. When one of the radio men was wounded by hostile fire, he advanced to the injured man, administered first aid and carried him back for evacuation....[141]

> for gallantry ... at Haman, Korea, on September 16, 1950. Colonel Corley's regiment launched a series of attacks against strong hostile positions. As his exhausted men organized for a final assault, he advanced to the line of departure to take personal command. Despite constant exposure to intense hostile fire, he rallied his men around him, led them in their successful assault and remained with the lead elements until recalled by the Division Commander....[142]

> for gallantry ... on November 30, 1950, near Pugwon, Korea. Strong hostile forces had penetrated friendly lines on the right flank of Colonel Corley's regiment. Advancing on foot to clarify the situation, he reorganized adjacent infantry elements in specifically assigned sectors and then proceeded to an important river crossing to ascertain if it was still in friendly hands. After reconnoitering the area without encountering hostile forces, he dispatched a platoon of tanks to re-enforce his forward battalion and remained at the crossing until assured that all friendly lines were firmly re-secured.[143]

DAVID H. HACKWORTH: FEBRUARY 6, 1951, AUGUST 8, 1951, NOVEMBER 4, 1951

David H. Hackworth received an unprecedented 10 Silver Stars during 20 years of soldiering and holds the record for the most Silvers Stars awarded to one individual. Hackworth received his first three Silver Stars in Korea and an additional seven Silver Stars in Vietnam (see below). His Korean War citations follow:

> for gallantry ... on February 6, 1951 near Soamni, Korea. The lead elements of Sergeant Hackworth's task force were subjected to heavy small arms and mortar fire. After organizing his men in advantageous positions, he mounted a tank and directed a heavy volume of machine gun fire at the hostile emplacements. When his ammunition was exhausted, he immediately moved to the exposed deck of another tank and directed its weapon against the foe. Although the enemy concentrated their firepower on his position, he continued his mission until he was severely wounded....[144]

> for gallantry ... on August 8, 1951. Lt. Hackworth volunteered to lead a reinforced patrol against well-defended positions near Pongmi, Korea. When the enemy began an intense small arms and automatic weapons barrage, he left his place of cover to emplace the tanks and halftracks and to direct their fire. Moving to the front, he led the infantryman in a furious grenade and bayonet assault to rout the hostile forces from the initial strongpoints. Although under direct observation of the enemy, he continued to direct an effective heavy weapons barrage on their positions. When the overwhelming numerical superiority of the foe forced a withdrawal, he manned a machine gun and gave supporting fire until the last of the patrol had reached safety....[145]

for gallantry ... in the vicinity of Kumhwa, Korea, on November 4, 1951. Lt. Hackworth's unit was engaged with a well-entrenched hostile force over the possession of a vital hill mass. While leading the assault squad up the slope through intense small arms, automatic weapons fire and bursting grenades, he was painfully wounded but refused evacuation and continued directing accurate concentrations on the main points of resistance. Finally leaving the impact area, he received medical aid. Quickly returning to his men, he led a spirited charge against the foe to overrun the position and rout the enemy. Unable to hold a weapon because of his broken arm, he accepted the assistance of an enlisted man, who held the carbine level while Lt. Hackworth placed heavy fire on the retreating enemy. He continued exposing himself to the withering crossfire in order to coordinate the tactics of his men and direct the evacuation of the wounded until he was called to his telephone and ordered to the rear for medical aid. Refusing to stay out of the impact area, he again went forward to assure himself that his men were well organized and all helpless soldiers were brought back to friendly positions.[146]

Born November 11, 1930, David Haskell Hackworth lied about his age and enlisted in the Army for three years on May 21, 1946, when he was still fifteen years old. After completing basic training as an infantryman, he served as a medium tank crewman with the 351st Infantry in Trieste, Italy.

After reenlisting in 1949, then Private First Class Hackworth deployed the following year to Korea as a member of Company G, 27th Infantry Regiment. He was promoted to sergeant and awarded his first Silver Star for combat heroism on February 6, 1951. He also received his first Purple Heart that same day (as he had received a gunshot wound to his head). Before his tour of duty in Korea had ended, Hackworth received a battlefield promotion to lieutenant and was awarded two more Silver Stars.

He remained on active duty after the Korean War and deployed to Vietnam in 1966, where Hackworth served in the 101st Airborne Division. During this combat assignment, he was awarded his fourth and fifth Silver Stars

(see below). In 1969, then Lt. Col. Hackworth returned to Vietnam and, while commanding the 4th Battalion, 39th Infantry, was awarded five more Silver Stars (see below).

Although under investigation for a variety of criminal offenses, Hackworth avoided trial by court-martial and retired as a colonel in 1971. He moved to Australia, where he was a successful businessman and restaurant owner. In the mid–1980s, Hackworth returned to the United States. After his autobiography, *About Face: The Odyssey of An American Warrior* (1989), became a bestseller, Hackworth embarked on a highly successful — but controversial — career as a writer and journalist.

"Hack" Hackworth died in Mexico in 2005, where he was undergoing treatment for bladder cancer. He was 74 years old.[147]

Congo

DONALD V. RATTAN: AUGUST 19, 1964

Lieutenant Colonel Rattan's Silver Star for gallantry in the Congo in 1964 is unique as the only combat heroism award for this military operation. His citation reads, in part:

for gallantry in action ... on 19 August 1964, while serving as Chief Observer of a Mobile Training Team during a violent uprising in the Republic of Congo. Colonel Rattan was participating in a reconnaissance mission with three other members of a joint team when they were suddenly attacked by an overwhelming force of Congolese rebels. Upon sustaining gunfire damage to his vehicle, he immediately directed the members of the team to flee to safety while he remained in his position, acting as a decoy although armed merely with a rifle in opposition to the onslaught of twelve hostile warriors wielding automatic weapons. Despite the extreme danger, he steadfastly covered the withdrawal of the team through two kilometers of hazardous terrain and succeeded in keeping the hostile force pinned down until his associates were hidden safely in the dense bush. Through his determination, indomitable courage, and complete disregard for his own safety to protect the lives of his fellow men, he prevented possible casualties and capture of the team.[148]

Vietnam

JOHN C. BAHNSEN, JR.: FEBRUARY 2, 1966, OCTOBER 17, 1968, FEBRUARY 3, 1969, MAY 29, 1969 AND SEPTEMBER 6, 1969

John C. "Doc" Bahnsen was awarded five Silver Stars during two combat tours in Vietnam. His citations follow:

for gallantry ... on 2 February 1966 while serving as aircraft commander and fire team commander on an armed UH-1B helicopter near Vuc Lien ... after making visual reconnaissance and providing overhead cover for the ground forces, Captain Bahnsen landed his fire team in a supposedly secure area. While being briefed by the ground commander, a Viet Cong force ambushed the unit. At this time Captain Bahnsen fearlessly led his fire team through intense automatic weapons fire to their aircraft, took off, daringly attacked the enemy forces, and saved the Marine force from having heavy casualties. When another company was ambushed, Captain Bahnsen aggressively made low-level attacks on the Viet Cong positions and, while receiving intense hostile fire, evacuated three critically wounded Marines. Upon returning from the evacuation mission, intense hostile fire was received during a low level reconnaissance flight. Captain Bahnsen dauntlessly made three firing passes on the insurgent positions, called for artillery fire and, after exhausting his ordnance, rearmed and returned to support the Marine force. Captain Bahnsen's courage during ten hours of intense hostile fire was an inspiration to his men and the Marine ground force....

for gallantry ... on 17 October 1968 while serving as the Commanding Officer of the Air Cavalry Troop of the 11th Armored Cavalry Regiment ... elements of the 11th Armored Cavalry Regiment engaged a company-sized North Vietnamese force within the Ba Da secret zone. During the firefight, the friendly force began receiving an intense concentration of automatic weapons fire from the numerically superior enemy force and immediately called for reinforcements. With the arrival of the friendly reinforcements, the hostile elements began withdrawing into the dense jungle terrain. One platoon from the 2d Mechanized Infantry Regiment and one aero rifle platoon pursued the enemy elements for two kilo-

meters, until they were suddenly engaged by heavy automatic weapons fire from well-concealed positions. Observing the enemy force from the air, Major Bahnsen began directing highly-accurate suppressive fire into the North Vietnamese Army positions. After making a number of passes, Major Bahnsen landed and positioned himself in front of the friendly forces, in full view of the enemy elements, and began directing his troop's advancement on the hostile positions. He was forced to seek cover when his position was raked by a barrage of automatic weapons fire, but after directing his gunship's fire onto the enemy force, he again exposed himself to the enemy fire and with shouts of encouragement to his men, led them on an all-out assault on the North Vietnamese positions, completely overrunning and destroying the hostile elements....

for gallantry ... on 3 February 1969 while serving as the Commanding Officer of the Air Cavalry Troop of the 11th Armored Cavalry Regiment ... while he was conducting a routine reconnaissance mission, his aircraft suddenly began receiving heavy automatic weapons fire from a well-concealed and heavily-fortified enemy base camp. Reacting instantly, Major Bahnsen returned to his base of operations, quickly assembled his Aero Rifle Platoon, and returned to the contact area. After beginning an assault upon the hostile position, he realized that the hostile fire was larger than he had anticipated. He therefore called his troops back and established a cordon around the hostile fortification. For the next three hours, Major Bahnsen, under constant enemy fire, directed air and artillery strikes against the enemy forces from his low flying aircraft. While directing the bombardment of the area, he requested a tank company. After armored cavalry assault vehicles arrived, he directed them into an assault formation and, disregarding his personal safety, flew his aircraft at treetop level over the enemy positions in order to effectively direct the final assault on the enemy base camp. When the hostile fortifications had been overrun, Major Bahnsen observed a number of enemy troops attempting to flee from the friendly forces. He immediately landed his helicopter and directed an assault upon the retreating enemy soldiers, killing one and capturing another....

for gallantry ... on 29 May 1969 ... while serving as Commanding Officer of the 1st Squadron, 11th Armored Cavalry Regiment ... when one of his troops was stopped by heavy enemy fire and dense jungle, Major Bahnsen directed the ground action as he made low passes over the contact area directing artillery, air strikes and helicopter gunships against an entrenched enemy bunker complex. Although his aircraft was repeatedly hit by ground fire, he refused to leave the area or fly at a higher altitude. After being forced to make an emergency landing at his base camp, he mounted a mechanized flame thrower and with his headquarters command group of cavalry assault vehicles moved under an air strike and through intense enemy fire to the point of heaviest contact. There he reorganized his ground teams by shouting instructions and encouragement to his troops. After expending his flame thrower against bunkers, Major Bahnsen led a dismounted attack against one bunker, clearing it with his rifle. Realizing the need for additional force, he then called in air strikes. As the enemy broke contact, Major Bahnsen then organized a hasty defensive position for the night among the enemy bunkers....

for gallantry ... on 6 September 1969 while serving as Commanding Officer of the 1st Squadron, 11th Armored Cavalry Regiment ... Major Bahnsen was flying in his command and control helicopter when he was informed of contact involving one of the squadron's troops nearby. He made low-level flights over the area while helping to direct the ground forces. Learning that the troop commander had been seriously wounded, he directed his pilot to land. When he landed, he discovered five prisoners had been captured and he helped to load them on the ship with the commander. Major Bahnsen remained on the ground to direct the forces. Mounting an armored cavalry assault vehicle, he led his men, forcing the enemy to break contact and resulting in sixty-nine enemy killed in action.

For Bahsen's Distinguished Service Cross, see above; for his Bronze Star Medals, see Chapter 3.

Lawrence L. Friedman: September 2, 1967

Major Friedman was awarded his Silver Star for aerial heroism over North Vietnam on September 2, 1967. His citation reads, in part:

Major Friedman was the pilot of an F-105F Thunderchief tasked to protect a large strike force from hostile surface-to-air missile sites. During the course of 20 minutes in the target area he was instrumental in neutralizing two missile complexes and one hostile antiaircraft site while under the awesome attack of 14 surface-to-air missiles, and extremely heavy antiaircraft fire.[149]

David H. Hackworth — March 4, 1966, June 12, 1966, February 29, 1969, March 4, 1969, March 22, 1969, May 22, 1969, May 22, 1969.

Hackworth received seven Silver Stars during two combat tours in Vietnam. He was awarded two in 1966 and five in 1969 and, as Hackworth had received three Silver Stars in Korea (see above), he left Vietnam with the record for most Silver Stars awarded to one individual. Note that Hackworth's last two awards were for gallantry occurring on the same day: May 22, 1969. His Vietnam citations read, in part:

for gallantry ... on March 4, 1966, near My Phu, Vietnam. Upon entering the operational area, Major Hackworth's unit made contact with a numerically superior Viet Cong force. During the early stages of the battle, Major Hackworth was airborne in a command and control helicopter. Later, he dauntlessly landed in the operation amidst intense hostile fire to personally direct his men. Undaunted by the intense machine gun fire, Major Hackworth remained with his men, exposed himself to hostile fire, and then assaulted the hostile emplacements. After the platoon seized its objective, Major Hackworth joined another rifle platoon which had sustained heavy casualties among its officer personnel and was virtually ineffective. He went from squad to squad in the most forward positions and rallied the disorganized platoon. He rendered first aid, directed evacuation of the wounded, and insured that ammunition was redistributed while continuously subjecting himself to an intense volume of VC fire. Later, as the platoon was inadvertently strafed by friendly aircraft, Major Hackworth braved the heavy machine gun and rocket fire while moving to a radio to call the aviation units to cease their attack on the friendly force. He then arranged for a medical evacuation of the seriously wounded. Again he exposed himself to intense hostile fire while running through a rice paddy to give visual landing guidance to the incoming aircraft. Due to the intensity of the hostile fire, the evacuation attempt was aborted. When darkness fell, reinforcements were brought in while Major Hackworth stood in the middle of an insecure landing zone with a flashlight guiding the landing of 10 aircraft. He then supervised the evacuation of the wounded....[150]

for gallantry ... on June 12, 1966 ... during a combat operation near Dak To, Vietnam. When a friendly company was assaulted by a Viet Cong force, Major Hackworth immediately proceeded to their assistance in his command and control helicopter. Unable to see the ground action below, Major Hackworth ordered the pilot to land him in a hastily prepared landing zone. As the aircraft hovered 15 feet above the ground and received intense hostile fire, Major Hackworth jumped from the helicopter and moved to the company command post. After a quick briefing, Major Hackworth sped to the defensive perimeter. Ignoring the intense VC fire raking the ground around him, he moved from position to position, directing his men and giving them words of encouragement. After observing the fanatical insurgents penetrate a section of the perimeter, Major Hackworth personally charged the breached position, killed three VC and wounded another. He then successfully reorganized the defenses which held throughout repeated insurgent attacks....[151]

for gallantry ... on February 26, 1969 while serving as a battalion commander on a reconnaissance mission near Fire Base Moore. Disregarding his own safety, Lt. Col. Hackworth exposed himself to intense enemy fire as he had his helicopter land in an insecure area where 16 men of an 18-man unit lay wounded. He maneuvered throughout the embattled area setting up a defensive perimeter with the men who were still able to fight. He then called in a support element and led them in a sweep of the area, routing the enemy. As a result of his courageous actions, the lives of several men were saved....[152]

for gallantry involving close combat on March 4, 1969. While on a mission near My An, Vietnam, Lt. Col. Hackworth learned that one of his companies was pinned down in a heavily mined area by intense hostile fire. He courageously directed his pilot to land in the area. After landing, Lt. Col. Hackworth received word that the company commander had been seriously wounded and immediately went into the minefield, picked up the wounded man, and carried him to a relatively safe position. He then reorganized the company and led them through a fusillade of fire to a point where they could be evacuated by helicopter....[153]

for gallantry ... on March 22, 1969, while on a reconnaissance mission near Fire Support Base Danger. After gunships had engaged an enemy element, Lt. Col. Hackworth directed his pilot to land in the isolated area in order to recover the enemy weapons. Upon landing, he detected movement in a nearby bunker and braved intense hostile fire to maneuver to the emplacement and destroy it. He then provided covering fire as his operation officer engaged and silenced a second bunker and, after recovering the weapons, provided suppressive fire as the helicopter lifted off....[154]

for gallantry ... on May 22, 1969, while on a reconnaissance mission in Dinh Tuong Province. After elements of his battalion came in contact with a large enemy force, Lt. Col. Hackworth braved intense hostile fire to fly over the hostile positions and direct artillery supporting fires onto them. Then, realizing that the enemy element was, in actuality, a main force battalion, he skillfully directed the insertion of reinforcements in blocking positions around the enemy. After surrounding the enemy, he repeatedly exposed himself to the murderous fusillade of hostile fire to direct his forces and mark targets for gunship strikes. His valiant actions resulted in the decimation of the large and important enemy unit....[155]

for gallantry ... on May 22, 1969. During the late afternoon, elements of his battalion encountered stiff enemy fire. From his light observation helicopter, which was under continual ground fire, Lt. Col. Hackworth directed effective artillery strikes. He then rapidly gathered all available intelligence and initiated a vigorous offensive against the large enemy forces. As the battle progressed, Lt. Col. Hackworth, ignoring the fire his helicopter was receiving, directed the gunships and ground elements toward enemy targets, at one time throwing smoke to mark an enemy position. The net effect of his tactical decisions and personal gallantry was a complete rout of the enemy.[156]

MALCOLM J. HOWARD: MAY 19, 1966

Captain Howard was awarded his Silver Star while he was serving as a company commander during a search and destroy mission in the Boi Loi Woods. His citation reads, in part:

> As his company was moving though the dense jungle, they received intense Viet Cong fire from well-fortified positions, sustaining numerous casualties. Captain Howard immediately moved forward to advise his platoon leader and supervise the deployment of two platoons. Under his outstanding leadership, the lead elements of his company charged the Viet Cong bunkers, killing the insurgents and destroying their positions. Although he was slightly wounded during the battle, he continued his mission until the company had taken its objective, evacuated the wounded, and moved back to the base area.[157]

Born in North Carolina on June 24, 1939, Malcolm Jones Howard was commissioned as an infantry officer after graduating from West Point in 1962. After completing training at Fort Benning, he joined the 25th Infantry Division in Hawaii. He then deployed twice to Vietnam. Howard's first tour — four months in 1964 — was followed by a second tour in 1966 as an infantry company commander. During this second tour, while in command of Company B, 27th Infantry, he was awarded the Silver Star, two Bronze Star Medals (one with "V" for valor), and the Purple Heart. When Howard returned to the United States, he taught for a short period at the U.S. Engineer School at Fort Belvoir, Virginia and then attended law school at Wake Forest University. After graduating in 1970, then Major Howard served two more years before resigning his Regular Army commission and leaving active duty.

Howard subsequently served as an Assistant U.S. Attorney and as White House Deputy Special Counsel during the Watergate Hearings. After more than 10 years in private practice, he was nominated by President Reagan and confirmed by the Senate as U.S. District Judge for the Eastern District of North Carolina in 1988. In 2005, Howard was appointed by Chief Justice William Rehnquist to the Foreign Intelligence Surveillance Act court for a term of seven years; he was the last Rehnquist appointment to this court.

Grenada
STEPHEN TRUJILLO: OCTOBER 27, 1983

Staff Sgt. Stephen Trujillo received the Silver Star for heroism while serving as a medical aidman with A Company, 2nd Battalion (Ranger), 75th Infantry Regiment. This was the first Silver Star awarded to a soldier since the war in Vietnam.

On October 27, 1983, Trujillo was participating in a four-helicopter air assault mission near the town of Calivigny. After fast-roping into a Cuban-held compound, Trujillo came under intense fire — as did the helicopters. Two of the aircraft crashed into each other and plunged to the ground. Trujillo, "exposing himself to intensive enemy fire, flying shrapnel and the possible explosion of the burning aircraft," sprinted twenty-five meters across open terrain to the downed helicopter. He then triaged casualties and directed treatment being administered by two other medics. Sgt. Trujillo continued to give first aid under gunfire until a physician's assistant arrived. He then returned to the crash site several times and carried soldiers out of danger. His actions "directly resulted in the saving of at least one life."[158]

The Balkans (Serbia)
SONNY P. BLINKINSOP: MAY 2, 1999

Air Force Captain Blinkinsop was awarded the Silver Star for "gallantry in connection with military operations against an opposing armed force" near Obrva, Yugoslavia, on May 2, 1999. His citation reads, in part:

> Captain Blinkinsop led a flight of F-16CJ aircraft into the heavily defended Obrva Airfield area, defended by a robust array of SA-3 batteries and heavy caliber anti-aircraft artillery. Minutes after establishing their combat air patrol, several SA-3 launches were visually detected from the target area. Recognizing the danger, Captain Blink-

insop directed his Number Three man to employ a reactive high-speed anti-radiation missile. As Number Three turned to fire, Captain Blinkinsop's flight came under fire from subsequent salvos of SA-3s. With no personal regard to his own safety, he immediately turned his aircraft to engage the SA-3s. Captain Blinkinsop fired a reactive, high-speed anti-radiation missile to suppress the SA-3, silencing the site. While reforming his flight, the second wave of strikers entered the Obrva SA-3 rings. Captain Blinkinsop again turned and fired his last missile as two more SA-3 missiles were launched at the strikers. His action forced the SA-3 to shut down allowing all strikers to make a safe recovery to friendly territory.[159]

ADAM B. KAVLICK: MAY 2, 1999

Air Force Captain Kavlick was awarded the Silver Star for his gallantry in the air near Novi Sad, Serbia, on May 2, 1999. He was flying as element leader on a mission to destroy known SA-3 and SA-6 sites. His citation reads, in part:

> During the attack, Captain Kavlick's wingman was struck by an SA-3 and forced to bail out behind enemy lines. Captain Kavlick took command of the combat search and rescue efforts. For over two hours, with complete disregard for his personal safety, Captain Kavlick stayed over his downed wingman and twice avoided surface-to-air missiles fired at his flight. Captain Kavlick continued to provide top cover as well as coordinating the rescue effort until his wingman was located and picked up.[160]

Iraq

LEIGH A. HESTER: MARCH 20, 2005

Then Sergeant Hester was the first female recipient of the Silver Star since World War II. She also is probably the first woman to be cited for gallantry in close combat.

On March 20, 2005, while her squad was

Air Force Chief of Staff General Norton A. Schwartz pins the Silver Star on Staff Sergeant Evan Jones during a medal ceremony for air combat controllers on April 29, 2010. Jones also received the Bronze Star with Valor (U.S. Air Force).

Army Sergeant Leigh A. Hester was the first woman to be decorated with the Silver Star since World War II. She received the decoration for her gallantry in action in Iraq on March 20, 2005 (U.S. Army).

shadowing a supply convoy near Baghdad, that convoy was attacked by insurgents. In the 25-minute firefight that followed, Hester and her fellow soldiers "moved to the side of the road, flanking the insurgents and cutting off their escape route." Hester then "led her team through the 'kill zone' and into a flanking position, where she assaulted a [enemy] trench line with grenades and M203 rounds." When it was all over, Hester had personally killed three insurgents.

Leigh Ann Hester was born in Bowling Green, Kentucky and enlisted in the Army National Guard in April 2001. She had been working as the floor manager in a shoe store in Nashville, Tennessee at the time she deployed to Iraq with her unit, the 617th Military Police Company. For her gallantry in action on March 20, Hester was awarded the Silver Star in a ceremony at Camp Liberty, Iraq, on June 16, 2005. She did not, however, think that her conduct had been particularly noteworthy. As Hester put it: "Your training kicks in and the soldier kicks in," she said. "It's your life or theirs ... You've got a job to do — protecting yourself and your fellow comrades."[161]

2

Decorations and Medals
for Noncombat Valor

At the end of World War I, the only military medals that could be awarded to soldiers and airmen for gallantry were the Medal of Honor and the Distinguished Service Cross. These two decorations, however, could be awarded only if the heroism occurred in conflict with an enemy. Consequently, wartime acts of valor that did not occur in the face of the enemy went unrewarded. So did peacetime acts of bravery.

Recognizing that there was a need to reward non-combat acts of valor, Congress authorized the Soldier's Medal for Army personnel in 1926. Soldiers and airmen who distinguished themselves "by heroism not involving actual conflict with an enemy" were awarded this decoration until 1960, when the Air Force obtained authorization for the Airman's Medal and began awarding it to airmen for non-combat valor.

THE SOLDIER'S MEDAL

Overview

Establishing Authority and Effective Dates: The Soldier's Medal was established by an act of Congress (Public Law 446, 69th Congress) on July 2, 1926.[1] It may be awarded for acts occurring after that date.

Criteria: The Soldier's Medal is awarded to any person of the Armed Forces of the United States or of a friendly foreign nation who, while serving in any capacity with the Army of the United States (including a Reserve Component soldier not in a duty status at the time of the heroic act), distinguishes himself or herself by heroism not involving actual conflict with an enemy. Civilians are ineligible for the Soldier's Medal.

The degree of heroism required for the Soldier's Medal is the same as that required for the award of the Distinguished Flying Cross. Additionally, the non-combat valor "must have involved personal hazard or danger and the voluntary risk of life under conditions not involving conflict with an armed enemy. Awards will not be made solely on the basis of having saved a life."[2]

Order of Precedence: The Soldier's Medal is worn after the Distinguished Flying Cross and before the Bronze Star Medal.

Devices: Subsequent awards of the Soldier's Medal are denoted by an oak leaf cluster.

Designer: The Soldier's Medal was designed by Gaetano Cecere (1894–1985), a New York City sculptor and the founder of Medallic Art Company.

Description and Symbolism

Obverse

On a bronze octagon-shaped planchet (1⅜ inches in circumscribing diameter) sits an eagle, standing on a fasces, between two groups of stars of six (left) and seven (right), and above the group of six stars a spray of leaves. The planchet is suspended by a solid rectangular-shaped ring. Medals manufactured in the 1920s and 1930s were serially numbered (on the bottom edge of the planchet) but this was discontinued during World War II and today the medal is unnumbered.

Top: Soldier's Medal (obverse). *Above:* Soldier's Medal (reverse).

Reverse

On the reverse of the eight-sided planchet is a shield consisting of thirteen stripes. At the chief of the shield are the letters "U.S.," supported by sprays of laurel and oak. Around the upper edge of the planchet is the inscription "Soldier's Medal" and across the face the words "For Valor." At the base of the reverse is a panel for engraving the recipient's rank, name and organization.

Ribbon

A silk moiré ribbon, 1⅜ inches in length and 1⅜ inches in width, composed of two outside stripes of blue ⅜ inches in width, the center containing thirteen white and red stripes of equal width (seven white and six red).

The octagon shape was chosen to distinguish the Soldier's Medal from all other U.S. awards and decorations. The symbolism in the medal and ribbon are typical of the period immediately following World War I. The eagle represents the United States of America. The bundle of rods, or fasces, is an old Roman symbol of authority and unity. The thirteen stars on the obverse, and thirteen stripes on the reverse, represent the original thirteen colonies. The alternating red and white stripes on a blue ribbon echo the American flag.

Historical Background

In the early 1920s, the War Department, recognizing the appropriateness of commending non-combat acts of heroism, began publishing details of such valor in War Department General Orders. On June 24, 1924, for example, Corporal Frank O. Staples received a "Commendation for heroic conduct" in rescuing "a 6-year-old child from a buggy drawn by a runaway horse."[3]

But while the need for a more substantial award for non-combat heroism must have been obvious to many in the Army, the impetus for the Soldier's Medal came not from the Secretary of War or the military establishment, but from Hiram Bingham, U.S. Senator from Connecticut.

Bingham, an airpower advocate and veteran World War I pilot, wanted the U.S. Army to have a Distinguished Flying Cross similar to that of Great Britain. Using his position as a member of the Aircraft Board, to which he had been appointed by President Calvin Coolidge, Bingham proposed to Congress that it create an award "for heroism of outstanding achievement while participating in aerial flight." While this new Distinguished Flying Cross could reward either combat or non-combat heroism, the aerial flight requirement made ground personnel ineligible for the new medal. This meant that a comparable decoration had to be created for soldiers. Consequently, legislation introduced in Congress to establish the Distinguished Flying Cross also included a provision for the creation of the Soldier's Medal.

On July 2, 1926, an Act of Congress authorized the President to award a "Soldier's Medal" to any person serving in the Army, National Guard, or Organized Reserves who "distinguish[es] himself, or herself, by heroism not involving actual conflict with an enemy."[4] The Act further provided that those men and women receiving the Soldier's Medal were entitled to a pay bonus of $2 per month. Given that pay for a private was $21 per month in the early 1920s, this was a considerable reward.[5] While this monthly pay bonus no longer exists, an *enlisted* Soldier's Medal recipient retiring today is eligible for a ten percent increase in retired pay, but only if his non-combat heroism was "equivalent to that required for the award of the Distinguished Service Cross."[6]

Although then President Calvin Coolidge could have announced the new Soldier's Medal — and promulgated criteria for it — by Executive Order, he did not. Rather, the War Department announced the new award in its Bulletin No. 8 and published the award standards for the new decoration on May 27, 1927, in Army Regulation 600-45, *Personnel:*

Award and Supply of Decorations for Individuals.

In the meantime, the Army already was working on a design for the Soldier's Medal. On August 11, 1926, the Secretary of War, in a letter signed by the Adjutant General, directed that the Quartermaster General prepare and submit designs for the new decoration. Some five months later, however, on January 18, 1927, the Secretary of War requested help in preparing a design for the Soldier's Medal from the Secretary of the Treasury. The latter wrote to the Secretary of War on January 22, 1927, that the Director of the Mint had asked the Engraver of the Mint in Philadelphia to submit a design. As a result, a proposed design was completed and forwarded from the Mint on June 22, 1927.

The Philadelphia Mint's design was sent to the Commission of Fine Arts for comment and approval. Its members, however, thought little of the design, for they wrote to the Secretary of War on February 27, 1928, that

it would be a very serious disappointment to this Commission, if after all its struggles to obtain good medals, to have to rely on work of this character. One of the fundamental objections to the designs submitted is a lack of simplicity which would characterize all medals of the highest class. The designs and casts are disapproved and returned.[7]

Either the War Department or the Mint submitted additional designs to the Commission in November 1929. These also were rejected. As a result, in a letter dated January 20, 1930, the Quartermaster General requested Mr. Gaetano Cerere of New York City to design the Soldier's Medal. The War Department agreed to pay up to $1500 for an *approved* design and cast. In April 1930, Cerere submitted his design. The Commission of Fine Arts approved it on May 5, 1930, and the Army finally had its Soldier's Medal.

Since the Soldier's Medal was created by legislation, the criteria for its award are fixed by the wording of the statute. There has, however, been some evolution in the standards governing its award. For example, Army regulations originally prohibited posthumous awards of the Soldier's Medal. This prohibition, however, was rescinded in 1937, and the first award to a soldier who lost his life while performing a peacetime act of valor was made in 1938.[8]

But the most significant change to the award criteria for the Soldier's Medal arguably occurred in 1943. A new phrase, contained in paragraph 15*b*, Army Regulation 600-45, now required the act of heroism to involve "voluntary risk of life." Given that the legislation establishing the Soldier's Medal has no such requirement, the War Department's decision to add these words is most interesting. Certainly, a look at awards of the Soldier's Medal from 1927 to 1942 shows that voluntary risk of life generally was an element of the heroism involved. The decision to add this new phrase, however, institutionalized what until then was probably an unspoken rule. These words now signaled to commanders that not all acts of non-combat gallantry merited an award of the Soldier's Medal. A soldier might well save another's life, or a number of lives, but if he did not put his own life at risk during the rescue, no Soldier's Medal could be awarded. On the other hand, since paragraph 15*b* implied that saving a life as not an absolute requirement, a Soldier's Medal might be awarded for a risky, but unsuccessful attempt to save another's life. It also might be awarded for saving or attempting to save valuable Government property, provided the heroic deed had this same risk of life.

The Army underscored the import of this "voluntary risk of life" language when publishing a new Army Regulation 600-45 in 1950. This new version stated that "[a]wards will not be made solely on the basis of having saved a life"—wording that continues in Army Regulation 600-8-22, *Military Awards*, the current regulation governing the award of the Soldier's Medal.[9]

Note: although a soldier may not receive the Soldier's Medal for an act of lifesaving alone, that soldier is eligible for the either the gold or silver Treasury Lifesaving Medal if the rescue involved drowning, shipwreck, or other peril of the water.[10]

First Recipients

The Army publicized the first four awards of the Soldier's Medal on October 17, 1927. Note that, as the design of the medal was not approved until May 1930, the recipients did not receive any decoration at the time their awards were announced.

CLEOPHAS C. BURNETT: AUGUST 16, 1926

Private Burnett received his Soldier's Medal for "heroism displayed in rescuing two women from drowning in the Roosevelt Park swimming pool, San Antonio, Texas, on August 16, 1926."[11]

JOHN F. BURNS: AUGUST 18, 1926

Private First Class Burns was awarded the Soldier's Medal for his heroism at the Pig Point Ordnance Reserve Depot, Pig Point, Virginia, on August 18, 1926.

Despite having no experience as a firefighter, when he saw "a fire in the high explosive area hastened to the fire house and gave the alarm." Then, "with utter disregard for his personal safety and acting beyond the call of duty, he mounted the fire truck and started for the fire alone." Enroute, Burns passed the regular fire truck, whose driver warned him that it was too dangerous to try to fight the fire. "Pvt. Burns nevertheless proceeded to the fire and laid fire hose which was successfully used in preventing the spread of the fire to adjacent magazines which he knew contained loaded bombs and high explosive shell." Burns' "fearless action served to strengthen the morale of a group of soldiers who saw him and practically all of them hastened to the magazine area" to assist him.[12]

JAMES P. MARTIN: AUGUST 18, 1926

Private First Class Martin was awarded the Soldier's Medal for his heroism "during a fire at the Pig Point Ordnance Reserve Depot, Pig Point, Virginia." On duty at the fire house at the time of the fire in the high explosive area, Martin "drove a truck into the area which was threatened with devastation, he being fully aware at the time that the buildings surrounding the burning magazine contained loaded bombs and loaded shell." Martin's "heroic and fearless conduct" inspired other soldiers to join in fighting the fire.[13]

JAMES K. WILSON: AUGUST 12, 1926

Warrant Officer Wilson was awarded the Soldier's Medal for "heroism displayed in saving the life of a boy from drowning in Cooper's Lake near Ft. McPherson, Georgia." On August 12, 1926, Wilson was serving as a scoutmaster of Troop No. 1, Boy Scouts of America, at Fort McPherson when, "upon hearing the cries of several of the boys that Scout Clyde Quigley was in distress, ran to the lake and without removing his clothing jumped in and with much difficulty succeeded in bringing the drowning boy to safety."[14]

Selected Recipients (Chronological)

LEONARD L. BARTON: AUGUST 2, 1942

Sergeant Leonard Lawrence Barton, a member of the Royal Australian Air Force stationed in North Africa, was awarded the Soldier's Medal for risking his life to save injured American airmen. Barton's citation reads, in part:

> Shortly after midnight on August 2, 1942, Sergeant Barton was present when a four-engine bomber of the U.S. Army Air Force, attempting to land after completing an operational mission, crashed into a building at the edge of its airdrome, spread gasoline over a wide area, and burst into flames. Eight members of the crew were known to be in the airplane, and several persons in the building. All were in seriously

injured condition and were struggling to escape from the burning wreckage. Tracer, incendiary, and ball ammunition, scattered by the impact, began to explode from the heat of the flames. With complete disregard for his safety and at great risk to his life, Sergeant Barton repeatedly fought his way into the flaming area and aided in extricating the injured personnel.[15]

While thousands of Soldier's Medals were awarded to U.S. personnel during World War II, probably fewer than one hundred went to United Kingdom, Commonwealth, or other allied military personnel; only a handful went to Australians like Barton.[16]

GREGOR BARCASE: SEPTEMBER 11, 1946

Private First Class Barcase received his Soldier's Medal for "voluntary risk of life" at Lanier Flying Field, Sendai, Honshu, Japan. During a jump operation on September 11, 1946, the foot of a parachutist "became entangled in the suspension lines of his parachute, causing him to descend head down and unable to extricate himself." Barcase guided his own parachute "close to the helpless victim and attempted to free him. Although unable to disentangle him, Private Barcase skillfully supported his fellow jumper and, despite shouted warnings from ground observers of great danger to himself, landed in such a way as to save the other man from probable death or injury."[17]

THOMAS E. MCKEMEY: JANUARY 21, 1966

Then Specialist Five McKemey was decorated for attempting to save the life of a Vietnamese woman near Dong Tre, Republic of Vietnam. At about 9:15 A.M. on January 21, 1966, "while enroute to the Vietnamese Army hospital at Qui Nhon, Specialist McKemey noticed that the woman, who had been diagnosed with suffering from a severe case of [bubonic] plague, was suddenly grasping for breath." Despite the risk to his own life, McKemey "elected to administer mouth to mouth resuscitation ... for thirty minutes ... until reaching the hospital, whereby the woman's breathing had been stabilized and her life saved."[18]

COLIN L. POWELL: NOVEMBER 16, 1968

Major Colin Luther Powell was decorated for non-combat heroism in Vietnam. On November 16, 1968, a helicopter transporting Americal Division personnel, including Powell and the division's commanding general, crashed. "With complete disregard for his own safety and while injured himself, Powell returned several times to the smoldering aircraft which was in danger of bursting into flames." Despite having to "break away part of the wreckage in order to get to a trapped individual," Powell's personal bravery and devotion to duty meant that the lives of "all personnel were saved."[19]

Powell subsequently had a distinguished career as a soldier and, after retiring as the chairman of the Joint Chiefs of Staff in 1993, General Powell returned to public service as U.S. Secretary of State from 2001 to 2005.[20]

GEORGE T. FLYNN: MAY 21, 1971

Major Flynn was serving at the 24th Evacuation Hospital at Long Binh when he performed a remarkable surgery that earned him a Soldier's Medal.

On May 21, 1971, Specialist Four Thomas J. Dalton arrived at the hospital with "a live M-79 grenade round" embedded in his left shoulder. "With disregard for his own safety and with no other protection than a flak jacket and steel helmet, Major Flynn stayed with the patient in order to reassure the patient and to keep him calm while preparations were being made to perform the surgery outside the hospital." Flynn then "performed surgery under extremely adverse conditions which included excessive heat, very poor lighting, and the wearing of uncomfortable and unfamiliar clothing." Despite these adverse conditions, Flynn successfully removed the live M-79 round. His heroism "saved the life of one person and protected numerous others from bodily harm."[21]

DAMIAN T. HORNE: OCTOBER 10, 1987

Then First Lieutenant Horne saved the life of a soldier while on a field training exercise at Fort Wingate, New Mexico, on October 10, 1987.

While in full uniform and gear, Horne "responded to a call for help from a soldier who had been seized by cramps in frigid lake waters." Despite being a weak swimmer, Horne swam to the drowning soldier. Although "the much larger man was in a state of panic" and continued to struggle against Horne, he nevertheless pulled the drowning soldier to shore and saved him from certain death.[22]

Commissioned in 1978 after graduating from Officer Candidate School as a teenager (he was 19 years old), Horne subsequently served as an infantry officer until leaving active duty in 1982. He was a Reserve officer assigned to 2nd Battalion, 12th Special Forces Group, at the time of the Soldier's Medal incident. Horne later left the Army Reserve but, after the September 11, 2001 attacks, re-enlisted as a sergeant in the New Mexico National Guard. Today, Horne is a judge advocate captain in the Colorado National Guard.

JAMES R. VELEZ: NOVEMBER 8, 1988

Staff Sergeant Velez was decorated for heroism while assigned to the 224th Military Intelligence Battalion (Aerial Exploitation), Hunter Army Airfield, Savannah, Georgia. His citation reads, in part:

> With total disregard for his own safety, Staff Sergeant Velez forced open the door of a burning automobile and extracted an unconscious teenager only moments before the wreckage exploded. Were it not for Staff Sergeant Velez' courage and quick thinking in the face of certain danger, the young driver surely would have suffered a tragic and untimely death.[23]

STEPHEN M. BADGER: OCTOBER 27, 1995

MATTHEW LEWIS: OCTOBER 27, 1995

GUY A. LOFARO: OCTOBER 27, 1995

Majors Badger and Lofaro, and Staff Sergeant Lewis, were awarded the Soldier's Medal for risking their lives to stop a sniper on a shooting rampage. Major Badger, who was killed while trying to stop the shooter, received a posthumous award.

On October 27, 1995, the three soldiers, all assigned to 82d Airborne Division at Fort Bragg, North Carolina, were in a stadium in the division area when a lone gunman opened fire from a concealed position. The shooter, Sergeant William J. Kreutzer, was hiding in the tree line adjacent to the housing area. Firing his rifle into a field where some 1,300 soldiers were about to start a four-mile run, Kreutzer killed one soldier (Badger). Nineteen other paratroopers were wounded before Lewis, Lofaro, and a number of other paratroopers managed to tackle Kreutzer and subdue him.[24]

CHRISTINE ROBERTS: JUNE 25, 2000

Sergeant Roberts, an Army flight medic, received the Soldier's Medal for rescuing a fellow soldier from a minefield in Kosovo.

On June 25, 2000, a twenty-two-year-old cavalry scout with the 1st Cavalry Brigade Reconnaissance Troop was on a mission near Basici, Kosovo, when he entered a minefield and stepped on a landmine. In the explosion that followed, the soldier lost his right foot.

Roberts was part of the UH-60 Black Hawk crew sent rescue the injured man. Carrying 80 pounds of gear, Roberts was lowered from the helicopter into the minefield. She "dangled from the steel hoist cable [and] dropped through a canopy of trees and vegetation so thick that she could no longer see the hovering chopper." The wounded soldier had lost a lot of blood and was going into shock. Despite the danger posed by the minefield —

a "demining team later found 14 mines between where Roberts initially landed and her patient"—Roberts treated his injuries and helped him into the helicopter."[25]

Army Chief of Staff General Eric K. Shinseki presented the Soldier's Medal to Roberts on October 5, 2001.

THE AIRMAN'S MEDAL

Overview

Establishing Authority and Effective Dates: The Airman's Medal was established by Public Law 86-593 on July 6, 1960. This law, however, did not create a new decoration. Rather, Congress amended the statute authorizing the Soldier's Medal (first enacted in 1926) so that the Air Force could have its own version of the Soldier's Medal ("of appropriate design with accompanying ribbon") and be permitted to call this new version the "Airman's Medal."[26]

Criteria: The Airman's Medal may be awarded to any person who, while serving in any capacity with the Air Force (including a member of the Ready Reserve who was not in a duty status when he committed an act of heroism), distinguishes himself by heroism not involving actual conflict with an enemy. Civilians are ineligible for the Airman's Medal.

The act of heroism must involve "voluntary risk of life," but the success of the voluntary heroic act is not essential. There also is no requirement that heroism involve lifesaving.[27]

Order of Precedence: The Airman's Medal is worn after the Distinguished Flying Cross and before the Bronze Star Medal.

Devices: Subsequent awards of the Airman's Medal are denoted by an oak leaf cluster.

Designer: Thomas Hudson Jones (1892–1969) designed and sculpted the Airman's Medal. On December 12, 1962, Jones obtained a patent (No. 194,212) for the design of the new medal. But, as he was a civilian employee at the Army Institute of Heraldry and had done the design for the Airman's Medal as a part of his official duties, Jones assigned his patent to the United States of America.

Jones was a nationally known artist. He is probably best known for sculpting the Tomb of the Unknowns in Arlington National Cemetery.

Description and Symbolism

Obverse

At the center of a bronze disc measuring 1⅜ inches in diameter is the profile figure of the Greek god Hermes, son of Zeus. He is facing to the left, resting on one knee, and

releasing an American bald eagle from his open hands. At nine o'clock is the word "AIR-MAN'S" and at three o'clock is the word "MEDAL."

Hermes represents "youthful vigor and boldness." The eagle being released symbolizes "the aspirations and ideals of the American Airman."[28]

Reverse

Centered on the reverse, in two lines, are the words "FOR VALOR." Surrounding this inscription, at the edge of the disk, is a laurel wreath, which denotes achievement.

Ribbon

The alternating stripes of blue (six) and gold (seven), bordered by stripes of pale blue,

Left: Airman's Medal (obverse). *Right:* Airman's Medal (reverse).

intentionally echo the ribbon of the Soldier's Medal, with its alternating red and whites stripes.

Historical Background

After becoming an independent and separate branch of the Armed Forces in 1947, the Air Force continued to award Army decorations, including the Soldier's Medal, to airmen. General Orders published by the Department of the Air Force in the 1950s, for example, routinely announce awards of the Soldier's Medal to airmen who risked their lives to save valuable equipment or the lives of fellow airmen. In 1953, for example, Technical Sergeant Fred A. Masterson received a Soldier's Medal for risking his life in saving a B-45 jet aircraft that had caught fire. When firefighters were unable to control the flames engulfing the jet, Masterson re-entered the burning aircraft and extinguished the fire by closing its fuel valves. That same year, Captain Peter T. Macy also was awarded the Soldier's Medal after he risked his life to enter a burning house to successfully rescue an unconscious man who had been overcome by heat and smoke poisoning.[29]

By the end of the 1950s, however, as the Air Force developed its own identity and culture, it began looking at replacing these Army awards with medals of its own design. In fact, although the Air Force did not get statutory authority for the Airman's Medal until July 1960, it was working with the Army's Institute of Heraldry to design a new decoration more than two years earlier.

In early 1958, the Air Force "informally transmitted" two possible designs for an Airman's Medal to the Army's Heraldic Branch for comment; both designs apparently had originated in the Air Force's Awards Branch. The first design featured the Wright Brothers' airplane and the words "AIRMAN'S MEDAL" and "FOR VALOR" on the obverse; the reverse was blank except for a laurel wreath. The second design depicted the profile of an airman, looking upward into the sky, on the obverse;

the words "FREEDOM IS THE FRUIT OF VALOR" were inscribed on the reverse.

The Army suggested that both designs were ill-advised for the Airman's Medal. The Wright Brothers' airplane was "not considered appropriate" because the image had nothing to do with valor. The second design, with its airman gazing into the sky, also was "not considered appropriate" because "the composition, in its entirety, is not deemed suitable for a medal."[30]

At the same time that the Air Force was working with the Army to develop a design for the Airman's Medal, the Air Force also was working on a design for "a distinctive Air Force Distinguished Service Medal." In fact, the Commission of Fine Arts had seen a proposed design for the new Air Force Distinguished Service Medal, and had reacted "favorably." As a result, when the Air Force decided in June 1960 to "cancel all actions to establish" a new Distinguished Service Medal," it proposed that "the design tentatively earmarked for the new [Air Force] Distinguished Service Medal" now be used for the new Airman's Medal.[31]

The Army agreed that transferring the design of the "metal pendant" originally intended for the new Air Force Distinguished Service Medal to the Airman's Medal was a good idea. The Army then queried the Commission of Fine Arts and that organization concurred with the proposed substitution in September 1960. The following month, the Commission members met with Thomas "Tom" Hudson Jones, a civilian employee of the Army Institute of Heraldry, "to consider a revised design" of the Airman's Medal. Jones' modified design added the inscriptions AIRMAN'S MEDAL on the obverse and FOR VALOR on the reverse. The Commission, pleased with the placement of the lettering, now formally approved the design for the new decoration on October 18, 1960.

In March 1961, after the Commission approved plaster casts of the Airman' Medal, the Air Force had its new decoration. As Jones had sculpted the original pendant, and had designed and then sculpted the revisions to it, he was now credited as the designer of the new Airman's Medal.

A final point about the design of the Airman's Medal. Jones' medal pendant — a bronze circular disc featuring an eagle — had been intended for a Distinguished Service Medal for airmen that would complement the circular shaped Distinguished Service Medals of the Army and the Navy (both of which also feature an eagle). This explains why the Airman's Medal, in contradistinction to the eight-sided Soldier's Medal, Navy and Marine Corps Medal, and Coast Guard Medal, used by the Army and the sea services, respectively, to recognize non-combat valor, has a unique circular shape.

First Recipient

The first Airman's Medal was awarded to Captain John Burger on July 21, 1960. The award was for an act of non-combat valor that occurred on September 9, 1959.

Selected Recipients (Chronological)

MOSES E. WILLOUGHBY: NOVEMBER 19, 1968

Staff Sergeant Willoughby received the Airman's Medal for risking his life to save six men from a burning crashed aircraft.

Born in Winterville, North Carolina, Willoughby enlisted in the Air Force after graduating from high school. Some years later, on November 19, 1968, Willoughby was doing maintenance chores at Kadena Air Base, Okinawa, Japan.

After an explosives-laden B-52 bomber taking off for Vietnam crashed at the end of a runway, fire immediately consumed the airplane. Most the crew managed to escape before the full fuel tanks ignited. Although there was every reason to believe that the burning jet fuel would soon cause the ordnance in the aircraft to explode, Willoughby and another airman, noticing "human motion through the 450-foot

flames, jumped into an ordinary military pick-up" truck and drove to the burning B-52. While there were "fires all over the place," Willoughby and his fellow airman managed to rescue six of the crew, including the B-52's navigator, who had broken his leg and was "hobbling along an adjacent road." Some of the crew had been horribly burned, and two later died from injuries suffered in the fire.

After receiving the Airman's Medal, Willoughby became a transportation coordinator and later supervised the motor pool at Andrews Air Force Base. He retired from the Air Force in 1975 and died in 2008.[32]

JAMES J. CLOUSE: JANUARY 19, 1969
PHILIP J. CONRAN: JANUARY 19, 1969

Then Technical Sergeant Clouse and then Major Conran were awarded the Airman's Medal for saving the life of another airman in Thailand.

On January 19, 1969, Conran and his co-pilot, Captain Troy Lindabury, were in the process of refueling at Nakhon Phanom Royal Thai Air Force Base when they got a radio call that a B-26 had jettisoned its bombs somewhere northeast of the base. The pilots were ordered to find the location, check for casualties, and secure the area. After topping off their fuel tanks, Conran and Lindabury took off and soon found the fires started by the detonated bombs.

Lindabury initiated the aircraft's approach while Conran covered the pre-landing checklist. Lindabury, disoriented as a result of focusing exclusively on the ground fires, developed vertigo and went from a straight-in descending approach to a nose-high unusual attitude. Before Conran could take any corrective action, however, the helicopter settled into one hundred foot trees. The blades struck the trees and the aircraft then fell to the ground like a rock.

When it struck the ground, the helicopter rolled and caught fire. Conran, Lindabury and Clouse, who was aboard as part of the crew, escaped. But, after hearing screaming coming from the rear of the helicopter, Conran and Clouse returned to the fiery wreck. Although the flames were intense, and ammunition was exploding around them, the two Americans managed to extricate another crew member trapped in the helicopter. The helicopter blew up as soon as Conran and Clouse took the immobile crewman from the area. Both men were awarded the Airman's Medal for their "heroism involving voluntary risk of life."[33]

ALFREDO R. GUERRERO: JUNE 25, 1996

Staff Sergeant Guerrero received his Airman's Medal for saving dozens of lives in the aftermath of the Khobar Towers terrorist attack.

On June 25, 1996, members of the terrorist group Hezbollah al-Hejaz exploded a fuel truck next to an eight-story building at Dhahran Air Base, Saudi Arabia. The building, commonly referred to as "Khobar Towers," housed Air Force personnel and most were airmen assigned to the 4404th Wing (Provisional). The Khobar Towers bombing resulted in the death of nineteen Americans and one Saudi Arabian national. More than 370 men and women of various nationalities also were wounded.

At the time of the attack, Guerrero was atop the Khobar Towers building. It was around 10 P.M. and Guerrero, a security policeman, was asking another sentry "if everything was OK." As the two men talked, Guerrero saw a green-colored gas truck following a white car. After he saw the truck park near Khobar Towers, and the occupants of the vehicle run from the truck to the white car—which then sped

Staff Sergeant Terral A. Leak was awarded the Airman's Medal for his heroism in rescuing 70 elderly Japanese citizens from an apartment fire in April 2006 (U.S. Air Force).

away — Guerrero "knew that something pretty big was about to happen."

After radioing the control center about the threat, Guerrero began a floor-by-floor evacuation of the building. Many of the evacuees were in a protected stairwell when the bomb exploded and they owed their lives to Guerrero's quick actions. While the massive explosion sent shards of glass into Guerrero's face, he ignored his wounds and helped others who were more seriously injured.

For risking his own life to save his fellow Americans, Guerrero was awarded the Airman's Medal by then Air Force Chief of Staff Ronald R. Fogleman on July 3, 1996. He also received a Purple Heart.[34]

Chris Harlan: October 8, 2007

Staff Sergeant Chris Harlan was awarded the Airman's Medal in 2009 for heroism in rescuing four college students from drowning.

On October 8, 2007, Harlan was on leave from the 965th Airborne Air Control Squadron at Tinker Air Force Base when he and some friends saw a group of five college students wading into a pool of water adjacent to Turner Falls, a 77-foot natural waterfall located near Davis, Oklahoma. The men, all exchange students from India attending Oklahoma City University, entered the shallow water with their arms linked to one another. Then, when one of the students slipped into deeper water, the other men were dragged along. None could swim and were soon in danger of drowning.

Ignoring the risk posed by the frigid water, Harlan and his friends dove to the rescue. Within minutes they had pulled four of the five students from the water. Then, despite being cold and exhausted, Harlan continued to search for the fifth student for another 30 minutes until the police arrived. The fifth man's body was recovered shortly thereafter.

Harlan received his Airman's Medal in a ceremony at Tinker Air Force Base in September 2009.[35]

3

Dual-Purpose Decorations for Performance or Valor

The Distinguished Flying Cross, Bronze Star Medal, and Air Medal are different from all other decorations in that they were *intentionally* created to be awards for either valor or performance. Other medals — like the Army Commendation Medal and Air Force Achievement Medal — may today be awarded for an act of courage or achievement or service, but those medals were initially created as performance or service awards. The Distinguished Flying Cross was a peacetime creation, while the Bronze Star Medal and the Air Medal were both established during World War II.

THE DISTINGUISHED FLYING CROSS

Overview

Establishing Authority and Effective Dates: The Distinguished Flying Cross was established by an act of Congress (Public Law 446, 69th Congress) on July 2, 1926. President Calvin Coolidge implemented the law when he signed Executive Order 4576 on January 28, 1927.

While the wording of the original statute permitted awards to be made for acts occurring "since the 6th day of April, 1917" (thus covering World War I), President Herbert Hoover restricted the ability to make such awards when he signed Executive Order 4601, on March 1, 1927. Hoover's order provided that for "any act

of heroism or extraordinary achievement performed on or before July 2, 1926, the Distinguished Flying Cross shall not be awarded after July 2, 1929, nor unless the recommendation therefore shall have been made on or before July 2, 1928."

In 1950, President Harry S. Truman signed a similar executive order affecting World War II awards: no Distinguished Flying Cross could be awarded after May 2, 1952 for any act or achievement occurring between December 7, 1941 and September 2, 1945, unless the recommendation for the Distinguished Flying Cross was made before May 2, 1951. However, for any act or achievement occurring after September 3, 1945 and before December 31, 1946, the recommendation for the Distinguished Flying Cross had to have been made before June 30, 1947.[1]

Criteria: The Distinguished Flying Cross may be awarded to soldiers and airmen who, while serving in any capacity with the Armed Forces, distinguish themselves by heroism or outstanding achievement while participating in aerial flight. Foreign military personnel also are eligible if they are serving with U.S. forces.

According to the Army Regulation implementing the award criteria for the Distinguished Flying Cross, an act of heroism is eligible for the award only if it is "evidenced by voluntary action above and beyond the call of duty." Similarly, for the decoration to be awarded for "extraordinary achievement," the act "must have resulted in an accomplishment so exceptional and outstanding as to clearly set the individual apart from his or her comrades or from other persons in similar circumstances." Finally, a soldier may not be awarded the Distinguished Flying Cross for "sustained operational activities against an armed enemy." On the contrary, awards "will be made only to recognize single acts of heroism or extraordinary achievement."[2]

The Air Force Instruction controlling eligibility for the Distinguished Flying Cross states that an airman's "heroism or achievement must be entirely distinctive" and must involve aerial operations "that are not routine." As with the regulation governing awards to soldiers, the Air Force Instruction also states that the Distinguished Flying Cross may not be awarded "for sustained operational activities and flights."[3]

Order of Precedence: The Distinguished Flying Cross is worn after the Legion of Merit and before the Soldier's or Airman's Medal.

Devices: In both the Army and the Air Force, additional awards of the Distinguished Flying Cross to the same individual are denoted by a bronze or silver twig of four oak leaves with three acorns on the stem, commonly called "oak leaf clusters." The silver oak leaf cluster is worn instead of five bronze oak leaf clusters.

Only the oak leaf cluster is authorized on Army awards of the Distinguished Flying Cross. In the Air Force, however, the ¼ inch high "V" device (reflecting valor involving conflict with an armed enemy) is worn on any Distinguished Flying Cross awarded for heroism (as reflected in the citation, certificate or orders for the award). Use of the "V" device was authorized by the Secretary of the Air Force on June 30, 2004, retroactive to September 18, 1947.

Designers: The Distinguished Flying Cross was designed by Arthur E. DuBois and Elizabeth Will, both civilian employees of the Army's Institute of Heraldry. DuBois was the Chief, Heraldic Section, Office of the Quartermaster General. He and Will designed hun-

dreds of new military badges and heraldic insignia for the Army, especially during World War II.

Description and Symbolism

Obverse

A four-bladed propeller 1¹¹⁄₁₆ inches across is shown on a bronze cross pattée that is 1½ inches across. In the re-entrant angles of the cross, rays form a one inch square. The cross is suspended from a plain metal rectangle.

Reverse

The reverse is blank, leaving space for engraving the recipient's name.

Ribbon

The ribbon is predominantly blue, with a narrow band of red bordered by white in the center. The edges of the ribbon are outlined with bands of white, then blue.

Distinguished Flying Cross (obverse).

Distinguished Flying Cross (reverse), officially engraved (courtesy Jeffrey B. Floyd & FJP Auctions).

Historical Background

Most military decorations are designed to reward an extraordinary act of heroism or some notable achievement. Although the same is true of the Distinguished Flying Cross, it is unique because it is an aviation award that only rewards heroism or achievement occurring in the air.

The Distinguished Flying Cross traces its origins to World War I. During that conflict, many new techniques of warfare were introduced, including the use of poison gas, flamethrowers, tanks, and aircraft. Military aviation added a new dimension to combat and provided a new arena for feats of valor. The flyers who operated early military aircraft not only had to be skilled pilots, they also had to have considerable courage and endurance.

The first aviation decorations did not, however, originate in the United States. The British created a set of decorations in 1918 that recognized both combat and noncombat heroism in the air. One of the new British decorations was the Distinguished Flying Cross, which was awarded to officers who performed noteworthy acts of heroism while engaged against an enemy; the counterpart for enlisted aviators was the Distinguished Flying Medal. For noncombat heroism, British officers were awarded the Air Force Cross, while enlisted members received the Air Force Medal.

The United States did not create any comparable decorations during the First World War, but rather rewarded aviation heroism and achievement with existing decorations, namely the Medal of Honor, the Distinguished Service Cross, and the Distinguished Service Medal.

Senator Hiram Bingham

The Distinguished Flying Cross is the product of one man's vision and determination, Hiram Bingham III. Born in Honolulu, Hawaii, on November 19, 1875, and educated at Yale University, the University of California at Berkeley, and Harvard University, Bingham taught history at Harvard and Princeton University after earning his Ph.D.

Bingham's interest in the military began in 1916, when he served as a captain in the 10th Field Artillery, Connecticut National Guard. He was fascinated with the Army's new airplanes and became a military aviator in 1917. Bingham organized the U.S. School of Military Aeronautics in May 1917 and, the following month, he was commissioned as a major in the Aviation Section of the Signal Corps. He served in France during World War I, where he commanded the flying school at Issoudun, France, earning a promotion to lieutenant colonel in October 1917.

After the war, Bingham's interest turned to politics. He served as the lieutenant governor of Connecticut from 1922 to 1924, and he was elected Connecticut's governor in November 1924. The next month, however, he left this office to fill a seat in the U.S. Senate vacated by the death of Senator Frank B. Branegee. Bingham remained in the Senate until 1933, and he never ceased to be an aviation enthusiast. As his World War I experience had given him knowledge of Britain's aviation decorations, he wanted a similar decoration for U.S. aviators.

The Morrow Board

Following World War I, Brig. Gen. William F. "Billy" Mitchell became one of the most outspoken supporters of airpower. Mitchell's frequent writings and comments on the subject irritated many in authority, however, and in 1925 he was transferred to San Antonio, Texas. In September 1925 the Navy dirigible *Shenandoah* crashed, and Mitchell charged the War Department and the Navy Department with "incompetency, criminal negligence, and almost treasonable administration of the national defense."[4] He was court-martialed shortly thereafter and convicted of making statements prejudicial to good order and military discipline.

While Mitchell's court-martial was in progress and being closely followed by the public, President Coolidge appointed an Aviation Board and named Dwight W. Morrow, a lawyer and banker from New Jersey, to be its chairman. Bingham also was appointed to the board and, through it, found the ideal vehicle for advocating the creation of a Distinguished Flying Cross. Consequently, when the board issued a final report in December 1925, it recommended "that there be instituted a special aviation medal and ribbon for extraordinary heroism or achievement in either peace or war."[5]

Legislation to create a Distinguished Flying Cross and the Soldier's Medal, which the Army desired as an award for peacetime heroism, was introduced in the House of Representatives in 1926. Both the House and the Senate approved the proposed statute, and the Distinguished Flying Cross was established on July 2, 1926.

Early Awards

When the Distinguished Flying Cross was created, subsonic aviation was still in its early years. The limits of both men and machines were unclear, and there was little if any margin for error in piloting. Flying was difficult, dangerous, and demanding, and pilots were public heroes whose exploits thrilled the nation and excited public imagination. In those early days of aviation pioneering advances were most often made by individuals, and this kind of personal initiative and heroism was what the Distinguished Flying Cross was designed to reward.

As a result the first awards were made to individuals who set altitude records, made record-breaking long-distance flights, or performed acts of heroism during flight that clearly justified a high level of public recognition. The purpose of the new decoration, however, did not include recognizing general aviation competence or research and development efforts. Consequently, recommendations for the award of the Distinguished Flying Cross generally had to be based on acts of heroism or extraordinary achievement during a particular flight. Prior the World War II, fewer than a hundred were awarded, including the twelve that went to civilians by special acts of Congress such as the award to Charles Lindbergh.

Development of the Medal's Design: A Troubled Start

Following the passage of the legislation that created the Distinguished Flying Cross, a joint board composed of officers of the Army and Navy conferred on the medal's design and developed regulations covering its award. The board did not desire to design the medal itself, so its recorder wrote the chairman of the Commission of Fine Arts on September 20, 1926, and asked if the commission would "be good enough to have prepared and submit ... an appropriate design for this cross."[6]

Since no money was available to underwrite a design competition for the new award, the Army's Heraldic Section — now known as the Institute of Heraldry — was asked to prepare several designs for consideration by the Commission of Fine Arts. When several variations of the Heraldic Section's basic design were placed before the commission, the commissioners were urged to accept one of them without delay because "there was an immediate necessity for approval of a design in order to present a cross to Colonel Lindbergh." Bowing to this pressure, the commission tentatively selected what it believed was the best of the proposed designs, even though the members felt it was "not worthy in general conception and execution of the high honor it was intended to signify." On the contrary, the commission considered the design of the medal to be "commonplace and insignificant" and made some recommendations on how the design could be improved. When the design was revised somewhat and resubmitted, however, the commission decided that the revised design was actually worse than the original and let its initial, unenthusiastic decision stand.[7]

Senator Bingham had seen the original design, as well, and he also did not like it. In a letter to the Commission of Fine Arts dated November 30, 1928, he explained, "I feel that it is fair to state that I was the father of the idea [of a Distinguished Flying Cross] and also had more to do with getting the idea into form of a law than any one else." As such, he was "very much disappointed" in the design when he first saw it, and "that disappointment has not decreased as time has gone on. I spoke to several of my friends in the War and Navy Departments about the matter more than a year ago and was assured by them that my wishes would be respected and the design changed so as to render it less heavy and more appropriate for a flying cross." Bingham concluded by requesting that the Commission of Fine Arts again reconsider the design of the new decoration.

Bingham's letter received a prompt reply

from Charles Moore, the chairman of the Commission of Fine Arts. On December 1, 1928, Moore wrote, "You are the first person in authority to express dissatisfaction with a Government award — a subject which this Commission has been carrying on an almost hopeless struggle for many years. It is encouraging to learn that you are very disappointed."[8] But, while Moore was sympathetic, his letter did not offer much encouragement. Moore did, however, send a letter to the War Department and the Navy Department on January 14, 1929, expressing his displeasure with the design of the Distinguished Flying Cross. Bingham's and Moore's dissatisfaction, however, had no effect. Both the Army and the Navy were pleased with the design and eager to have the medal available as soon as possible. The services' views prevailed, and nothing else was done on the design.

World War II Awards

When the Distinguished Flying Cross was created, its intended use was clear: The medal was to be awarded for either heroism or for extraordinary achievement while participating in aerial flight. It was also understood that any "extraordinary achievement" should occur during a single flight. Unfortunately, the concept of "extraordinary achievement" was so broad that it left a great deal of room for interpretation, and this led to serious problems during World War II.

The Army decided that the Distinguished Flying Cross could be a morale builder for aviators and, as a result, began using a formula based on the number of hours in the air in a combat zone, regardless of whether contact was made with the enemy, to award the medal. In the Twelfth Air Force, for example, an Air Medal was awarded for completing five sorties of two and a half hours or for completing ten sorties of less than two and half hours. A Distinguished Flying Cross was then awarded after a pilot earned five Air Medals. Each time a pilot earned another five Air Medals, he was award an oak leaf cluster to attach to the ribbon of his Distinguished Flying Cross.

Automatic awards of the Distinguished Flying Cross to Army aviators became widespread and created problems for the Navy, which refused to implement an automatic awards system. This had two effects on naval aviators. Those who earned their Distinguished Flying Crosses "the hard way" took great pride in their awards, and their chief complaint was that there was no way to distinguish between Navy and Army awards of the same decoration. On the other hand, naval aviators who had not earned the Distinguished Flying Cross expressed dissatisfaction that Army personnel received them for the same routine duty for which they earned nothing.

Ultimately, the Navy relented and liberalized its criteria for awarding the Distinguished Flying Cross, but never to the extent that the Army did. This is reflected in award statistics: between December 7, 1941, and June 30, 1947, the Army awarded 126,318 Distinguished Flying Crosses (not including those awarded to foreigners), while the Navy awarded 21,537.[9] To many, this was clear evidence that the Army had cheapened the award but, to date, there are no uniform criteria for awarding the Distinguished Flying Cross.

First Recipients

The first recipient of the Distinguished Flying Cross was U.S. Army Reserve Capt. Charles A. Lindbergh. On June 11, 1927, in recognition of his daring flight across in the Atlantic in the *Spirit of St. Louis*, Lindbergh received cross No. 1 from President Coolidge in a special ceremony on the grounds of the Washington Monument.[10]

The first Air Force recipient of the Distinguished Flying Cross was Colonel James M. Gillespie, who earned the decoration for his participation in the first fully automated trans–Atlantic flight of an Air Force C-54 "Skymaster" in September 1947.

Selected Recipients (Chronological)

The record for the most Distinguished Flying Cross awards to an Air Force recipient — at thirteen — apparently belongs to Col. Francis S. "Gabby" Gabreski.

ORVILLE WRIGHT: DECEMBER 17, 1903
WILBUR WRIGHT: DECEMBER 17, 1903

While Lindbergh received the first Distinguished Flying Cross, Wilbur and Orville Wright subsequently received the decoration for an earlier event. On December 18, 1928, by an act of Congress (Private Law 313), the Wright brothers were awarded the Distinguished Flying Cross for having made the first manned flight at Kitty Hawk, N.C. in 1903. Their citations were mirror images of each other:

> for heroism and extraordinary achievement while participating in an aerial flight. By his vision, perseverance, courage, and skill, Orville Wright / Wilbur Wright, in collaboration with his brother ... designed, constructed, and operated the airplane at Kitty Hawk, North Carolina, on 17 December 1903, made the first successful flight under its own power and carrying a human operator thereby making possible achievements which are now stirring the emotions and pride of this world.[11]

Wilbur's award was posthumous, as he had died in 1912.

JAMES H. DOOLITTLE: SEPTEMBER 4–5, 1922, AND MARCH 1924

Medal of Honor recipient James H. "Jimmy" Doolittle received two Distinguished Flying Crosses for "extraordinary achievement" in the 1920s. Note that both awards were for peacetime piloting and occurred prior to the creation of the Distinguished Flying Cross. Doolittle's citations are as follows:

> On September 4–5, 1922, Lieutenant Doolittle accomplished a one-stop flight from Pablo Beach, Fla. to San Diego, Calif., in 22 hours and 30 minutes elapsed time, an extraordinary achieve-

ment with the equipment available at that time. By his skill, endurance, and resourcefulness, he demonstrated the possibility of moving Air Corps units to any portion of the United States in less than 24 hours....

During March 1924, at McCook Field, Dayton, Ohio, Lieutenant Doolittle, piloting a Fokker PW-7 pursuit airplane, performed a series of acceleration tests requiring skill, initiative, endurance, and courage of the highest type. In these tests a recording accelerometer was mounted in the airplane and the accelerations taken for the following maneuvers: Loops at various airspeeds; single and multiple barrel rolls; power spirals; tail spins, power on and power off; half loop, half roll, and Immelman turn; inverted flight; pulling out of a dive at various air speeds; flying the plane on a level course with considerable angle of bank; and flying in bumpy air. In these tests the airplane was put through the most extreme maneuvers possible in order that the flight loads imposed upon the wings of the airplane under extreme conditions of air combat might be ascertained. These tests were put through with that fine combination of fearlessness and skill which constitutes the essence of distinguished flying. Through them scientific data of great and permanent importance to the Air Corps were obtained.[12]

AMELIA M. EARHART: MAY 20, 1932

Amelia Earhart was the first woman recipient of the Distinguished Flying Cross. Her citation reads:

The President of the United States of America ... takes pleasure in presenting the Distinguished Flying Cross to Mrs. Amelia Mary Earhart Putnam, a United States Civilian, for heroic courage and skill as a navigator, at the risk of her life, by her nonstop flight in her plane, unnamed, from Harbor Grace, Newfoundland, to Londonderry, Ireland, on 20 May 1932, by which she became the first and only woman, and the second person, to cross the Atlantic Ocean in a plane in solo flight, and also establish new records for speed and elapsed time between two continents.[13]

Born in Kansas in July 1897, Amelia Earhart began flying in 1921 and set her first aviation record the following year (when she became the first female pilot to reach 14,000 feet). In 1928, she published *20 Hrs., 40 Min.:*

Our Flight in the Friendship, a book about her experiences as the first woman to fly across the Atlantic as a passenger in an airplane. While this critically acclaimed book brought Earhart to the attention of the American public, it was Earhart's fifteen hour solo flight across the Atlantic in 1932 that turned her into an international celebrity. Charles Lindbergh had been the first person to cross the Atlantic in a solo flight and Earhart now joined him as the first woman to accomplish the same feat. Earhart disappeared while attempting to circumnavigate the globe; her airplane most likely ran out of fuel and crashed into the ocean after it had taken off from Lae, New Guinea, in July 1937. Earhart was declared legally dead in 1939.[14]

JEROME G. SCHWEICKERT: MARCH 22, 1944

Flight Officer Schweickert (the rank is equivalent to Warrant Officer (junior grade)) was a pilot assigned to the 94th Fighter Squadron, 1st Fighter Group, in the Mediterranean Theater. He was awarded the Distinguished Flying Cross for "leading a squadron of P-38's on a bomber escort mission over Italy" on March 22, 1944." As his citation explains, when

twelve enemy fighters attempted to intercept the lead formation of B-17's ... Schweickert gallantly led his formation into those enemy fighters and engaged them in aerial combat. Through his excellent leadership and sound judgment Flight Officer Schweickert kept his formation intact, thus attaining maximum firepower and affording maximum protection to the bombers. So expertly did he control his offensive tactics that the enemy formation was completely broken up. The bombers then completed their bombing run unmolested, registering direct hits on their target and inflicting heavy losses upon the enemy. As the bombers turned for home he led his formation over the target through intense anti-aircraft fire in order to protect the rear formation of B-17's, after which he led the bombers safely back to friendly territory without loss. Flight Officer Schweickert's gallant leadership and sound judgment was largely responsible for the success of this mission.[15]

JOSEPH LUBAS: AUGUST 13, SEPTEMBER 9 AND NOVEMBER 21, 1944

Technical Sergeant Lubas was awarded the Distinguished Flying Cross for extraordinary achievement while serving as radio operator of a B-17 airplane on bombing missions over enemy occupied Europe on August 13, September 9 and November 21, 1944. His citation states:

On all these operations Sergeant Lubas exhibited exceptional proficiency and exemplary devotion to duty. In the face of the numerous hazards and difficulties inherent to combat operations, this soldier was never charged with an error on strike or other message transmissions. On one occasion, Sergeant Lubas expertly administered first aid to a wounded crew member. Despite innumerable adversities on many missions, this soldier tenaciously remained at his post, performing his duties in high commendable manner.[16]

JAMES M. GILLESPIE: SEPTEMBER 21, 1947

The first Distinguished Flying Cross awarded by the Air Force for extraordinary achievement went to James Milligan Gillespie.

On September 21, 1947, then Colonel Gillespie commanded "a crew of specially trained officers, non-commissioned officers and civilian engineers" aboard a C-54 transport as it flew a "pre-programmed and fully automated" mission from Stephenville, Newfoundland to Royal Air Force base Brize Norton, England. The successful journey proved that flying was no longer subject to adverse weather conditions because an "electro-mechanical 'brain'" operated the aircraft's throttles, propeller pitch, flaps and landing gear.[17]

The citation for Gillespie's award describes extraordinary achievement in aerial flight. As commander of the Air Forces' first fully automatic flight across the Atlantic Ocean, Colonel Gillespie displayed superior ability, judgment, and alertness in the performance of duties. He supervised the preparation of the aircraft and its equipment for this precedent setting flight. He organized and trained the crew and was chiefly instrumental in the development of the project

to its successful end. The efficient operation of the entire flight was due entirely to strict supervision and attention to duty. Despite severe weather conditions encountered over the North Atlantic, the flights were maintained in accordance with strict time schedules laid down by Headquarters, United States Air Force and the Royal Air Force. The effort expended by Colonel Gillespie and his ability in organizing and commanding this research flight to its successful end upholds the highest traditions of the United States Air Force.[18]

CHARLES E. YEAGER: OCTOBER 14, 1947

Captain "Chuck" Yeager was awarded his second Distinguished Flying Cross "for heroism and extraordinary achievement in aerial flight while testing an experimental aircraft." Yeager's citation reads:

Captain Yeager, piloting the XS-1, became the first man on record to fly a plane faster than the

Charles E. "Chuck" Yeager was awarded the Distinguished Flying Cross for being the first man to fly faster than the speed of sound (U.S. Air Force).

speed of sound. This accomplishment of this mission, which required superior professional ability, coolness and a determined courage by Captain Yeager, was a contribution to the advancement of aeronautical science and reflects great credit upon him and the United States Air Force."[19]

Born in Myra, West Virginia in February 1923, Charles Elwood "Chuck" Yeager is the most famous test pilot in American aviation history. During his Air Force career, Yeager flew more than 10,000 hours in more than three hundred different types and models of aircraft.[20]

James E. McInerney, Jr.: May 10, 1955

James Eugene McInerney was awarded the Distinguished Flying Cross seven times during his Air Force career. His first award was for attacking (and probably downing) a MiG in 1955, two years after fighting on the Korean peninsula had ended, the citation noted his

extraordinary achievement while participating in aerial flight on 10 May 1955 as Pilot of an F-86F type aircraft with the 84th Fighter Bomber Wing, Fifth Air Force. While flying the element lead on the lead flight of an eight aircraft formation on an essential patrol mission over international waters off the west coast of North Korea, the squadron was attacked by approximately sixteen MiG-type aircraft. Approximately sixteen additional MiG-type aircraft were circling above. Lieutenant McInerney immediately engaged with a flight of the attacking aircraft and by exercising superior flying ability and excellent judgment, did outmaneuver them and did fire at one inflicting severe damage on it. The aircraft was last seen smoking and heading downward indicating it was probably destroyed.

John C. Bahnsen, Jr.: May 22, 1966, October 29, 1968 and December 1, 1968

Major John "Doc" Bahnsen was awarded the Distinguished Flying Cross three times. The citations for his awards follow:

For heroism while participating in aerial flight ... on 22 May 1966 while serving as pilot of a UH-1D helicopter in support of a combat mission near Cu Chi. While flying with limited visibility

on a low level reconnaissance flight, Major Bahnsen observed a Viet Cong squad in the open approximately two miles from the perimeter of an American base camp. He immediately conducted five firing passes on the Viet Cong and directed the suppressive fire of his door gunners. As he continued his firing passes, Major Bahnsen discovered an estimated two Viet Cong companies who were directing fire at his aircraft. Although the fire became increasingly intense and his helicopter received several hits, Major Bahnsen fearlessly marked the insurgent position with smoke and directed a light fire team to engage the Viet Cong. After both helicopters of the light fire team were hit and departed the area, Major Bahnsen, with complete disregard for his safety, remained in the area to adjust artillery fire and air strikes on the hostile force. After refueling, Major Bahnsen piloted his helicopter back to the battle area and flew through intense Viet Cong ground fire while marking the insurgent positions for the advancing American ground force. Through his courage he disrupted a potential attack on the American base camp and contributed immeasurably to the defeat of the Viet Cong force.[21]

For heroism while participating in aerial flight ... on 29 October 1968 while serving as the Commanding Officer of the Air Cavalry Troop, 11th Armored Cavalry Regiment. On this date, in the vicinity of Chanh Buu, Major Bahnsen was leading the combined elements of his troop against an estimated Viet Cong platoon. While conducting the search operation the Aero Rifle Platoon came under intense automatic weapons fire from the hostile force. Despite the fact that two of the troop's scout helicopters had received hits, Major Bahnsen maneuvered his aircraft to an extremely low altitude and delivered highly-accurate machine gun fire upon the elements. He continued his courageous actions, inflicting numerous casualties and enabling the friendly ground forces to assault and overrun the enemy.[22]

For heroism while participating in aerial flight ... on 1 December 1968 while serving as the Commanding Officer of the Air Cavalry Troop, 11th Armored Cavalry Regiment. On this date, while serving as a helicopter commander, he directed an assault upon a well-entrenched force. After inserting the troop's Aero Rifle Platoon, Major Bahnsen directed his aircraft through intense enemy fire to mark the enemy positions for airstrikes. Upon completion of the airstrikes he

directed a ground assault on the hostile fortifications. When additional helicopters arrived at the
scene late in the day to resupply the ground
troops with ammunition, the supply ships immediately came under intense enemy fire and one
helicopter was shot down. Disregarding his personal safety, Major Bahnsen directed his helicopter through the heavy enemy antiaircraft fire in
order to locate the downed aircraft and direct the
evacuation of its crew. After ensuring that the
men were safe, he called for the adjusted artillery
fire upon the enemy positions.[23]

John A. Firse: March 12, 1968

John Firse's fourth Distinguished Flying
Cross is highly unusual because it is a Coast
Guard award to an Air Force pilot. The com-
plete citation reads:

The President of the United States of America
takes pleasure in presenting a Gold Star in addition to two previously awarded Bronze Oak Leaf
Clusters in lieu of a Fourth Award of the Distinguished Flying Cross (Coast Guard Award) to
Captain John Albert Firse ... for extraordinary
achievement while participating in aerial flight
on 12 March 1968 as Aircraft Commander of a
Coast Guard HH-52A helicopter engaged in the
evacuation of 11 crewmen from the floating oil
rig JULIE ANN, Dixilyn No. 8, located 110 miles
southwest of New Orleans, Louisiana, in the Gulf
of Mexico. Despite severe weather conditions
with 40-knot winds, 20-foot seas and blowing
spray, which constantly threatened to extinguish
the aircraft's engine, Captain Firse skillfully maneuvered the helicopter and hovered close aboard
the sinking rig with his rotor blades less than 10
feet from the superstructure. Although occasional
monstrous swells racked the rig even closer to the
hovering helicopter, Captain Firse persevered and
with utmost precision successfully hoisted seven
survivors, off-loaded them on a nearby stationary
oil rig platform and returned to the pounding rig
to hoist four more survivors under the same ar-
duous conditions. Captain Firse remained on
scene until his critical fuel state forced him to relinquish his post and proceed to a fueling site.
Captain Firse displayed expert airmanship and
dauntless valor throughout this perilous mission.
His aeronautical skill, courage, sound judgment
and unwavering devotion to duty reflect the
highest credit upon himself, the United States
Coast Guard and the United States Air Force.

Born in Ohio in November 1937, John
Albert Firse was commissioned after completing flight training in June 1958. He subsequently flew the H-21, H-43, CH-3C
helicopters before deploying to Southeast Asia
in October 1966. During this combat tour,
while assigned to the 38th Rescue and
Recovery Squadron, Udorn Air Base, Thailand,
then Captain Firse was awarded the Air Force
Cross for extraordinary heroism on June 11,
1967. On that date, Firse flew his HH-3E
"Jolly Green Giant" deep into North Vietnam
to successfully rescue two downed American
pilots.[24]

After returning to the United States in
December 1967, Firse was attached to the U.S.
Coast Guard. Until he returned to the Air
Force in January 1971, Firse flew the HH-52
Sea Guard helicopter; his heroism in evacu-
ating personnel from a floating oil rig in March
1968 resulted in the unusual Coast Guard
award of the Distinguished Flying Cross to
him.

Firse later served as the Chief, Air Force
Section, U.S. Military Group, Nicaragua, from
February 1977 to March 1979. He retired as a
lieutenant colonel in 1982.[25]

Ronald B. Yuss: April 28, 1971

Air Force First Lieutenant Yuss was
awarded the Distinguished Flying Cross for
heroism while participating in aerial flight as
an F-4D pilot in Binh Dinh Province,
Republic of Vietnam. On April 28, 1971, Yuss
"attacked a large hostile force that had occupied
five buildings in a friendly village and had
friendly troops pinned down by extremely accurate and heavy small arms fire." As his citation explains, despite "the close proximity of
the friendly villagers, heavy anti-aircraft fire,
and low clouds," Yuss "courageously assisted
his flight commander in extremely accurate
and devastating ordnance deliveries." Yuss
alone destroyed the five buildings occupied by
the enemy troops and inflicted "numerous casualties on the hostile force thus saving many
friendly lives."[26]

RICHARD L. PAULY: FEBRUARY 2, 1991

Then Air Force Major Pauly "distinguished himself by extraordinary achievement while participating in aerial flight as an A-10 fighter pilot in Kuwait."

On February 2, 1991, "Pauly displayed outstanding airmanship and courage under extremely hazardous conditions, while employing his aircraft against a heavily defended Iraqi radar site. Despite encountering accurate antiaircraft artillery and infrared surface-to-air missile fire that hit the cockpit of his aircraft ... he successfully disabled this high value target and ... was able to successfully land his crippled aircraft."[27]

TERRY K. KERR: FEBRUARY 13, 1991

Senior Master Sergeant Terry K. Kerr received his Distinguished Flying Cross for his heroism in aerial flight while working as a Boom Operator over the Gulf of Arabia in Operation DESERT STORM.

On February 13, 1991, while Kerr was flying as Boom Operator on a KC-135, his aircraft "experienced an explosion in the galley area of the fuselage." The explosion knocked Kerr to the floor of the plane and the fire that followed engulfed the KC-135 in heavy suffocating smoke. Although Kerr suffered "first and second degree burns on the face and scalp" and the fire "burned away over twenty-five percent of his hair," Kerr had "the presence of mind to run to the cockpit and don emergency oxygen equipment. After acquiring a fire extinguisher, he reentered the galley region, which by now was a raging fire, and extinguished the flames. His quick thinking and heroic reaction were directly responsible for saving the lives of his crew and allowing the safe recovery of the aircraft."[28]

AARON DOVE: OCTOBER 3, 2009

MICHAEL POLIDOR: OCTOBER 3, 2009

Captain Polidor and First Lieutenant Dove were awarded the Distinguished Flying Cross for their roles as an airborne tactical air controllers in Afghanistan on October 3, 2009.

On that date, "Mike" Polidor was flying an F-15E Strike Eagle when he arrived over Afghanistan's rugged Kamdesh Valley. He "looked to the ground and saw pure chaos" as some 250 Taliban insurgents had attacked two Army outposts. The enemy outnumbered the Americans and their Afghan National Army soldiers by 3-to-1 and they "were firing from all sides." Polidor remembered that "it looked just like the Fourth of July ... explosions going on everywhere — I'd never seen anything like it."[29]

Polidor, aided by his weapons systems officer, 1st Lt. Aaron Dove, immediately assumed the role of airborne tactical air controller. Over the next eight hours, Polidor and Dove coordinated the strikes and strafing runs of 19 aircraft. By the end of the day, the Air Force had expended 30,000 pounds of ordnance to repel the Taliban. While eight U.S. soldiers and three Afghan soldiers were killed in the fighting, the casualties would have been much higher had it not been for the efforts of Polidor and Dove.[30]

THE BRONZE STAR MEDAL

Overview

Establishing Authority and Effective Dates: The Bronze Star Medal was established by Executive Order 9419 on February 4, 1944. The medal may be awarded for acts occurring after December 7, 1941, the date of the Japanese attack on Pearl Harbor.

Criteria: The Bronze Star Medal may be awarded to individuals who, while serving in any capacity with the Armed Forces of the United States in a combat theater, distinguish themselves by heroic or meritorious achievement or service, not involving participation in aerial flight.

Order of Precedence: The Bronze Star

Medal is worn after the Soldier's Medal and Airman's Medal and before the Purple Heart.

Devices: Additional awards of the Bronze Star Medal to the same individual are denoted by bronze (and silver) oak leaf clusters, and the "V for Valor" device is authorized.

When the "V" device is authorized, it is worn in the middle of the Bronze Star Medal ribbon when there is only one award. When there is more than one award, the "V" remains centered, and oak leaf clusters are worn to the left and right of the "V," with the first cluster placed to the wearer's right.

Designer: The Bronze Star Medal was designed by Rudolf Freund (1878–1960), an employee of the Philadelphia jewelry firm Bailey, Banks and Biddle. Freund also designed the Silver Star medal.

Description and Symbolism

Obverse

The medal is a bronze, points-up five-pointed star that is 1½ inches in circumscribing diameter. In the center of the star there is a smaller, raised star that is ³⁄₁₆ of an inch in diameter. The center lines of the arms of both stars coincide. The design was suggested by the Silver Star.

Reverse

In the center of the star, in raised letters and forming a circle around the center, is the inscription "Heroic or Meritorious Achievement."

Ribbon

The ribbon is predominantly red. There is a white-edged blue band in the center; the outer edges are also white.

Historical Background

Colonel Reeder's Role

In the early years of World War II, Col. Russell P. Reeder Jr. was assigned to the Operations Division of the War Department's General Staff. After about a year in that post, Reeder noticed that many aviators had earned the Air Medal and "thought it too bad that the

Left: Bronze Star Medal (obverse). *Right:* Bronze Star Medal (reverse), officially engraved to "Wallace C. Wallace."

ground soldiers did not have a similar decoration." On June 27, 1943, Reeder "placed the idea in the form of a letter" to Army Ground Forces Commanding General Lt. Gen. Leslie McNair.

In his letter Reeder wrote that "it would be an aid to morale if the captain of a company or the captain of a battery had a medal he could award to deserving people under him." He noted that the recently created Air Medal "has proven to be a great morale factor in the Army Air Force" and that "a similar medal is needed for members of the Army Ground Forces, and members of other Forces who are attached to or are serving with Ground Troops." Reeder expressly recommended that the new award be called the "Ground Medal," which would clearly identify it as a counterpart to the existing Air Medal, and that it be established "for *meritorious* achievement for award to any person while serving in any capacity with United States Army Ground Forces in an operation against the enemy" (emphasis in original).[31]

Reeder had been in the Army long enough to know how to make things work. On one of his free afternoons he took his proposal to McNair and gave it to him in person because, "it seemed to me a good idea to carry the paper direct and not send it through channels where it might be harpooned."[32]

McNair was interested in the proposal and promised to have it referred for further action. Reeder's proposal was forwarded through channels and received support until it reached the Adjutant General's Office, where it foundered. This was because the adjutant general, Maj. Gen. James A. Ulio, had been directed by the Secretary of War Henry L. Stimson to write a letter to the commanding generals of the Army Service Forces, Army Ground Forces, and the Army Air Forces, stating in substance that Stimson was not willing to authorize any additional medals or ribbons "at this time." As a result, Ulio wrote to McNair on October 4, 1943, and formally rejected Reeder's proposal for a Ground Medal.

McNair, however, refused to drop the idea. He took Reeder's idea to Army Chief of Staff Gen. George C. Marshall, who immediately saw the benefit of such an award. On February 3, 1944, Marshall asked President Roosevelt to authorize a "Bronze Star Medal" that would serve the purposes outlined in Reeder's original proposal. Roosevelt agreed at once, and the following day signed an executive order creating the Bronze Star Medal.[33]

Marshall's feelings were eloquently expressed in a letter dated April 10, 1944 to U.S. Rep. Thomas E. Martin of Iowa, who had been critical of the number of decorations awarded by the Army. As Marshall noted, "I was so impressed with the effect of the Air Medal and for the long-suffering infantryman that I personally asked for and secured the President's approval to a corresponding decoration for the ground forces, to be known as the Bronze Star. I want to obtain the same effect with this among the ground troops, particularly the infantry who suffer such a high percentage of our casualties, and I intend that it shall be awarded with the same freedom as the Air Medal."[34]

The Bronze Star Medal's design reflects the intent that it be a junior companion to the Silver Star. When the Commission of Fine Arts was presented with the proposed design of the Bronze Star, it noted its similarity to the Silver Star medal but voiced no official objections.

Wearing the "V" for Valor Device on the Bronze Star Medal

To distinguish between Bronze Star Medals awarded for combat gallantry and those awarded for meritorious achievement or service, the Army announced in December 1945 that a ¼ inch high block letter "V" device would be affixed to the ribbon of the Bronze Star Medal when the decoration was awarded for valor in combat. The Air Force continued this practice after becoming a separate service in 1947. Today, the "V" may be worn by a soldier or airman on the Bronze Star Medal only if the decoration is being awarded for combat heroism and the "V" is expressly authorized in the citation for the award. For more on this history of this "V" appurtenance, see Appendix D.

Combat Infantryman Badge and Combat Medical Badge Retroactive Awards; Distinguished Unit Citation (Corregidor and Bataan) Retroactive Awards

In September 1947, the Army announced that any soldier who had been awarded the Combat Infantryman Badge or Combat Medical Badge between December 7, 1941 and September 2, 1945 could apply to The Adjutant General for a Bronze Star Medal.

This decision resulted from the Army's belief that too few awards of the Bronze Star Medal had been made to ground troops in World War II. A 1947 memorandum prepared for Gen. Jacob L. Devers, then commander of Army Ground Forces, showed that Marshall's chief purpose in creating the Bronze Star Medal had not been implemented by commanders in the field. Marshall wanted the Bronze Star Medal to boost morale, and this required liberal awards of the medal. Yet a statistical study showed that "the rate of Air Medals awarded was more than 20 times greater than that for Bronze Stars ... 1000 Air Medals per 95 air corps casualties versus 50 Bronze Stars per 105 casualties among ground troops."[35] Consequently, to fulfill Marshall's intended goal, the Army authorized the retroactive award of the Bronze Star Medal to all soldiers who had been awarded the Combat Infantryman Badge or Combat Medical Badge.

In 1983, the Secretary of the Army created a second category of retroactive awards when he announced that "conditions of the defense of the Philippines deserved special recognition."[36] Consequently, any soldier who performed military duties "on the island of Luzon or the Harbor Defenses in Corregidor and Bataan" between December 7, 1941 and March 10, 1942, and who had been awarded the Distinguished Unit Citation (now called the Presidential Unit Citation) were authorized the retroactive award of the Bronze Star Medal.[37]

These Combat Infantryman Badge/Combat Medical Badge/Distinguished Unit Citation conversion awards have no time limit and are still being made today surviving World War II veterans who apply for the Bronze Star Medal.[38] Note, however, that the medal awarded is for merit, not valor.

Purple Heart to Bronze Star Medal Conversions

Starting in 1947, the Army also authorized soldiers who had received a Purple Heart for meritorious service or achievement to exchange it for an "appropriate award."[39] But, as a total of 272 Purple Hearts were awarded *for merit* in World War II, only a few soldiers applied for this "appropriate award"—which The Adjutant General decided was the Bronze Star Medal for ground personnel and the Air Medal for airmen.[40]

Selected Recipients

World War II

AUDIE L. MURPHY: MARCH 2, 1944, AND MAY 8, 1944

Audie Leon Murphy was one of the most highly decorated soldiers of World War II. In addition to Bronze Star Medals, Murphy also was awarded the Medal of Honor, Distinguished Service Cross, two Silver Stars, the Legion of Merit, and three Purple Hearts.[41]

Murphy's citation for his Bronze Star Medal with "V" reads:

> On the night of 2 March 1944, on the Anzio Beachhead in Italy, First Lieutenant (then Staff Sergeant) Murphy crept 100 yards over flat, open terrain during a fire fight between his small patrol and a group of Germans, to a point 50 yards from a partly disabled enemy tank. Taking careful aim, he fired several rifle grenades at the tank, hitting and completely destroying it. Then, when a great many enemy machine guns in the sector opened up, he led his men through a bullet swept area to safety.[42]

Murphy's citation for his second Bronze Star Medal — for outstanding achievement or meritorious service — reads:

> For exemplary conduct in ground combat against an armed enemy while assigned to the 15th Infantry Regiment, on or about 8 May 1944, as Staff Sergeant, European Theater of Operations.[43]

HARRY BELCHER: MARCH 25, 1944

Harry Belcher, a Flight lieutenant in the Royal Australian Air Force, was awarded the Bronze Star Medal for heroism at Manus Island, on March 25, 1944. At the time, Belcher was in command of a bomb disposal unit and was attached to an American cavalry brigade advancing toward the village of Lorengau. When "a narrow road, forming the only advance for tanks, was blocked by a mine field covered by heavy small arms fire from well-entrenched enemy positions, Flight Lieutenant Belcher voluntarily crawled alone across the exposed road and located and removed the mines ... opening a route for a tank attack."[44]

RICHARD D. WINTERS: JUNE 6 TO DECEMBER 31, 1944

Captain Richard "Dick" Winters, whose exploits in the 506th Infantry Regiment, 101st Airborne Division, were immortalized in the bestselling book *Band of Brothers*, was awarded the Bronze Star Medal "for meritorious service in connection with military operations against the enemy ... in France, Holland, and Belgium ... from 6 June 1944 to 31 December 1944."[45]

Korean War

JAMES R. WHITE: AUGUST 31–SEPTEMBER 1, 1950

Corporal White was a member of Company A, 23rd Infantry Regiment, 2nd Infantry Division, and working in his company's rear command group in the vicinity of Changnyong, Korea, when he earned the Bronze Star Medal for heroism. His citation reads:

> On the night of 31 August 1950 ... a strong enemy force came around the left flank of the company and attacked his group from the rear. A defense perimeter was immediately organized. Corporal White, with complete disregard for his personal safety, constantly exposed himself to the intense hostile fire raking the perimeter in order to return the enemy fire. On one occasion, he voluntarily left the safety of his covered position and dashed through the enemy fire to an abandoned jeep. Aided by two comrades, he returned to the perimeter with a .50 caliber machine gun and two automatic rifles, thereby greatly increasing the firepower of the small defensive force and covering all avenues of approach. Although the group was surrounded, Corporal White courageously held his ground until, early in the morning of 1 September 1950, orders were received to withdraw. His fearless determination throughout this firefight contributed greatly to the success of the command group in preventing the forward elements of his company from being attacked from the rear.[46]

LESLIE M. RAY: MARCH 3, 1951

Leslie M. Ray was an American Red Cross field director serving with the 15th Infantry Regiment near Seoul, Korea. His citation reads:

> On 3 March 1951 ... displaying sympathetic understanding and consummate concern for the mental and physical wellbeing of the combat soldier, Mr. Ray selflessly braved withering hostile fire to locate seven enlisted men with advance elements deployed along the Han River to deliver messages of critical morale nature. Through his efforts, a link was established between them and their families, which relieved the strain and uncertainty created by emotional upsets involving personal problems and difficulties. Mr. Ray's unflinching courage and devotion to duty were highly inspirational, enhanced the esprit de corps and combat effectiveness of the command, and reflect distinct credit on himself and the American Red Cross.[47]

Vietnam War

JOSEPH L. GALLOWAY: NOVEMBER 14–15, 1965

Joseph "Joe" Galloway, who served as a civilian war correspondent for United Press International and co-authored the critically acclaimed *We Were Soldiers Once ... And Young*,[48] was awarded the Bronze Star Medal with "V" for his heroism at Ia Drang. While at least one source claims that Galloway's award is "the only such valor award made to a civilian during the Vietnam War,"[49] this is not true: John Paul Vann, a civilian State Department employee, was awarded the Distinguished Service Cross for extraordinary heroism in combat in 1972. Galloway's citation reads:

> for heroism while accompanying the 7th Cavalry Regiment. During the afternoon of 14 November 1965, a furious battle had been fought between the 1st Battalion, 7th Cavalry Regiment, and the 66th Regiment of the Peoples Army of Vietnam. Mr. Galloway voluntarily boarded a helicopter which landed at night on a hazardous resupply run into an active combat situation where he was determined to report to the world details of the first major battle of the Vietnam War. Early on 15 November 1965 in the fury of the action, an American fighter bomber dropped two napalm bombs on the Battalion Command Post and Aid Station area gravely wounding two soldiers. Mr. Galloway and a medical aid man rose, braving enemy fire, and ran to the aid of the injured soldiers. The medical aid man was immediately shot and killed. With assistance from another man, Mr. Galloway carried one of the injured soldiers to the medical aid station. He remained on the ground throughout the grueling three-day battle, frequently under fire, until the 1st Battalion, 7th Cavalry was replaced by other forces of the 1st Cavalry Division. Mr. Galloway's valorous actions under enemy fire and his determination to get accurate, factual reports to the American people reflect great credit upon himself and American War Correspondents.[50]

JOE M. O'GRADY: MARCH 19, 1967

Air Force Lt. Col. O'Grady distinguished himself in ground operations near Tan Lop, South Vietnam, on March 19, 1967. His Bronze Star Medal citation reads, in part:

> He led a ground reconnaissance mission into unfriendly territory and positively identified a suspected missile launch site which post a threat to the Bien Hoa Air Base/Long Binh Army Complex. In spite of the opposition, Colonel O'Grady was able to complete the mission successfully and provide valuable information to friendly forces which resulted in destruction of the missile launch site.[51]

JOHN C. BAHNSEN, JR.: OCTOBER 6, 1968, OCTOBER 16, 1968, AND JUNE 9, 1969

Major "Doc" Bahnsen was awarded three Bronze Star Medals with "V for Valor" in Vietnam. The citations follow:

> On 6 October 1968, while serving as the Commander of the Air Cavalry Troop, 11th Armored Cavalry Regiment ... while on a reconnaissance mission, Major Bahnsen received a report on enemy activity in the immediate area. Reacting instantly, he instructed his scouts to maintain visual contact while he inserted two squads of his aero-rifle platoon. Realizing that a thorough search was necessary, he joined the squads on the ground and personally directed the search by expertly deploying his men to cover the extremely difficult terrain. Spotting the enemy in a very dense thicket, he quickly decided that pursuit was necessary and rallied his men, leading them into the dense growth in order to chase the enemy from its well-concealed position. One enemy soldier was captured and indicated the presence of additional armed enemy soldiers nearby. Acting on this intelligence, Major Bahnsen led his men in their advance into the thicket and came upon an enemy soldier and bodily dragged him out. Subsequent searches in the extremely rough terrain resulted in the capture of six armed enemy soldiers with no losses to the friendly force....[52]
> on 16 October 1968 while serving as the Commander of the Air Cavalry Troop, 11th Armored Cavalry Regiment ... while securing a downed helicopter, a report was received that another OH-6A had crashed into an enemy position. Major Bahnsen immediately flew to the area and landed approximately 100 meters from the downed aircraft. He continued to the crash site to find the pilot mortally wounded and the crew chief severely burned. Realizing that the Viet Cong had their position pinpointed, he provided cover for the withdrawal as other members of the party carried the wounded pilot back to his aircraft. He then directed another OH-6A to land in the area and evacuate the wounded men while he waited for ground troops to arrive and directed them into the Viet Cong base camp....[53]

On 9 June 1969 while serving as the Commanding Officer of 1st Squadron, 11th Armored Cavalry Regiment ... elements of the 1st Squadron were conducting a reconnaissance mission near the Saigon River when they spotted an enemy soldier. Immediately they began pursuing him with armored vehicles and helicopter gunships until he disappeared along the riverbank. At this point Major Bahnsen landed his helicopter and pursued the enemy on foot. Disregarding the likelihood of more North Vietnamese being in the area, Major Bahnsen began searching along the riverbank for the enemy soldier. He suddenly spotted him beneath the water and grasped the enemy by the throat, lifting him to the surface.[54]

TIMOTHY J. RYAN: OCTOBER 3, 1993 AND AUGUST 2–DECEMBER 1, 1993

Second Lt. Ryan received two Bronze Star Medals while assigned to C Company, 2d Battalion, 14th Infantry Regiment, 10th Mountain Division. The first was awarded with the "V" device for an "exceptionally valorous act" in Mogadishu, Somalia; the second was awarded for "meritorious service." The two citations follow:

> serving as part of the United Nations Quick Reaction Force, Second Lieutenant Ryan displayed uncommon valor and commitment to mission accomplishment ... his valiant efforts allowed Charlie Company to succeed in rescuing fellow soldiers trapped by an overwhelming force.[55]
> for meritorious service ... while serving as 2d Platoon Leader ... during deployment to Somalia for Operation CONTINUE HOPE. He performed his leadership duties in an outstanding manner.[56]

The events of October 3–4, 1993 are thoroughly detailed in Mark Bowden's *Black Hawk Down*.[57]

THE AIR MEDAL

Overview

Establishing Authority and Effective Dates: The Air Medal was established by Executive Order 9158 on May 11, 1942. It may be awarded for acts occurring after September 8, 1939, the day President Roosevelt declared a "limited national emergency" because of the outbreak of fighting in Europe.

Criteria: The Air Medal may be awarded to any individual who, while serving in any capacity with the Armed Forces, distinguishes himself or herself by heroism, outstanding achievement, or by meritorious service while participating in aerial flight that is not of a degree that would justify an award of the Distinguished Flying Cross.

In the Army, the Air Medal may be awarded to recognize single acts of merit or heroism, or for meritorious service. Awards for *heroism* must be in connection with military operations against an armed enemy or while engaged in military operations involving conflict with an opposing armed force in which the United States is not a belligerent party. Awards made for *single acts of meritorious achievement* "involving superior airmanship" must be "accomplished with distinction beyond that normally expected." Finally, awards for *meritorious service* must be "for sustained distinction in the performance of duties involving regular and frequent participation on aerial flight for at least six months." However, "accumulation of a specified number of hours and missions will not serve as the basis for award of the Air Medal."[58]

As the Army regulation governing the award of the Air Medal explains, the decoration "is primarily intended to recognize those personnel who are on current crewmember or non-crewmember flying status which requires them to participate in aerial flight on a regular and frequent basis in the performance of their primary duties." But, the medal also may be awarded to persons "whose combat duties require regular and frequent flying in other than a passenger status, or individuals who perform a particularly noteworthy act while performing the function of a crewmember, but who are not on flying status." For example, a soldier whose combat duties require him to fly would include those in the "attack elements of units involved in air-land assaults" and those "directly involved in airborne command and control of combat operations." But, as the Army regulation states, the Air Medal will not be awarded "to individuals who use air transportation solely for the purpose of moving from point to point in a combat zone."[59]

Regulatory guidance for the award of the Air Medal in the Air Force is much less detailed: the applicable instruction states only that the Air Medal is awarded "for single acts of achievement while participating in aerial flight." The level of achievement required "is less than that required for the Distinguished Flying Cross," but nevertheless "must be accomplished with distinction above and beyond that expected of professional airmen." Finally, the Air Force prohibits awards of the Air Medal "for peace time sustained operational activities and flights."[60] Note the import of this prohibition: while the Army permits the Air Medal's award for some types of meritorious service involving frequent and regular participation in air operations, the Air Force does not.

Order of Precedence: The Air Medal is worn after the Bronze Star Medal and before Joint Service Commendation Medal. For Air Force personnel it is worn before the Aerial Achievement Medal.

Devices: In the Army, the Bronze "V" device was authorized for wear on Air Medals awarded for acts of heroism involving conflict with an armed enemy, effective February 29, 1964. Arabic numerals, starting with "2," are used to signify second and subsequent awards made for achievement while participating in sustained aerial fight operations, with the number indicating the times the individual has received such an award. The bronze colored metal numerals are 3/16 of an inch in height.

In the Air Force, the V device is not authorized for wear on the Air Medal. Additionally, only oak bronze and silver oak leaf clusters are authorized to denote second and subsequent awards; the Air Force does not use numerals.[61]

Designer: The Air Medal was designed and sculpted by Walker Hancock. Born in

1901, Hancock taught at the Pennsylvania Academy of Fine Arts from 1929 to 1967. He produced hundreds of realistic sculptures during his lifetime, including a 39-foot bronze angel in Philadelphia that commemorates railroad employees killed in World War II and a statue of James Madison in the Library of Congress. Hancock won the national competition to design the Air Medal in 1942 and, while later serving as an Army captain, participated in efforts to identify and reclaim art stolen by the Nazis. He published an autobiography a year before his death in 1998.[62]

Description and Symbolism

Obverse

The obverse is a bronze compass rose with sixteen points that is 1.6875 inches in circumscribing diameter. The compass rose is suspended by a fleur-de-lis. In the center of the obverse there is an eagle in flight, swooping

Air Medal (obverse).

Air Medal (reverse).Officially hand-engraved S[taff]. Sgt. Robert A. Cochrane, A[ir] C[orps].

downward and carrying a lighting bolt in each talon. The compass rose reflects the global capacity of American airpower, which is itself represented by the American bald eagle. The lightning bolts in the eagle's talons allude to the ability of the United States to wage war from the air. The fleur-de-lis, the French symbol of nobility, represents the high ideals of American airmen.

Reverse

The central portion of the reverse side has been left plain for the inscribing the recipient's name.

Ribbon

The ribbon is predominantly ultramarine blue, and two orange-gold stripes are set just inside each edge. The colors were those of the Army Air Force.

Historical Background

On March 9, 1942, Secretary of War Henry L. Stimson sent a proposed executive order for the creation of an Air Medal to Director of the Bureau of the Budget Harold Smith. Stimson pointed out that the Distinguished Flying Cross was available only for heroism or extraordinary achievement in aerial flight, but that it was his desire "to have available for morale purposes a decoration with less stringent qualifications." He went on to note that the new and unusual flight duties "now being performed by the Air Force Combat Command and the Air Force Ferrying Command illustrate the need for such an award." In a separate letter dated April 13, 1942, Secretary of the Navy James Forestall concurred with Stimson's recommendations. The package was forwarded to President Roosevelt, who scribbled "approved" on the bottom, which he signed as "C in C," indicating "Commander-in-Chief." A formal executive order was signed on May 11, 1942.

The Problem of Automatic Awards

The Air Medal was to be awarded for essentially the same kind of acts that were recognized by the Distinguished Flying Cross but which involved a lesser degree of heroism or achievement. This made the Air Medal a morale-builder and had the added benefit of maintaining the value of the Distinguished Flying Cross. Certainly, some commands believed the Air Medal should be liberally awarded, and airmen soon saw the medal as almost automatic. For example, any pilot who destroyed an enemy aircraft in flight received an Air Medal, as did any pilot who completed five sorties of two and one-half hours each or ten sorties of shorter duration.

As a result of these practices the Air Medal lost its value as an award for individual achievement and, in time, was criticized as a glorified campaign medal for airmen. The numbers would seem to support this criticism. During World War II the Army awarded 1,166,471 Air Medals, accounting for 65 percent of all Army decorations awarded during the war. This high rate of Air Medal awards — at least in the Army — continued in Vietnam: the Army awarded 31,665 Air Medals with "V" device and 1,007,459 for achievement or service, for a total of 1,039,124.[63] Many of these Air Medals were automatic awards based on the number of "aerial missions" performed. For example, then Captain John B. Whitehead (whose Air Medal with "V" device is featured below) received 21 Air Medals in a single citation for "meritorious achievement" in having "actively participated in more than twenty-five aerial missions over hostile territory" between December 23, 1971 and December 11, 1972.

While a number of individuals have been awarded more than 100 Air Medals, no one knows who holds the record. A contender for the record is William J. Maddox, who served on active duty from 1943 to 1976 and retired as a major general. Maddox "amassed more than 10,600 flying hours, including 4,000 in combat in Korea, Vietnam, and Cambodia" and was awarded 127 Air Medals.[64]

Today in the Army, the Air Medal continues to be awarded for individual heroism, achievement, or service. In the Air Force, however, the Air Medal is restricted to heroism and "single acts of achievement while participating in aerial flight." Service awards are prohibited.

Selected Recipients (Chronological)

PHILIP J. CONRAN: MARCH 25, 1969

Captain Conran received nine Air Medals for "meritorious achievement while participating in aerial flight over Southeast Asia." The citation for his second award was:

> on 25 March 1969 ... he superbly accomplished a highly intricate mission to support Free World forces that were combating aggression. His energetic application of his knowledge and skill were significant factors that contributed greatly to furthering United States goals in Southeast Asia.[65]

JOHN B. WHITEHEAD: AUGUST 7, 1972

Captain John Whitehead was awarded a total of 32 Air Medals "while engaged in aerial flight in connection with military operations against a hostile force" in Vietnam. The citation for his last award — "Air Medal Thirty-Second Award with 'V' Device" — is

> for exceptionally valorous actions while serving as pilot of a light observation helicopter which was part of a flight assigned the task of locating elements of a Viet Cong regiment which had ambushed a popular forces company in the vicinity of Long Thanh. As Captain Whitehead began his reconnaissance, his aircraft was subjected to enemy automatic rifle and rocket fire. Captain Whitehead maneuvered his aircraft through the hostile fire and marked the enemy positions with smoke grenades, for strikes by the cobra gunships. These strikes forced the enemy to retreat leaving behind their dead and wounded soldiers.[66]

L. TAMMY DUCKWORTH: NOVEMBER 12, 2004

Major Ladda "Tammy" Duckworth, an Illinois Army National Guard officer, was awarded the Air Medal after a rocket propelled grenade hit her helicopter on November 12, 2004. Duckworth had flown more than 120 combat hours in a UH-60 Blackhawk in Iraq at the time of the attack. She lost both legs and almost lost her right arm as well. Today, Duckworth serves as an assistant secretary in the Department of Veterans Affairs.[67]

4

Awards and Decorations for Outstanding Achievement or Meritorious Service

Soldiers and airmen are eligible for a wide array of decorations and medals for outstanding achievement or meritorious service. Those described in this chapter are, in order of precedence, as follows:

- Defense Distinguished Service Medal
- Army Distinguished Service Medal
- Air Force Distinguished Service Medal
- Defense Superior Service Medal
- Legion of Merit
- Defense Meritorious Service Medal
- Meritorious Service Medal
- Purple Heart
- Aerial Achievement Medal
- Joint Service Commendation Medal
- Army Commendation Medal
- Air Force Commendation Medal
- Joint Service Achievement Medal
- Army Achievement Medal
- Air Force Achievement Medal

While some of these awards have a long and distinguished history, most are recent arrivals. This is particularly true of the many Defense Department awards that may be awarded to soldiers and airmen serving in U.S. Department of Defense billets or participating in joint operations. The oldest Defense Department award dates to 1963. While those awards have a different design and ribbon and outrank their

Army and Air Force counterparts, the medals have the same or similar names and are awarded using the same criteria for the relevant Army or Air Force award. For example, an Air Force sergeant serving at U.S. Central Command who receives the Defense Meritorious Service Medal or the Joint Service Achievement Medal has been awarded the Defense Department's equivalent of the Meritorious Service Medal or the Air Force Achievement Medal, respectively.

DEFENSE DISTINGUISHED SERVICE MEDAL

Overview

Establishing Authority and Effective Date: President Richard M. Nixon established the Defense Distinguished Service Medal when he signed Executive Order 11545 on July 9, 1970. The medal has been in effect since that date.

Criteria: The Defense Distinguished Service Medal is awarded by the secretary of defense to any person who performs exceptionally meritorious service in a duty of great responsibility with the Office of the Secretary of Defense, the Joint Chiefs of Staff Organization, a specified or unified command, a

Defense Department agency, or such other joint activity as may be designated by the secretary.

Order of Precedence: The Defense Distinguished Service Medal is worn after the Distinguished Service Cross or Air Force Cross, depending on the service of the recipient, and before the distinguished service medals of the separate services.

Devices: Additional awards of the Defense Distinguished Service Medal to the same individual are reflected by oak leaf clusters.

Designer: The Defense Distinguished Service Medal was designed by Mildred Orloff and sculpted by Lewis J. King Jr., both of the Army's Institute of Heraldry.

Description and Symbolism

Obverse

The Defense Distinguished Service Medal is gold in color and 1⅞ inches in overall height. It features a medium-blue enameled pentagon with points up that is superimposed

Defense Distinguished Service Medal (obverse).

with a gold eagle with outspread wings. The eagle's breast is charged with the shield of the Great Seal of the United States, and the eagle is shown grasping three crossed arrows in its talons. The pentagon and eagle are enclosed within a gold, pierced circle consisting of thirteen stars in the upper half and a branch of laurel leaves (on the left) and olive leaves (on the right) in the lower half. At the top of the medal is a suspender composed of five graduated gold rays that extend above the stars.

The Defense Distinguished Service Medal is rich in symbolism. The eagle grasping the arrows is taken from the seal of the secretary of defense and is the American bald eagle. The pentagon in the background alludes to the five branches of the Armed Forces. It also alludes to the headquarters of the Department of Defense, which is housed in the Pentagon. The thirteen stars represent the thirteen original colonies and, through them, all of the fifty states. The olive branch represents the goal of defense — peace — while the laurel branch represents achievement.

Reverse

Centered on the reverse of the pentagon of the Defense Distinguished Service Medal is the inscription "From / The Secretary / Of Defense / To," with space beneath for inscribing the recipient's name. On the reverse of the ring bearing the stars and above the pentagon is the inscription "For Distinguished Service."

Ribbon

The ribbon bears a central stripe of red flanked on either side by stripes of gold and blue. The red represents zeal and courageous action, the gold represents excellence and the knowledge and guidance provided through senior leadership, and the blue represents the Department of Defense.

Historical Background

Many senior-ranking soldiers and airmen have held assignments that placed them in a

Defense Distinguished Service Medal (reverse).

position of authority over elements of other branches. In fact, the so-called unified or "joint commands," consisting of personnel from all the services, are the standard organizations through which most major military operations are conducted today. In the past, it was accepted practice for each military branch to award its own medal for distinguished service to senior officers of other service branches when those individual's leadership in a joint command justified the award. For example, General Eisenhower, who was the Supreme Commander of Allied Forces Europe during World War II, received both the Army and the Navy Distinguished Service Medals.

It has also become customary for the chairmen of the Joint Chiefs of Staff to be awarded the Distinguished Service Medals of each military service when they retire. For example, on September 1, 1969, General Lyman Lemnitzer received the Army, Navy, and Air Force Distinguished Service Medals at the ceremony marking his retirement from

his position as Supreme Allied Commander, Europe. This reportedly led Secretary of Defense Melvin Laird to remark that the use of the multiple decorations seemed improper and that a single decoration should be created for individuals who serve in duties of unusual responsibility.[1] Thus, the idea of a "senior" medal for distinguished military service was born.

Although this concept seemed simple, it raised a number of questions. Could a new award be created administratively, or would this require an executive order or legislation from Congress? Could the award rank above the service Distinguished Service Medals? Should it? When the decision was made to create a new award — tentatively called the "Joint Distinguished Service Medal" — a number of offices within the Office of the Secretary of Defense began exploring these and other questions.

In 1970, Assistant Secretary of Defense for Manpower and Reserve Affairs Roger D. Kelly was tasked with developing the new decoration. On March 26, 1970, his office contacted the Army's Institute of Heraldry and told it that Secretary Laird wanted the medal designed, developed, and ready for presentation by July 3, 1970. The assistant secretary's office also suggested to the institute that some elements from the seal of the secretary of defense be incorporated into the design of the medal.[2]

On the same day that the Institute of Heraldry was first contacted about the new decoration, a legal opinion issued by the office of the Department of Defense General Counsel concluded that authority for the new award could be obtained through congressional legislation, an executive order, or a Defense Department regulation.

The disadvantage of the executive order was that the president might be criticized for creating a Distinguished Service Medal by executive fiat when the Army, Navy and Air Force Distinguished Service Medals had been created by Congress. But an executive order had the advantage of being more easily promulgated than a statute, as well as the prestige of coming from the president. Finally, although a Department of Defense regulation was the easiest way to get the new decoration authorized, it was also the least prestigious. The Office of the General Counsel recommended that authority be sought under an executive order, even though such a move would establish a precedent by creating a decoration that ranked above several highly regarded, long-standing decorations that had been established by acts of Congress.

On March 27, 1970, a memo announced that the secretary of defense had directed that the "Joint Distinguished Service Medal" be created and that the new medal was to rank as the highest award for meritorious service within the Department of Defense. At the same time, the Army's Institute of Heraldry was formally tasked with designing and procuring the medal no later than June 15, 1970. On April 15, 1970, the Commission on Fine Arts approved the design proposed by the Institute of Heraldry. Finally, on July 9, 1970, President Nixon signed Executive Order 11545, establishing the Defense Distinguished Service Medal.

On June 21, 1971, D. O. Cooke, the administrative assistant to the secretary of defense, visited Vice Admiral Nels C. Johnson, the director of the Joint Staff, to discuss the proposed award of the new Defense Distinguished Service Medal to General Earle G. Wheeler upon his upcoming retirement as chairman of the Joint Chiefs. At this meeting, Cooke gently suggested "that the DDSM should be presented only." Johnson and the chiefs of the separate services, however, indicated that they intended "to give additionally the DSM of the Army, Navy and the Air Force." As a result, despite Secretary Laird's original desire to create a senior medal for distinguished service that would to preclude multiple Distinguished Service Medal awards, Cooke was told that "we can expect on the retirement ceremony at Andrews [Air Force Base]

... General Wheeler will receive not only the DDSM but three others as well."[3]

The first Defense Distinguished Service Medal — along with the Distinguished Service Medals of the Army, Navy and Air Force — was awarded to Wheeler the same day that he retired as chairman of the Joint Chiefs of Staff. Today, the Army, Navy, and Air Force continue to award their respective Distinguished Service Medals to certain senior military and naval officers of other services even though the Defense Distinguished Service Medal was created to eliminate that practice.

One of the unique features of the Defense Distinguished Service Medal is that it is awarded by the secretary of defense and has no delegated authority: that is, the separate branches of the Armed Forces cannot award the medal in the secretary's name. It is not within the authority of the military services to even initiate a recommendation for an award of the Defense Distinguished Service Medal or to provide supporting comments in favor of such a recommendation. The Defense Distinguished Service Medal is awarded solely at the initiative and pleasure of the secretary of defense.

First Recipient

The first recipient of the Defense Distinguished Service Medal was Air Force Gen. Earle G. Wheeler, who received it upon his retirement as chairman of the Joint Chiefs of Staff on July 9, 1970.

Selected Recipients

COLIN L. POWELL: OCTOBER 1989 TO SEPTEMBER 1993

General Powell was awarded his fourth Defense Distinguished Service Medal for his "exceptionally distinguished service as Chairman, Joint Chiefs of Staff. His citation reads:

> General Powell's tireless dedication to the best interests of the United States and its Allied Forces helped two Presidents and two Secretaries of De-

fense to chart the safest course for the Nation. As principal military advisor to the President, the Secretary of Defense and the National Security Council, General Powell confronted rapid and profound change. He was the first Chairman in history to deploy over 540,000 troops to a combat zone while at the same time overseeing the most dramatic restructuring of the Nation's Armed Forces since World War II. Moreover, in the wake of the Cold War, General Powell advised national leaders as they responded to a number of crises that resulted in military operations ranging from major conflict to peacekeeping and humanitarian operations. In a time of decreasing resources and mounting demands on America's Armed Forces, General Powell forged a team of Service leaders that cooperated in the best spirit of the military tradition. His dealings with foreign leaders enhanced United States national security relationships worldwide. The distinctive accomplishments of General Powell culminate a long and distinguished career in the service of his country and reflect great credit upon himself, the United States Army, and the Department of Defense.

Born in Harlem, New York, in 1937, Colin Luther Powell graduated from the City College of New York in 1958. Having been enrolled in the ROTC program, Powell was commissioned as an infantry second lieutenant. He subsequently had a stellar career in the Army, which culminated in his service as the Chairman, Joint Chiefs of Staff, from 1989 to 1993. Operations *Desert Shield* and *Desert Storm* occurred during his tenure. Although Powell retired from active duty in 1993, his service to the United States was not at an end; he served as Secretary of State from 2001 to 2005.[4]

T. MICHAEL MOSELEY: MARCH 19 TO MAY 3, 2003, NOVEMBER 2005 TO NOVEMBER 2006

General Moseley received his first Defense Distinguished Service Medal for his "exceptionally meritorious and distinguished achievement as the commander of U.S. Central Command Air Forces; his second award recognized General Moseley's exceptional service as Air Force Chief of Staff. Both citations follow:

General Moseley's vision, stellar leadership, and precise execution of joint doctrine was key to the success of combat operations, dominating across the full spectrum of warfare by incorporating joint and coalition forces to decisively apply airpower against the Iraqi regime and over 360,000 ground forces in Operation IRAQI FREEDOM. He wisely focused the leadership of 18 wing commanders and over 45,000 warfighters as forces flew over 38,000 sorties employing 26,000 plus munitions, air-refueling 55 million gallons, and moving 61,000 short tons of cargo. The architect for every aspect of aerial operations to include mission planning, air tasking orders, requests for forces, aircraft beddown, and airspace management, he brilliantly interacted with four unified commands, thirteen regional bases, Royal Saudi Air Force, Royal Air Force, Royal Australian Air Force, United States Embassies, and six carrier battle groups....

for exceptionally meritorious and distinguished service in a position of great responsibility ... as Chief of Staff, United States Air Force. While continuing to excel in traditional mission areas, General Moseley's strategic vision became a catalyst for expanding the Air Force's combat roles into non-traditional areas in support of the Global War on Terrorism. Under General Moseley's direction, Airmen contributed to meeting the Department's challenges in unprecedented ways, allowing traditional ground forces greater flexibility in managing and projecting a sustained level of long-term combat presence that allowed more focus on directly confronting hostile forces and conducting counter-insurgency operations. General Moseley's transformation of the Air Force led to innovative and responsive solutions to joint warfare challenges with a renewed emphasis on the Air Force's expeditionary heritage. In the Central Command area of responsibility, Air Force personnel played an indispensable role in intra-theater logistics under demanding combat conditions, greatly increasing theater airlift capacity through higher tempo operations, assuming a lead role in truck convoy movement, and exploiting new tactics and technologies to continually counter and detect an evolving Improvised Explosive Device threat. General Moseley re-defined Airpower for the 21st Century by setting "fly and fight in air, space, and cyberspace" as the Service's core mission while concurrently providing direct, invaluable combat and combat support assistance to traditional ground forces.

Born in 1949 in Grand View, Texas, Teed Michael "Buzz" Moseley graduated from Texas A&M University in 1971. He served as the 18th Chief of Staff of the Air Force and retired as a four-star general in July 2008.

ARMY DISTINGUISHED SERVICE MEDAL

Overview

Establishing Authority and Effective Dates: The Army Distinguished Service Medal was established by Congress (Public Law 253, 65th Congress) on February 4, 1919. It may be awarded for service after April 6, 1917, which was the date of U.S. entry into World War I.

Criteria: The Army Distinguished Service Medal is awarded "to any person who, while serving in any capacity with the Army, has distinguished himself by exceptionally meritorious service to the government while holding a position of great responsibility."[5] The performance must be such as to merit recognition for service which is clearly exceptional. The exceptional performance of normal duty will not alone justify an award of this decoration.

"For service not related to actual war, the term 'duty of great responsibility' applies to a narrower range of positions than it does in time of war, and requires evidence of conspicuously significant achievement." However, a Distinguished Service Medal may be justified "by exceptionally meritorious service in a succession of high positions of great importance."[6]

Order of Precedence: The Army Distinguished Service Medal is worn after the Defense Distinguished Service Medal and before the Silver Star.

Devices: Additional awards of the Army Distinguished Service Medal to the same individual are denoted by bronze (or silver) oak leaf clusters.

Designer: Captain Aymar Embury, a well-known New York architect then serving in the Army in Washington, D.C., designed the Distinguished Service Medal. The plaster model of the medal was sculpted by Gaetano Cecere, who would later design and sculpt the Soldier's Medal.

Description and Symbolism

Obverse

The coat of arms of the United States in gold is centered on a gilt-bronze medallion, and this coat of arms is surrounded by a circle of dark blue enamel, 1½ inches in diameter, bearing the inscription "For Distinguished Service MCMXVIII." Each medal was originally numbered on the rim at the bottom and a record maintained that matched each num-

Army DSM (obverse).

bered medal with each recipient. This practice ceased in World War II.

Reverse

On the reverse is a blank scroll (for engraving the name of the recipient) which is centered on a trophy of flags and weapons.

Ribbon

The medal is suspended from by a bar attached to the ribbon, which is 1⅜ inches wide and consists of the following stripes: 5/16 inch scarlet; 1/16 inch ultramarine blue; ⅝ inch white; 1/16 inch ultramarine blue; and 5/16 inch scarlet. These colors are meant to echo those of the U.S. flag.

Historical Background

When the United States entered World War I, the Army had only the Medal of Honor as an award for combat heroism, and there was no decoration for achievement or meritorious service.[7] After American troops began arriving in France, General John J. Pershing, the American Expeditionary Force commander, realized that the Army needed some sort of award for outstanding performance, especially for those officers serving in a position of great responsibility.

Pershing requested that the War Department create such an award — a Distinguished Service Medal — and Secretary of War Newton D. Baker forwarded Pershing's request to President Woodrow Wilson for action. Pershing, who had also requested that the Army create a new decoration for combat heroism — a Distinguished Service Cross — was certainly pleased when he learned that Wilson had authorized both medals on January 9, 1918. The two new decorations were announced in War Department General Orders No. 6 on January 12, 1918.

Six months later, on July 9, 1918, Congress enacted a statute creating the Distinguished Service Medal. According to the War Department's Annual Report for 1918, this leg-islation (which also created the Distinguished Service Cross) "authorized the issue of the ... medal under the same conditions as those set forth in" General Order No. 6.[8] The original wording of the statute reads:

> The President ... is ... authorized to present, but not in the name of the Congress, a distinguished-service medal of appropriate design and a ribbon, together with a rosette or other device, to be worn in lieu thereof, to any person who, while serving in any capacity with the Army of the United States since the 6th day of April 1917, has distinguished, or who hereafter shall distinguish, himself or herself by exceptionally meritorious service to the Government in a duty of great responsibility.[9]

The original statute was amended in 1956 to delete several unnecessary phrases. For example, the prohibition on presenting the medal in the name of the Congress was omitted as surplusage since a medal may be presented in the name of the Congress only if the law so directs. Similarly, the word "herself" was deleted as surplusage, as words importing the masculine gender include the feminine. The reference to the start date of U.S. involvement in World War I was also omitted as no longer necessary with the passage of time.

Today, the Distinguished Service Medal is awarded almost exclusively to general officers, although occasionally a long-serving colonel may receive it. The award of the decoration to a non-commissioned officer, however, is very rare.

First Recipient

General John J. Pershing was the first American recipient of the Army Distinguished Service Medal. He received this decoration in an October 21, 1918 ceremony in which the Distinguished Service Medal also was awarded to Marshall Foch, Marshall Joffre and General Petain (all of France), Field Marshall Sir Douglas Haig (Great Britain), Lieutenant General Diaz (Italy) and Lieutenant General Gillian (Belgium).

Selected Recipients (Chronological)

ALLEN W. GULLION: MAY 4, 1917– MARCH 26, 1918

After the United States entered World War I, Congress enacted the first war-time draft since the Civil War. This monumental task was overseen by Major General Enoch Crowder, who temporarily relinquished his position as Army Judge Advocate General to become Provost Marshal General and supervise the registration, classification, and induction of nearly three million young men into the armed services. Then Major Allen W. Guillion, a lawyer in the Judge Advocate General's Department in Washington, D.C., was part of these efforts, and his hard work was recognized with a Distinguished Service Medal. His citation reads:

> for exceptionally meritorious and distinguished services in the national administration of the Selective Service Law from May 2, 1917 to March 26, 1918. As chief of publicity and information under the Provost Marshal General, he successfully conducted the campaign to popularize selective service. Later, as acting executive officer to the Provost Marshal General, he solved many intricate problems with firmness, promptness and common sense. Finally, as the first Chief of the Mobilization Division of the Provost Marshal General's Office, he supervised all matters relating to making and filling of calls and the accomplishments of individual inductions. To each of his varied and important duties he brought a high order of ability and remarkable powers of application. His services were of great value in raising our National Army.[10]

EDGAR M. HALYBURTON: NOVEMBER 1917–NOVEMBER 1918

Sergeant Halyburton, a member of Company F, 16th Infantry, 1st Division, was the only enlisted soldier to be awarded the Distinguished Service Medal in World War I. His citation reads:

> While a prisoner of war in the hands of the German Government ... he voluntarily took command of the different camps in which he was located and under difficult conditions established administrative and personnel headquarters, organized the men into units, billeted them systematically, established sanitary regulations and made equitable distribution of supplies; he established an intelligence service to prevent our men giving information to the enemy and prevent the enemy introducing propaganda. His patriotism and leadership under trying conditions were an inspiration to his fellow prisoners and contributed greatly to the amelioration of their hardships.[11]

CARRIE L. HOWARD: SEPTEMBER TO NOVEMBER 1918

First Lieutenant Howard was awarded the Distinguished Service Medal for her work as the chief nurse at the port of embarkation, Hoboken, New Jersey during World War I. Her citation reads, in part:

> She held a position of great responsibility. To her fell the duty of supervising the nursing departments of all the hospitals at the port of embarkation and the mobilization stations for nurses destined for overseas duty. By her efficiency, energy, and knowledge of administrative detail she added greatly to the proficiency of the Medical Department of the Army at those trying stations.[12]

Born in California in 1874, Carrie Leona Howard joined the Army as a contract nurse in July 1900. After a few months at the General Hospital of the Presidio of San Francisco, she was deployed to Manila, Philippines, where she remained until mid–January 1901. Thousands of U.S. troops were in the Philippines fighting insurgents, and Howard nursed the sick and wounded at the First Reserve and Santa Mesa hospitals in Manila.

Howard returned repeatedly to the Philippines: she was a nurse at the Convalescent Hospital, Corregidor Islands in 1904, and served at the Division Hospital in Manila from 1905 to 1906. From 1910 to 1912, Howard worked as a nurse and chief nurse in Manila, and at Fort McKinley and Pettit Barracks on the island of Mindanao.

From 1901 to 1918, she also served in the

United States as a nurse in the general hospitals at Fort Bayard, New Mexico, in San Francisco and at Walter Reed General Hospital in Washington, D.C.

When the United States entered World War I, Howard was chief nurse in Manila. She returned to the United States in mid–1918 and, in September of that year, assumed duties as the chief nurse of Army Embarkation Hospital No. 1, Hoboken, New Jersey, where she supervised the nursing departments of the hospitals at the port of embarkation and at mobilization stations for nurses destined for overseas duty with the American Expeditionary Force in France. For her service, Howard received the Distinguished Service Medal.

After the war ended, Howard continued to serve and, from 1923 to 1935, she was the chief nurse at Letterman General Hospital, San Francisco. When she retired as a first lieutenant in December 1935, Major General C.R. Reynolds, then–Army surgeon general, wrote to Howard: "[Y]ours has been a unique service, for no member of the Corps has ever served so long or with such a health record. As one of the pioneers in the Corps you greatly assisted in establishing a record which may serve as a standard for the members of the Nurse Corps and which has brought prestige to the Medical Service of the Army." Howard died in 1951.[13]

JOSEPH L. LOCKARD: DECEMBER 7, 1941

Staff Sergeant Lockard was the first — and apparently the only — enlisted recipient of the Distinguished Service Medal in World War II. His award was "for exceptionally meritorious and distinguished services in a position of great responsibility" and the citation reads:

> Staff Sergeant Lockard was the operator in charge of the detector unit operating by his organization on the island of Oahu, Territory of Hawaii, on the morning of December 7, 1941. In order that instruction in the operation of aircraft warning equipment might be given to another soldier under training, he, in devotion to duty, remained

at his station upon completion of the scheduled operating period. At approximately 7:02 A.M., a signal was detected on his instruments which, in the opinion of Staff Sergeant Lockard, signified a large number of airplanes in flight approximately 132 miles distant, azimuth three degrees. At that moment Staff Sergeant Lockard was placed in a position of great and grave responsibility to his country. After rechecking the distance and azimuth, Staff Sergeant Lockard promptly contacted the duty officer of the information center and furnished him with complete particulars of the readings. Subsequent investigations have proven conclusively that the airplanes reported by Staff Sergeant Lockard were the large Japanese Air Force which attacked the island of Oahu at approximately 7:55 A.M.[14]

This unusual award was personally presented to Lockard by Under Secretary of War Robert P. Patterson in Washington, D.C. in March 1942. It reflects official recognition that Lockard and Private George E. Elliott, his fellow oscilloscope operator at Opana Mobile Radar Station on the north shore of Oahu, were — unlike the rest of the Army and Navy in Hawaii on December 7, 1941 — alert to the danger of a surprise attack on Pearl Harbor.[15]

CLINTON A. PIERCE: DECEMBER 8, 1941–MARCH 11, 1942

Clinton A. Pierce was awarded the Distinguished Service Medal for "exceptionally meritorious service" as commander of the 26th Cavalry (Philippine Scouts). Pierce was the only Army general to be both wounded in action and taken prisoner by the enemy in World War II. His Distinguished Service Medal citation reads, in part:

> As commander of the 26th Cavalry (Philippine Scouts), Brigadier General (then Colonel) Pierce occupied with his regiment a position in the reserve of the North Luzon Force. When the enemy effected a landing in force in Lingayen Gulf, he moved his regiment rapidly to oppose the landing and with it, bore the brunt of the initial resistance to the hostile advance, covering the right flank of the North Luzon Force against which the enemy directed his major effort. His aggressive leadership of this veteran regiment, which fought

brilliantly in spite of heavy losses, was of major importance in the successful withdrawal of the force to the Bataan Peninsula. Later, as a part of the I Philippine Corps, he led his regiments, ahead of the forward defensive position, in successful harassing action against enemy forces. Assigned to command a sector of the west coast of Bataan, Brigadier General Pierce, with Air Corps units of the United States Army and of the Philippine Army, acting as Infantry, first limited the advance, and then with battalions of the 45th Infantry (Philippine Scouts) from the general reserve, destroyed strong enemy landing parties in his sector. His brilliant personal leadership in combat was an inspiration to his command.[16]

The Army Decorations Board recommended that Pierce receive this Distinguished Service Medal on October 19, 1942 and the Secretary of War approved the award on October 26, 1942.

Born in Brooklyn, N.Y. on June 15, 1894, Clinton Albert Pierce served as an enlisted soldier in the Illinois National Guard in 1916 before being commissioned as a Regular Army second lieutenant in the 12th Cavalry in March 1917. He subsequently served in a variety of cavalry assignments in the United States until May 1940, when then Lt. Col. Pierce was assigned to Fort Stotsenburg, Philippine Islands.

When the Japanese attacked on December 8, 1941, now Colonel Pierce (he had been promoted in October) was in command of the 26th Cavalry Regiment. He and his fellow troopers fought valiantly against the enemy while covering the withdrawal of U.S. and Filipino forces into the Bataan Peninsula, and Lieutenant General Jonathan Wainwright lauded "this devoted little band of horsemen" in his official report of operation.[17]

On January 24, 1942, Pierce was promoted to one-star rank and, in a front-line ceremony, Wainwright took the stars from his own shoulders and presented them to Pierce. Now Brigadier General Pierce took command of the 71st Division, Philippine Army and continued to fight until the fall of Bataan on April 11, 1942. He was awarded two Silver Stars for

gallantry in action and the Purple Heart (his toe was shot off by a Japanese sniper).

Pierce spent the rest of the war as a prisoner of war. After being liberated in September 1945, Pierce served at Fort Riley, Kansas and in Augsburg, Germany before retiring in February 1951. He died in August 1966 in Eureka Spring, Arkansas.

GEORGE I. BACK: SEPTEMBER 1944– AUGUST 1945; JUNE 1950–APRIL 1951

George Irving Beck was awarded two Distinguished Service Medals during his career as an Army Signal Corps officer. His first was for his work in the Mediterranean Theater of Operations (1944–1945) and his second was for his service in the Far East Command (1950–1951).

Born in February 1894 in Sioux City, Iowa, Back graduated from high school in 1912. In 1914, he entered Morningside College in his home town and studied physics and mathematics for three years before enlisting in the Army in August 1917. Two months later, Back was commissioned as a second lieutenant, Signal Officers' Reserve Corps.

While today's Signal Corps is chiefly concerned with computers and information systems, in Back's day the Corps was focused on telephones and radios. This explains why then 1st Lt. Back studied at the Signal Corps radio school at the University of Maryland and at the Signal Corps telephone school at the University of Michigan. After World War I, Back — who had remained on active duty after the armistice — also studied communications engineering at Yale University.

In the 1920s, Back emerged as one of the Corps' foremost technical experts and was assigned to the Chief Signal Officer's Research and Engineering Division. In 1929, he was detailed to conduct transmission tests of a newly installed command and fire control cable in Hawaii. Back subsequently joined the crew of the U.S. Army Transport Cable Ship *Dellwood*, sailed to England with that vessel to pick up submarine cable, and then went to the Philippine Islands where the cable was laid.

Back spent most of the 1930s at the Signal Corps' laboratories at Fort Monmouth, New Jersey. Soon after the United States entered World War II, Back was promoted to colonel and assigned to Washington, D.C., where he worked signal supply and procurement issues. In 1944, Back deployed to the Mediterranean Theater of Operations, where he served first as deputy chief signal officer of the Allied Forces Headquarters and then as the Chief Signal Officer. During this assignment, Back had overall responsibility for setting up radio communication at the Big Three Power Conference at Yalta. This was a difficult task because Back's signal personnel were required to set up a secure but speedy radio-teletype system that would allow President Roosevelt to communicate with officials in Washington, D.C. while the president was thousands of miles in the Soviet Union. Then Colonel Back's success at Yalta was an important factor in his being awarded his first Distinguished Service Medal in August 1945.[18]

In March 1947, then Brig. General Back was assigned as the signal officer of the Far East Command. In July 1950, when the United Nations Command in the Far East was established, Back assumed the additional duty of signal officer of that command. He was awarded an oak leaf cluster to his Distinguished Service Medal for his superlative performance between June 1950 and April 1951. The citation describes

> exceptionally meritorious service ... in a position of great responsibility from June 1950 to April 1951. As Signal Officer, United Nations Command ... he demonstrated superior leadership, sound judgment and outstanding professional and administrative competence in directing the various complex operations of his offices. He provided in a minimum of time, an enormously expanded fixed plant communications system essential to the efficient conduct of United Nations operations in the Far East and swift reliable contacts with the outside world. General Back assured the inspection and re-equipping of combat

units with communications equipment, the coordination of communications required to serve each of the many United Nations in Korea and the providing of comprehensive photographic coverage required for intelligence, news and historical purposes. His comprehensive grasp of the vast range of communications requirements and his quick accomplishment of his many missions were exceptional. General Back's outstanding professional ability, initiative, resourcefulness and unremitting devotion to duty made a marked contribution to the successful accomplishment of the mission of the United Nations' forces in Korea.[19]

Major General Back's final assignment was as the Army's Chief Signal Officer. He retired in 1955 and died in 1972.

JOHN T. CORLEY: JANUARY 1963–SEPTEMBER 1966

When John Thomas Corley retired as a brigadier general in 1966, he had already been awarded two Distinguished Service Crosses, eight Silver Stars, two Legions of Merit, the Soldier's Medal, four Bronze Star Medals, and the Purple Heart. Upon leaving active duty, however, he received his first Distinguished Service Medal. The citation for that award reads in part:

> Brigadier General John T. Corley served with exceptional distinction in positions of great responsibility from January 1963 to September 1966. These were important years of devoted service to the United States. Their importance lies in the internationally significant problems that faced the Army during this period and the contribution General Corley made in our nation's quest for world peace. Early in this period, General Corley demonstrated his dynamic leadership and professional acumen while serving as Assistant Division Commander, 2d Infantry Division. He displayed his ability to elicit the best performance from soldiers and from tactical units when he organized, trained and deployed a brigade force. Later as Chief of Staff, First Army, General Corley consistently and effectively guided the staff through a difficult period of retrenchment, maintaining a high state of morale and effectiveness. General Corley culminated his brilliant career as

Officially machine-engraved Army DSM and Legion of Merit to Army Brigadier General Lynn D. Smith.

Deputy Commanding General, U.S. Army Training Center, Fort Jackson, S.C., where his extensive background and outstanding leadership ability were directed to the training of soldiers to meet the Army's worldwide commitments. A grateful nation recognizes that General Corley's outstanding achievements and his distinguished service for over 28 years continues the highest military traditions.

JOHN W. VESSEY, JR.: AUGUST 1975– JUNE 1982

General John W. Vessey received three awards of the Distinguished Service Medal. The citation for his second decoration says, in part, that he

has distinguished himself by exceptionally meritorious service in successive positions of great responsibility and trust during the period August 1975 to June 1982. As Deputy Chief of Staff for

Operations and Plans ... he was a prime mover in shaping and providing direction to the Army during the challenging period following the cessation of hostilities in Vietnam and the transition to an all-volunteer force. Attuned to the needs of field commanders, General Vessey overwatched Army-wide activities ensure timely staff response to operational requirements and contingency situations. Later, as Commanding General, Eighth U.S. Army, General Vessey demonstrated consummate wisdom, strategic vision, and tireless leadership in directing a highly effective program of combined training and readiness activities which brought the command to peak levels of preparedness and furthered it credibility as a deterrent force. As Army Vice Chief of Staff, General Vessey deftly orchestrated the multifaceted and diverse activities of the Army Staff. In particular, he was instrumental in assuring that significant additions to the Army arsenal of weaponry were developed, procured and fielded in a timely, technically sound and economic manner, and through his efforts he played a key role in molding the Army of the future and enhancing the security of the Nation. In his capacity as the Army Vice Chief of Staff, General Vessey's advice to the Joint Chiefs and senior Defense officials was consistently well-reasoned and demonstrated his superb judgment, capacity for innovation, and outstanding professional ability, earning him the respect and admiration of the Nation, our allies and his associates. General Vessey's execution of all responsibilities has been marked by an unprecedented degree of humility and selflessness which has brought honor and distinction to the Army during a difficult and changing era in our Nation's history.

Born in Minneapolis, Minnesota, in June 1922, John William Vessey, Jr. enlisted in the Minnesota National Guard in May 1939, when he was sixteen years old. Throughout World War II, he served with the 34th Infantry Division. Vessey fought in North Africa and Italy and was serving as a first sergeant at the Anzio beachhead on May 6, 1944 when he received a battlefield commission as a field artillery second lieutenant.

After the war, Vessey remained on active duty. From 1951 to 1954, he served as a field artillery battery commander and staff officer with the 4th Infantry Division in Germany.

He subsequently served twice as a field artillery battalion commander: first with the 3rd Armored Division in Germany from 1963 to 1965 and later with the 25th Infantry Division in Vietnam from 1966 to 1967. His extraordinary heroism in this last assignment — while in command of 2d Battalion, 77th Artillery — resulted in Vessey's being awarded the Distinguished Service Cross.

Vessey's first assignment as a general officer was as Commander, U.S. Army Support Command, Thailand in December 1970. He left this assignment in January 1972 to assume duties as the Chief, Military Assistance Advisory Group for Laos and served there until the cease-fire was signed in Laos in February 1973.

After his return from Southeast Asia, Vessey served in a variety of increasingly important assignments. After receiving his second star in August 1974, Vessey commanded the 4th Infantry Division (Mech) at Fort Carson, Colorado. Promoted to lieutenant general in September 1975, he returned to the Pentagon to assume duties as Deputy Chief of Staff for Operations and Plans. Promoted to full general in November 1976, Vessey became Commander-in-Chief, United Nations Command and Commander, U.S. Forces, Korea. In 1978, he became the first Commander-in-Chief of the newly formed Republic of Korea-United States Combined Forces Command.

In July 1979, General Vessey was appointed Vice Chief of Staff of the Army and in July 1982 became the 10th Chairman of the Joint Chiefs of Staff. He retired in 1985 when he was 63 years old.

When Vessey retired, he was the last four-star World War II combat veteran on active duty and had served an unprecedented 46 years in uniform. In addition to his two Army Distinguished Service Medals and Distinguished Service Cross, Vessey also was awarded two Defense Distinguished Service Medals, the Navy Distinguished Service Medal, the Air Force Distinguished Service Medal, two Legions of Merit, two Bronze Star Medals, four Air Medals, the Joint Service Commendation Medal, the Army Commendation Medal with "V" for valor, and the Purple Heart. He also wears the Army Aviator Badge — having completed the Army Aviation School in 1970, when he was 48 years old.[20]

In 1992, General Vessey was awarded the Presidential Medal of Freedom. This award — the highest American civilian decoration — is awarded to any person who has made "an especially meritorious contribution to the security or national interests of the United States, world peace, cultural or other significant public or private endeavors."[21] Vessey's award was in recognition of his efforts to account for military personnel missing in action from the Vietnam War.

AIR FORCE DISTINGUISHED SERVICE MEDAL

Overview

Establishing Authority and Effective Dates: The Air Force Distinguished Service Medal was established by an act of Congress (Public Law 86-593) on July 6, 1960. This law, however, did not create a new decoration. Rather, Congress amended the July 1918 statute creating the Army Distinguished Service Medal to authorize the Air Force to have its own version "of appropriate design."

The Air Force Distinguished Service Medal has been awarded since November 1, 1965; airmen awarded a Distinguished Service Medal prior to this date received the Army version of the decoration.

Criteria: The Air Force Distinguished Service Medal is awarded to any "person who, while serving in any capacity with the Air Force, distinguishes himself by exceptionally meritorious service to the United States in a duty of great responsibility."[22]

Order of Precedence: The Air Force

Distinguished Service Medal is worn after the Defense Distinguished Service Medal and before the Silver Star.

Devices: Additional awards of the Air Force Distinguished Service Medal to the same individual are denoted by bronze (or silver) oak leaf clusters.

Designer: The Air Force Distinguished Service Medal was designed and sculpted by Frank H. Alston, Jr., a painter, lithographer and etcher who worked for many years as a civilian illustrator and designer at the Army's Institute of Heraldry. Alston was born in Providence, Rhode Island and graduated from the well-known Rhode Island School of Design in 1937. After retiring from the Army, he worked at Howard University's Art Gallery in Washington, DC.

Description and Symbolism

Obverse

The 2¼ inch wide obverse of the Air Force Distinguished Service Medal consists of a dramatic sunburst of 13 gold rays separated by 13 white enameled stars; a semiprecious blue stone is centered in the sunburst. The medal is suspended from its ribbon by a wide slotted bar which consists of stylized wings.

The sunburst design was a radical departure from the Army and Navy Distinguished Service Medals, both of which are circular in shape and whose designs incorporated traditional military and naval motifs. According to the Air Force, the thirteen stars "represent the thirteen original colonies and man's chain of achievements" while the rays "depict man's quest for light and knowledge." As for the sunburst, it reflects "the glory that accompanies great achievements." The blue stone in the center "represents the vault of the heavens."[23]

Reverse

The reverse of the Air Force Distinguished Service Medal is plain and is suitable for engraving the recipient's name.

Air Force Distinguished Service Medal, obverse (courtesy Jeffrey B. Floyd).

Ribbon

The ribbon consists of a wide center stripe of white flanked on either side by a thin stripe of old gold, a wide stripe of ultramarine blue and a narrow stripe of old gold at the edges.

Historical Background

After becoming an independent service in 1947, the Air Force continued to award Army decorations to airmen. By the end of the 1950s, however, Air Force leaders recognized that it was time for airmen to have their own distinctive awards and medals and this led to the development of an Air Force version of the Army Medal of Honor, Distinguished Service Cross (called the Air Force

Air Force DSM (reverse) (courtesy Jeffrey B. Floyd).

reacted favorably to Jones' proposed design (and tentatively approved it), the Air Force decided in June 1960 to re-start the entire design process. As a result, Jones' medal design was modified slightly and adopted as the new Airman's Medal.

As for the Air Force Distinguished Service Medal, a radical design proposed by Frank H. Alston, Jr. ultimately was adopted as the Air Force's highest award for service.

Today, the Air Force Distinguished Service Medal is awarded principally to general officers — on the rationale that only an individual wearing stars serves in "a duty of great responsibility." However, a colonel occasionally may receive the decoration. For example, Colonel Buzz Aldrin, who was the second man to walk on the surface of the moon, was twice awarded the Air Force Distinguished Service Medal. Colonel Lawrence Nicholas Guarino, who spent seven years as a prisoner of war, also was awarded the Air Force Distinguished Service Medal for his service as the senior ranking officer of the largest prison camp in North Vietnam. Finally, the Chief Master Sergeant of the Air Force — the top enlisted airman — also now typically receives the Air Force Distinguished Service Medal upon retirement.

First Recipient

Major General Osmond J. Ritland was the first recipient of the Air Force Distinguished Service Medal. He was awarded it when he retired on December 1, 1965.

Born in October 1909 in Berthoud, Colorado, Osmond J. Ritland studied mechanical engineering at San Diego State College before enlisting in the Army Air Corps as a flying cadet in 1932. Riltland flew with the Army Air Corps Mail Operation from 1933 to 1935 before leaving active duty to work as a pilot for United Airlines.

Returning to the Army in 1939, Ritland served as an experimental test pilot at Wright Field, Ohio, before transferring to the China-

Cross), and Soldier's Medal (called the Airman's Medal) — and an Air Force Distinguished Service Medal.

In the late 1950s — anticipating that it would soon be given authorization from Congress for its own distinctive Distinguished Service Medal — the Air Force began working with the Army's Institute of Heraldry on a design for the new decoration. Thomas Hudson Jones, a civilian employee at the Institute, looked to the Army and Navy Distinguished Service Medals as a guide and proposed that the Air Force adopt a bronze circular disk featuring an eagle for its new Distinguished Service Medal.

While the Commission of Fine Arts had

Burma-India Theater in December 1944. He served as the commander of the Assam Air Depot, India, until returning to the United States in February 1946.

In February 1950, Ritland organized— and then commanded—the 4925th Test Group (Atomic). This unit was responsible for testing all equipment needed for the Air Force's nuclear weapons capability. Then Colonel Ritland later was the Air Force's project manager for the U-2 spyplane and, after his promotion to brigadier general, was responsible for the Air Force's first ballistic missile program. In the early 1960s, then Major General Ritland was responsible for all Air Force participation in the Mercury and Gemini manned space flight programs.

Ritland died in Rancho Santa Fe, California, in March 1991.

Selected Recipients (Chronological)

DONAVON F. SMITH: OCTOBER 23, 1966–MARCH 1, 1968

Brigadier General Smith received his Distinguished Service Medal for his work as Chief, Air Force Advisory Group, U.S. Military Assistance Command, Vietnam, and as Senior Air Force Advisor to the Commander, Vietnamese Air Force. His citation reads, in part:

> In this important and sensitive assignment, General Smith provided ingenuity, leadership, and persuasive guidance to the entire United States Air Force advisory efforts to make the Vietnamese Air Force an effective air arm for eventual self-defense of its homeland. The significance of this great task in accomplishing and meeting established goals of teaching, training, and modernizing an antiquated and undersized Air Force, while actually engaged in armed conflict with a hostile force, further underscores the exceptional abilities and fortitude of this outstanding leader.

Donavon Smith was an ace in World War II.

EDWIN E. (BUZZ) ALDRIN, JR.: JULY 16–24, 1969, JUNE 1, 1951–FEBRUARY 29, 1972

Colonel Buzz Aldrin received two Air Force Distinguished Service Medals. His first award was for his extraordinary service as an astronaut; his second decoration was a retirement award. His citations read, in part:

> for an exceptionally outstanding achievement in a position of great responsibility as Astronaut with the National Aeronautics and Space Administration, Manned Spacecraft Center, Houston, Texas, during the period 16 July 1969 to 24 July 1969. During this period he served as Lunar Module Pilot on the Apollo XI spacecraft. This mission successfully landed the first earthman on the moon, culminating in man's ages-old desire to travel to other planets. Colonel Aldrin overcame all obstacles encountered in the new and strange lunar environment and with painstaking thoroughness and great physical effort successfully completed his assigned mission. He deployed a solar wind composition experiment, conducted an extensive evaluation of lunar environment, set up various experiments to remain behind on the moon's surface, and collected lunar samples for scientific evaluation upon return to earth...

> for exceptionally meritorious and distinguished service in a position of great responsibility to the Government of the United States from 1 June 1951 to 29 February 1972. Colonel Aldrin demonstrated remarkable skill and bravery as a combat pilot in the Korean War. He later completed an arduous technical program and obtained the degree of Doctor of Science and Astronautics. Colonel Aldrin's outstanding and dedicated efforts gave direction to the National Space Program and resulted in the development of vastly improved orbital rendezvous and lunar descent procedures. These efforts were instrumental in the accomplishment of the national objective of landing men on the moon and culminated in his being second man to set foot on the lunar surface. His contributions to the space shuttle and space station programs have also played a significant role in formulating advanced mission planning for those important programs.

Born in Glen Ridge, New Jersey, in January 1930, Edwin Eugene (Buzz) Aldrin, Jr.

(he later legally changed his first name from Edwin to Buzz) graduated from the U.S. Military Academy in 1951. He was third in his class. During the Korean War, Aldrin was credited with shooting down two enemy airplanes in air combat and destroying a third on the ground. He is best known for his service as an astronaut, and for being the second person to walk on the surface of the moon.

LAWRENCE N. GUARINO: APRIL 28, 1968–JUNE 1, 1970

Colonel Guarino was awarded his Distinguished Service Medal for his service as the Senior Ranking Officer of the largest prison camp in North Vietnam. His citation reads, in part:

> From 28 April 1968 to 1 June 1970 ... the enemy was attempting to convert this camp into a progressive camp of Americans conditioned to make written or oral statements contrary to the best interests of the United States and its allies. Colonel Guarino, recognizing his duties as Senior Ranking Officer, set the resistance posture against the enemy by outlining policy, rebuilding and strengthening the camp communications system, and counseling cell block senior officers in resistance activities. Despite the continuous enemy program of harassment and torture, the prisoners of war maintained a solid front of resistance under the leadership of Colonel Guarino. His courage in the face of great adversity and torture had few equals in prisoner history, and his personal resistance offered a rallying point.[24]

Born in April 1922 in Newark, New Jersey, Lawrence "Larry" Nicholas Guarino served as a fighter pilot in both Europe and the Pacific in World War II, and is credited with shooting down three enemy aircraft. He remained in the Air Force after the war and was leading a fighter-bomber strike when his F-105 aircraft was shot down over North Vietnam on June 14, 1965. Released on February 12, 1973, after nearly seven years in captivity, Guarino recorded the story of his imprisonment in *A POW's Story: 2801 Days in Hanoi*. He retired as a colonel in July 1975.

GEORGE E. DAY: APRIL 1968–FEBRUARY 1973

The most highly decorated living American — he holds every single combat decoration that may be awarded to an airman — Colonel "Bud" Day was awarded the Distinguished Service Medal for his meritorious service in North Vietnam. His citation describes

exceptionally meritorious service in duties of great responsibility. Colonel Day distinguished himself as one of the senior ranking officers in the prison camps of North Vietnam where he was interned from April 1968 to February 1973. During this period, Colonel Day performed his duties in accord with the Code of Conduct and exhibited leadership with courage and determination, regardless of the cost in the many cruel tortures and beatings which he had to endure because he refused to desert his duties as the senior ranking officer. The execution of these responsibilities was a vital factor in setting the standards for the other

Lieutenant General Terry L. Gabreski was awarded her second Air Force Distinguished Service Medal when she retired in 2010 (U.S. Air Force).

Former Secretary of the Air Force Michael Wynne decorates General T. Michael Moseley with the Air Force Distinguished Service Medal during Moseley's retirement ceremony on July 11, 2008 (U.S. Air Force).

prisoners and the successful resistance met by the enemy. The singularly distinctive accomplishments of Colonel Day reflected the highest credit upon himself and the United States Air Force.

ERIC W. BENKEN: NOVEMBER 1996–OCTOBER 1999

Eric Benken received his Air Force Distinguished Service Medal when he retired as the 12th Chief Master Sergeant of the Air Force in 1999. His citation states that he

distinguished himself as Chief Master Sergeant of the Air Force ... his unparalleled leadership and tremendous concern for the enlisted men and women of the United States Air Force led to numerous positive initiatives that will have enduring impact. He joined the Chief of Staff in providing impassioned and persuasive testimonies before Congressional committees that were instrumental in increasing military compensation and quality

of life initiatives, to include military pay raises, pay table reform, and a proposal to repeal the 1986 Redux Retirement System. He strongly battled opposition to gender-integrated training through congressional testimony and constant media input, insisting that Air Force women should have the same opportunity to train for military service as their male counterparts, thus preserving twenty-three years of progress. Chief Benken placed a strong focus on the professional development of the enlisted force resulting in the implementation of professional development seminars across the entire Air Force.

DAVID M. EDGINGTON: SEPTEMBER 16, 2002–JUNE 10, 2005

Brigadier General Edgington was awarded his medal for "exceptionally meritorious and distinguished service" during Operation IRAQI FREEDOM while working as Deputy Commander, North Atlantic Treaty Organization (NATO) Combined Air Operations Center 6 and as Deputy for Support, Air Armament Center, Eglin Air Force Base, Florida. Edgington "exhibited tremendous leadership and masterful diplomacy" and "through sheer determination, will of effort, and enlightened leadership ... developed a dynamic multinational team of combat mission-ready warriors, turned Combined Air Operations Center 6 into a major weapon system, and led the Southern Region by achieving full operational capability four months ahead of schedule." According to the citation for his award, Edgington initiated Operation DISPLAY GUARDIAN to protect Turkey against air and missile threats from Iraq, and consequently made history since this was the first ever NATO defensive operation. But Edgington's work in Operation IRAQI FREEDOM was only part of his distinguished service: "as offsite commander during HURRICANE IVAN, the area's worst natural disaster in ten years, General Edgington provided invaluable guidance and coordination to have Eglin up and running 48 hours after landfall."

DEFENSE SUPERIOR SERVICE MEDAL

Overview

Establishing Authority and Effective Dates: The Defense Superior Service Medal was established by Executive Order 11904 on February 6, 1976, and it may be awarded for service after that date.

Criteria: The Defense Superior Service Medal is awarded by the secretary of defense to any member of the Armed Forces of the United States who, after February 6, 1976, renders superior meritorious service while holding a position of significant responsibility while assigned to a joint activity.

Order of Precedence: The Defense Superior Service Medal is worn after the Silver Star but before the Legion of Merit.

Devices: Additional awards of the Defense Superior Service Medal to the same soldier or airman are denoted by bronze (or silver) oak leaf clusters.

Designer: The design of the Defense Superior Service Medal was adapted from that of the Defense Distinguished Service Medal, which was designed by Mildred Orloff and sculpted by Lewis J. King Jr., both of the Army's Institute of Heraldry.

Description and Symbolism

Obverse

The medal is silver in color and is 1⅞ inches in overall height. It matches the Defense Distinguished Service Medal in design, except for color, and features a medium-blue enameled pentagon with its point up. A silver eagle with outspread wings is superimposed on the pentagon. Centered on the eagle's breast is the shield from the Great Seal of the United States, and the eagle is grasping three crossed arrows

Defense Superior Service Medal (obverse).

in its talons. The pentagon and eagle are enclosed within a silver pierced circle consisting of thirteen stars in the upper half and a branch of laurel leaves (on the left) and olive leaves (on the right) in the lower half. At the top of the medal is a suspender composed of five graduated silver rays that extend above the stars.

The Defense Superior Service Medal is rich in symbolism. The eagle grasping the arrows is taken from the seal of the secretary of defense and is the American bald eagle. The pentagon in the background alludes to the five branches of the Armed Forces. It also alludes to the headquarters of the Department of Defense, which is housed in the Pentagon. Additionally, the conjoined stars and silver rays signify unity and excellence in the performance of the mission of the Department of Defense on behalf of the United States. The thirteen stars represent the thirteen original colonies and, by extension, all of 50 states. The olive branch represents the goal of defense (i.e., peace), while the laurel branch represents achievement.

Reverse

In the center of the back side of medal is the inscription "From / The Secretary / Of Defense / To," with space beneath for inscribing the recipient's name. On the reverse of the ring bearing the stars, and above the pentagon, is the inscription "For Superior Service."

Ribbon

The ribbon consists of a central stripe of red, flanked on either side by stripes of white, blue, and gold.

Historical Background

In the summer of 1975, Deputy Secretary of Defense William Clements requested that the Army award the Legion of Merit to an Army officer assigned to the Office of the Secretary of Defense. The recommendation had to be forwarded through Army channels

Defense Superior Service Medal (reverse).

because the secretary of defense does not have the authority to award the Legion of Merit. The recommendation moved forward until it reached the Secretary of the Army Martin R. Hoffman, who refused to make the award.

On September 23, 1975, as a direct result of the Army's refusal to approve his recommendation, Clements wrote to William K. Brehm, Assistant Secretary of Defense for Manpower and Reserve affairs. Clements told Brehm that the Defense Department needed "a new *Defense* medal to recognize exceptional performance of duty by members of the Armed Forces assigned to the OSD (Office of the Secretary of Defense) and other joint activities," and he wanted this new medal to be "comparable to the Legion of Merit."[25]

Clements' military assistant subsequently provided more guidance on the new medal. It was to be called the "Defense Superior Service Medal" and was to be established by an executive order. To save time and money, the new medal would use the same design as the existing Defense Distinguished Service Medal except that the new award would be finished in silver rather than gold, and it would have its inscription properly modified.[26]

On November 18, 1975, Clements formally approved the design of the proposed Defense Superior Service Medal and its ribbon. On February 6, 1976, President Gerald R. Ford formally established the Defense Superior Service Medal when he signed Executive Order 11904.

First Recipient

The first Defense Superior Service Medal was awarded to U.S. Army Brig. Gen. John G. Jones in March of 1976 for "exceptionally superior service as Military Assistant to the Deputy Secretary of Defense from February of 1972 to July of 1975."[27]

Selected Recipients (Chronological)

CHARLES M. FERGUSON: AUGUST 1984–JULY 1994

Air Force Reserve Colonel Ferguson received his Defense Superior Service Medal for his ten years of "exceptionally superior service" in Reserve military competitions. His citation recognizes

> exceptionally superior service as United States delegate to the Sixth Commission, Interallied Confederation of Reserve Officers (CIOR) from August 1984 to July 1994. Colonel Ferguson's superior abilities as a diplomat enabled him to spearhead several successful interallied projects, including publishing a multi-lingual, comprehensive CIOR competitions manual, and organizing a flawless, impromptu orienteering competition at Athens, Greece. Colonel Ferguson performed in diverse leadership positions ranging from Committee Chair to Vice President, and was often requested by host nations to be a consultant or juror for interallied competitions. He was instrumental in the addition of women to CIOR yearly competitions, and was responsible

for a shift in focus of the competitions from "athletic event" to "military development," furthering officer professional development in small unit leadership, proper military bearing, appearance and behavior.

Born in South Carolina in July 1941, Charles Marvin Ferguson grew up in North Carolina and graduated as a Morehead Scholar from the University of North Carolina at Chapel Hill in 1963. Having participated in the Air Force Reserve Officer Training Corps program, Ferguson was commissioned as a second lieutenant. He subsequently served two tours in Vietnam, including 82 combat missions as an air intelligence officer.

After leaving active duty in 1968, Ferguson received a Ph.D. at the University of South Carolina and began a career as a college professor. He continued his Air Force Reserve career as an intelligence officer and a historical officer, and also as a participant and coach of the U.S. team to the yearly Interallied Confederation of Reserve Officers military competitions. Ferguson retired as a colonel in 2001 and as Vice President of Academic Affairs at Marine Corps University in 2005.

DALE E. STOVALL: JULY 11, 1991–JUNE 30, 1993

Air Force Brigadier General Stovall was awarded his Defense Superior Service Medal for "exceptionally superior service while serving as Deputy Commanding General, Joint Special Operations Command." According to his citation, his "dynamic leadership, vision and professional competence contributed directly and positively to the successful conduct of numerous special operations contingencies."

Born in Toppenish, Washington in February 1944, Stovall entered the U.S. Air Force Academy in 1963. He was a good student and an excellent athlete (a three-year letterman in track, Stovall qualified for the 1966 All-American Indoor Track Team). After graduating in 1967, he completed fixed-wing pilot training and then flew the C-141A Starlifter on long-range transport missions.

After transitioning to helicopters, Stovall flew the HH-53C at Patrick Air Force Base, Florida as part of the recovery team for the Apollo 14 and 15 Lunar space flights. Then, he joined the 40th Aerospace Rescue and Recovery Squadron at Nakhon Phanom Air Base, Thailand. In this squadron, Stovall told an interviewer, "four out of 40 pilots were killed in combat, a loss of ten percent, something most units wouldn't be able to handle. Our rescue missions were very much combat first, rescue second."[28]

On June 1–2, 1972, then Captain Stovall's extraordinary heroism resulted in the award of the Air Force Cross. Despite attacks from enemy missiles and gunfire, Stovall ultimately was able to rescue an F-4 Phantom weapons officer, Roger Locher, who had been shot down deep inside North Vietnam and had evaded capture for 23 days.[29]

Stovall spent a career in the Air Force and spent most of his time in rescue and special operations. He commanded the 1st Special Operations Wing at Hurlburt Field, Florida, from 1987 to 1989. In his final two assignments between 1990 and 1993, Stovall was vice commander of Air Force Special Operations Command and deputy commanding general of Joint Special Operations Command at Fort Bragg, North Carolina. When he retired in 1993, Stovall was widely viewed as one of the Air Force's most respected special operations leaders.

WILLIAM S. REEDER: APRIL 28, 1993– DECEMBER 8, 1994

Army Colonel William S. Reeder was awarded the Defense Superior Service Medal for his superior service as the Deputy Chief of Staff, U.S. Southern Command, in Panama. His "sound judgment, superb organizational skills and gifted leadership contributed immeasurably to the effectiveness of the Joint Staff in support of the Commander-in-Chief and to the success of the command throughout the theater." According to the citation

for Reeder's award, his efforts were critical in counter-drug planning and operations in Central and South America. Reeder also played a key role in implementing the required drawdown of the U.S. military presence in Panama mandated by the Panama Canal Treaty of 1978.

Born in Lake Arrowhead, California, in December 1945, William Spencer "Bill" Reeder, Jr. enlisted in the Army in 1965 and was commissioned after completing Artillery Officer Candidate School in 1966. He subsequently qualified as a fixed-wing pilot and served as an OV-1 Mohawk pilot in Vietnam from October 1968 to October 1969.

After qualifying as a rotary-wing pilot in 1971, now Captain Reeder returned to Vietnam as an AH-1 "Cobra" pilot with the 361st Aerial Weapons Company. He was shot down in South Vietnam on May 9, 1972 and was taken prisoner by the Viet Cong. Reeder subsequently spent 320 days as a combat captive in Kontum Province, near the border of Laos, Cambodia and South Vietnam. Reeder was released on March 27, 1973.[30]

After returning to the United States, Reeder served in a number of increasingly important assignments, including commander, 3rd Squadron, 5th Cavalry Regiment at Fort Lewis, Washington, and commander, 5th Squadron, 17th Cavalry Regiment, Fort Hood, Texas. His last assignment before retiring in 1995 was in Panama.[31]

DANA K. CHIPMAN: JUNE 2000–JUNE 2002; JUNE 2003–JUNE 2006; JULY 2006–JANUARY 2008

Lieutenant General Chipman has been awarded three Defense Superior Service Medals during his Army career. The three citations follow:

Colonel Dana K. Chipman ... distinguished himself by exceptionally superior service while serving as Legal Advisor, Joint Special Operations Command, Fort Bragg, North Carolina from June 2000 to June 2002. During this period, the outstanding leadership and ceaseless efforts of Colonel Chipman resulted in major contributions to the national security of the U.S. Colonel Chipman orchestrated legal support to joint special operations forces in operations and exercises to ensure the task forces could accomplish their assigned sensitive missions of national importance. His superior legal acumen and experience were essential to the development of Department of Defense policy positions on matters of national importance, from Presidential decision directives addressing threats to national security to sensitive military support of national security special events and civilian law enforcement operations.[32]

Colonel Dana K. Chipman ... distinguished himself by exceptionally superior service while serving as Staff Judge Advocate, Headquarters, U.S. Special Operations Command, MacDill Air Force Base, Florida, from June 2003 to June 2006.During this period, Colonel Chipman's outstanding leadership, superior managerial skills, and superb legal abilities were essential to the success of a world-class legal organization. He ensured the highest level of proficiency and professionalism among the USSOCOM legal staff composed of military lawyers and paralegals from different Services. Colonel Chipman's guidance, advice, and assistance ensured the command's compass was focused within legal, moral and ethical boundaries.[33]

Colonel Dana K. Chipman ... distinguished himself by exceptionally superior service while serving as Staff Judge Advocate, United States Central Command, MacDill Air Force Base, Florida, from July 2006 to January 2008. As Senior Legal Advisor for U.S. Central Command, Colonel Chipman had a keen understanding of the command's wide spectrum of complex legal issues and activities. Time and again, through diligence, dedication and self-sacrifice, he proved his unparalleled mastery of the issues and legal authorities by coordinating and directing legal services in the three theaters of operations in the Command's Area of Responsibility. Colonel Chipman always provided succinct, valuable and thoughtful analysis while maintaining allegiance to the integrity of the Rule of Law and advocating correct, yet sometimes unpopular, courses of action. His intellect, results-oriented style of leadership, communication skills, and warrior focus, instilled a proactive mission-focused climate within the Office of the Staff Judge Advocate. As a personal advisor to the commander, he operated with ease to resolve problems and eliminate roadblocks for successful Operations ENDURING FREEDOM and IRAQI FREEDOM.[34]

Born in California in 1958, Dana Kyle Chipman graduated from the U.S. Military Academy in 1980. He then served as an infantry officer before attending Stanford University's law school, from which he graduated in 1986. After entering the Army Judge Advocate General's Corps, Chipman served in a variety of increasingly important assignments. In 2007, he was selected for promotion to brigadier general and two years later made history as the first in his West Point class to wear three stars. Chipman also has the distinction of being the only Army officer in modern history to go from colonel to lieutenant general in less than two years. He now serves as The Judge Advocate General.

THE LEGION OF MERIT

Overview

Establishing Authority and Effective Dates: The Legion of Merit was created by an act of Congress (Public Law 671, 77th Congress) on July 20, 1942, and implemented by Executive Order 9260, signed by President Roosevelt on October 29, 1942. Awards of the Legion of Merit are retroactive to September 8, 1939, the date Roosevelt declared a "limited national emergency" in response to the war in Europe.

Criteria: The Legion of Merit is awarded to members of the Armed Forces of the United States or a friendly foreign nation who have exhibited exceptionally outstanding conduct in the performance of meritorious service to the United States. The performance of duties that are *normal* to the recipient's grade, branch, specialty, or assignment and experience is not an adequate basis for this award. In peacetime, service meriting a Legion of Merit should be in the nature of a special requirement or an extremely difficult duty performed in an unprecedented and clearly exceptional manner. The award, however, may be justified by virtue of exceptionally meritorious service in a succession of important positions.

Order of Precedence: The Legion of Merit is worn after the Defense Superior Service Medal and before the Distinguished Flying Cross. Awards to members of foreign militaries may be made to individuals in the grades of chief commander, commander, officer, and legionnaire, and those awards are worn by recipients according to their own nation's regulations governing decorations and medals.

Devices: Additional awards of the Legion of Merit to the same individual are bronze (or silver) oak leaf clusters.

Designer: The Legion of Merit was designed by Army Colonel Robert Townsend Heard and sculpted by Katherine W. Lane.

Description and Symbolism

Obverse

The Legion of Merit is a five-armed white, enameled cross of ten points, with each point tipped with a gold ball. The cross is bordered in red enamel. In the center of the cross, thirteen stars on a blue field are surrounded by a circle of clouds. Between the arms of the cross, a laurel wreath is tied in a bow between the two lower arms of the cross. Between the wreath and the center of the medal, situated in each reentrant angle of the cross, are two crossed arrows pointing outward.

Both the shape and the name of the Legion of Merit were inspired by the French Legion of Honor, which also is a white enameled cross whose arms are tipped with balls. The field of thirteen stars surrounded by clouds is taken from the reverse of the Great Seal of the United States and represents the "new constellation," which was a description of the young U.S. republic used by the Founding Fathers. The laurel wreath alludes to achievement, and

Legion of Merit (obverse).

the arrows pointing outward represent armed protection of the nation.

Reverse

The cross shown on the obverse also appears on the reverse of the Legion of Merit, except it is not enameled. In the center of the cross on the reverse is a blank circular space defined by a rope border that is to be used for engraving the recipient's name. Contained within a second rope border, which forms a space between the two ropes, is the raised inscription "*Annuit Coeptis* MDCCLXXXII;" each word is separated by a bullet. In place of the wreath that appears on the obverse, there is a band bearing the raised inscription, "United States of America," with each word also being separated by a bullet. In the reentrant angles of the cross, in the space between the band and the center of the medal, are two crossed arrows pointing outward.

The words *Annuit Coeptis*, meaning "He

(God) Has Favored Our Undertaking," is taken from the front of the Great Seal of the United States, and the date "MDCCLXXXII" (1782) refers to the year Gen. George Washington established the Badge of Military Merit, from which the Legion of Merit is descended.

Ribbon

The ribbon is purple-red and edged in white. The color is modified from that of the Purple Heart, which is also derived from General Washington's Badge of Military Merit.

Historical Background

The Desire for a "Meritorious Service Medal"

In 1919, General of the Army John J. Pershing suggested that a "meritorious service medal" be created as an award to recognize service that was not sufficient to qualify for the Distinguished Service Medal. Although the Army Judge Advocate General, Maj. Gen. Enoch H. Crowder, was of the opinion that the president could establish such an award, no further action was taken on Pershing's request at that time.

In 1938, the topic was raised again when both the Army and Navy voiced the need for a medal junior to their respective Distinguished Service Medals. Both services wanted an award that could be given for meritorious service in positions of "considerable" responsibility, as opposed to the "great" responsibility required for the award of a Distinguished Service Medal. The War Department recommended that the president sign an executive order creating a decoration to be known as the "Meritorious Service Medal," that would be awarded to military and naval personnel for especially meritorious service.

Before an executive order could be submitted for the president's signature, however, a bill was introduced in Congress to create and authorize the president to bestow upon any officer or employee of the United States a medal to be known as the "Meritorious Service Medal." The Navy opposed this legislation because, while it agreed that civilians in government service should be recognized, the Navy believed that awards for military service should be restricted to military personnel and not also used to reward civilian service. The Navy was of the opinion that it would be better to create separate military and civilian awards.

Colonel Heard and the Legion of Merit

In summer 1940, Colonel Robert Townsend Heard, a decorated veteran of the World War I and chief of the American Intelligence Command, became involved in the controversy over the proposed Meritorious Service Medal. Heard agreed that there was a need for such a decoration, but he was also interested in establishing a decoration for recognizing foreign personnel, both military and civilian. Having served abroad in diplomatic posts, Heard was well aware of the political value that a high-level award could have, and he wanted a medal that would draw on the prestige of the Prussian *Pour le Mérite* and the French *Legion of Honor* but which nonetheless would trace its lineage through purely American lines.

Under Heard's guidance all previous proposals for a Meritorious Service Medal were withdrawn, and the War Department instead drafted legislation to create a new decoration to be known as "The Legion of Merit." The original concept was to create a new decoration and award it to uniformed members of the U.S. Armed Forces, military personnel of friendly foreign nations, and to American civilians directly involved with national defense.

The Navy agreed with Heard's approach, but a problem arose when Heard testified about his proposed decoration at congressional hearings. Some members of Congress were reluctant to create a *single* decoration that would recognize both civilians and military personnel. As a result of this reluctance, Heard now followed the Navy's earlier recommendation and suggested separate medals for military personnel and civilians. His new suggestion was accepted, and Congress enacted legislation in July 1942 that created the Legion of Merit for military personnel and the Medal for Merit for civilians.

While Congress had authorized the creation of the Legion of Merit for four groups of military personnel, it left the details of specifying those groups to Roosevelt and the Army and the Navy. Officials from the Navy Department and the War Department met several times to arrive at regulations that would meet the requirements of the law and establish procedures common to both services. The services agreed that the medal should have four degrees: chief commander, commander, officer, and legionnaire. The first draft regulation, at the Army's suggestion, contained a clause that made the award dependent on the rank of the recipient, as follows:

- Chief commander: To commanders-in-chief of large armed forces, either army or naval
- Commander: To officers of or above the rank of brigadier general or rear admiral
- Officer: To field grade officers, meaning majors in the Army or Marine Corps and lieutenant commander in the Navy through colonel in the Army or Marine Corps and captain in the Navy
- Legionnaire: To members of the Armed Forces of the United States and the Philippines and friendly foreign nations not included in the higher categories

Roosevelt rejected this proposal, however, because he did not want the degree of award to be based in any way on the rank of the recipient. Rather, Roosevelt wanted the level of award to be based on the recipient's conduct and service. He also was adamant in his wish to make enlisted personnel eligible for the highest degree, and he likewise insisted that general and flag officers receive the lowest degree if their conduct and service so warranted. On September 15, 1942, Roosevelt noti-

fied the Army and Navy Departments that he wanted all recommendations for the Legion of Merit to be submitted to him for approval because "during the early awards and until we get the thing running smoothly, I want to keep a personal eye on just what is being done."[35] Both the Army and the Navy complied with this directive, even though doing so proved both awkward and time-consuming. On February 1, 1943, Army Chief of Staff Gen. George C. Marshall sent a memorandum to Roosevelt in which Marshall pointed out that when he visited North Africa, both Generals Eisenhower and Patton stressed the importance of being able to make prompt awards of the Legion of Merit to U.S. personnel. Marshall went on to say that

> all the officers with whom I discussed the matter of awards ... were unanimous in stating that the fact that the award was made virtually on the field of battle had a profound effect; also that there

Extremely rare Legion of Merit, Legionnaire, with enameled reverse.

was far less likelihood of misuse of the decoration if bestowed at the time of the deed rather than at some later period when many outside influences are brought to bear. Favoritism is not likely during a campaign, it too quickly reacts on the troops for a commander to dare indulge in it. However, in the months and years following the event, individuals can draw up quite a statement as to their prowess and frequently it finally becomes a matter of political pressure. Therefore I strongly recommend that we be permitted to award to *U.S. personnel* the Legion of Merit just as we do the Distinguished Service and Distinguished Flying Crosses, the Soldier's Medal and the Distinguished Service Medal.[36]

On February 5, 1943, Roosevelt wrote back to Marshall, "I entirely approve the award of the Legion of Merit to U.S. military personnel in the field without further reference to me." The president went on to state, "It should be noted ... however, that the Legion of Merit grades are not to be awarded on the basis of rank but must be awarded as a result of an evaluation of the degree of performance."[37]

The matter of awarding the Legion of Merit U.S. personnel in the posts of commander-in-chief and commander continued to be a problem for both pragmatic and political reasons. Finally, on May 26, 1943, the secretary of war and the secretary of the Navy addressed a joint letter to the president requesting that the Legion of Merit be awarded to personnel of the Armed Forces of the United States and the Philippines without reference to rank or post while reserving the higher degrees for members of the military of friendly foreign nations. The secretaries based their recommendation on the premise that four separate levels of award were unnecessary for U.S. services and that the award without degree would fill the need for a service medal that was just below the Distinguished Service Medal in prestige and would occupy the position originally recommended for the Meritorious Service medal that was proposed before the war. At the same time both secretaries believed that the retention of degrees for foreign personnel would fill a long-felt need for an award in several degrees,

particularly since most of the friendly foreign nations awarded many of their orders and decorations in various degrees. The secretaries also proposed that the medal and ribbon of the lowest degree used for member of the U.S. Armed Forces be referred to simply as the "Legion of Merit." Their letter further proposed that the Army's and the Navy's Distinguished Service Medal be awarded to personnel of foreign nations only in very exceptional cases. The president approved these proposals on May 27, 1943.

Between the time that the Legion of Merit was authorized and when the president agreed to limit its award at the lowest grade to U.S. personnel, a small number of awards in the grade of officer — and none in the two higher grades — had been made. Those awards were allowed to stand and were the last of their kind.

Design of the Legion of Merit

Colonel Heard, acting on behalf of the War Department, had previously prepared and submitted proposed designs for the degrees of the Legion of Merit. His design followed the basic concept of the French Legion of Honor but, to make it more "American," Heard described it as a descendant of the George Washington's Badge of Military Merit, which had been established in 1782. This badge had been revived in a modified form as the Purple Heart in 1932, and Heard wanted to tie his proposed decoration to that lineage while taking advantage of the form suggested by the French Legion of Honor.

In July 1942, a plaster model of the Legion of Merit medal sculpted by Katherine W. Lane was sent to the Commission of Fine Arts, along with a request for early consideration. Gilmore D. Clarke, who was then the chairman of the Commission of Fine Arts, replied on August 3, 1942. He said, in part, that "the design is an inferior imitation of the French Legion of Honor" and went on to criticize numerous features of the medal. Clarke also said that "medals of the United States of America should be distinctive in form and character and not in any way resemble medals of other countries." He thought it would be better to use a star rather than a cross. After officially disapproving the design submitted by Lane, Clarke said: "It is respectfully suggested that these gentlemen be requested to submit examples of medallic art which they have designed previously, before they are requested to restudy the design for this medal. Thus we may determine whether or not they are sufficiently competent to carry out an important commission."[38]

Shortly thereafter Clarke met with Heard and several others to discuss the proposed design for the Legion of Merit. Heard explained that the project had been in the works for longer than two years and the design had been approved by the War Department, the Navy Department, and the State Department. The result of this meeting was a compromise in which Heard and Clarke agreed that certain features of the medal's design would be modified without significantly altering its overall design.

After the revised design was approved by the Commission of Fine Arts, now Brigadier General Heard provided the necessary materials to Bailey, Banks and Biddle of Philadelphia, and sample medals were made. After a sample was shown to the secretary of war on January 5, 1943, Chief of Staff George C. Marshall approved it. Full scale production of the decoration got under way shortly thereafter.

Awards of the Legion of Merit from World War II to the Present

Given the size of the Army and Army Air Force in World War II (some eight million men and women served on the ground or in the air) awards of the Legion of Merit were relatively few: a total of 20,273 awards, with most being for achievement rather than service. Of these, 3,114 (15.3 percent) went to enlisted personnel and 2,185 (10.8 percent) were awarded to company grade officers. The majority—13,648 (67.3 percent)—went to field grade officers, with general officers receiving the remainder.[39]

During the Korean War and the Vietnam War, the Legion of Merit continued to be sparingly awarded in the Army and the Air Force. By the 1980s, however, the Army and Air Force had decided that that the Legion of Merit should be primarily an award for ser-vice rather than achievement. As a result the Legion of Merit is now most often awarded for exceptionally meritorious service in a succession of difficult and increasingly important jobs; it is often a retirement award for lieutenant colonels and colonels. The Legion of Merit is seldom awarded to enlisted personnel. When it is, those awards are generally made to the most senior enlisted personnel — and even then, the awards are usually only given upon retirement.

Selected Recipients (Chronological)

ELY J. KAHN: FEBRUARY 12, 1944–OCTOBER 7, 1945

Chief Warrant Officer Kahn was awarded his Legion of Merit for "exceptionally meritorious conduct in the performance of outstanding services."[40] The award of the decoration was based, in part, on his research and writing of *Fighting Divisions: Histories of Each U.S. Combat Division in World War II*, which was published by Infantry Journal in 1945. But, as Kahn had previously published two other well-received books about soldiering, these other publications almost certainly influenced the award process.[41]

Born in New York City in December 1916, Ely Jacques Kahn graduated Phi Beta Kappa from Harvard in 1937 and then embarked on a career as a writer and journalist. Seven months after Pearl Harbor, Kahn was inducted into the Army and assigned to the 32d Infantry Division. In January 1943, while stationed in Australia, Kahn was discharged to accept an appointment as a Warrant Officer (junior grade). He finished the war as a Chief Warrant Officer and, after being honorably discharged, returned to civilian life.

Until his death in New York City in 1994, Kahn published a variety of books and articles. He was a regular contributor to *The New Yorker* and other national magazines.

CURTIS G. CULIN III: JUNE 1944

Curtis "Bud" Culin, an Army sergeant serving as a tanker with the 102d Cavalry Reconnaissance Squadron in France in June 1944, was awarded the Legion of Merit for inventing a plow-like cutter that, when attached to the front of a tank, would slice through a hedgerow. Since these six to 10-foot-high hedgerows surrounding farms and roads were wreaking havoc on the Allied advance in Normandy, Culin's invention was the perfect solution.

Culin had made the four-pronged plow from scrap steel and, after General Omar Bradley saw a demonstration of the "rhino" device (as troops had nicknamed Culin's invention), Bradley directed that the plow be produced immediately; almost three hundred of them were manufactured. Eisenhower later credited the invention with saving many Allied and American lives.[42]

Born in 1915 in Cranford, New Jersey, Culin served in France and Germany in World War II. He was badly wounded in the Huertgen Forest (he lost a leg to a landmine) but survived to return to New Jersey and civilian life. "Bud" Culin died in 1963.

PAUL W. AIREY: APRIL 3, 1967–AUGUST 1, 1970

Chief Master Sergeant of the Air Force Airey was awarded the Legion of Merit for his leadership as the first chief master sergeant of the Air Force.

Born in December 1923 in New Bedford, Massachusetts, Airy dropped out of high school to enlist in the Army Air Corps in 1942. He subsequently served as a gunner on B-24 bombing missions over North Africa, Italy, Germany and Austria. In July 1944, Airy bailed out of his flak-damaged aircraft and was taken prisoner by the Germans.

After being released from a Luftwaffe-run prisoner of war camp in May 1945, Airey remained on active duty. During the Korean War, he was stationed at Naha Air Base, Okinawa, Japan. During this assignment, Airey "constructed equipment from salvaged parts that improved corrosion control of sensitive radio and radar components."[43] This innovative work so impressed his superiors that Airey was awarded the Legion of Merit, a very high honor for an enlisted airman in the 1950s.

Airey had a series of assignments as a first sergeant before he was selected to be the first chief master sergeant of the Air Force by Chief of Staff John P. McConnell in April 1967. Airey served two years as the "voice and advocate of enlisted airmen" and made a number of important contributions, including pushing for an Air Force-level Senior Noncommissioned Officer Academy and laying the groundwork for the Weighted Airman Promotion System, which is still used today. Airey left the Air Force's top enlisted job in July 1969. He remained on active duty one more year until re-

Chief Master Sergeant of the Air Force Paul W. Airey was awarded two Legions of Merit.

tiring in August 1970. Airey died in Panama City, Florida in March 2009. He was 85 years old.[44]

JOHN K. SINGLAUB: AUGUST 1968–OCTOBER 1969

Brigadier General John K. Singlaub was awarded his second Legion of Merit for his "exceptionally meritorious conduct in the performance of outstanding service in Europe" while serving as Assistant Division Commander (Maneuver), 8th Infantry Division. His citation reads, in part:

Brigadier General Singlaub's creative leadership, personal drive, initiative and organizational skill enabled him to produce outstanding results in every assignment. His creative generalship produced the historic non-stop flight from Germany to Spain for an airborne assault conducted during Exercise PATHFINDER EXPRESS III. This new concept significantly increased the capabilities of the division. Brigadier General Singlaub

Major General John K. Singlaub's uniform reflects two awards of the Legion of Merit, as well as two Distinguished Service Medals, the Silver Star, the Soldier's Medal, two Bronze Star Medals, two Air Medals, the Army Commendation Medal, and two Purple Hearts (courtesy Jon Vastine).

held a succession of extremely important and influential positions. In every case he sought additional responsibility and achieved outstanding results. His personal leadership was an example to all who met him. His deep desire to insure the best sustained performance at all levels of command and his concern for the individual soldier enabled him to transmit a sense of urgency to the work at hand, together with inspiring a fierce pride in accomplishment resulting in repeatedly outstanding achievements.[45]

Major General John Singlaub served from 1943 until 1978, when he retired from active duty. He served in the OSS in World War II, was an early member of the Central Intelligence Agency, and spent many years in Army covert operations. Singlaub published an account of his years as a soldier in 1991.[46]

THE DEFENSE MERITORIOUS SERVICE MEDAL

Overview

Establishing Authority and Effective Dates: The Defense Meritorious Service Medal was established by Executive Order 12019 on November 3, 1977. The medal is for service performed after that date.

Criteria: The Defense Meritorious Service Medal is awarded in the name of the secretary of defense to members of the Armed Forces who, while serving in a joint activity, distinguish themselves by achievement or meritorious service in noncombat activities that do not warrant award of the Defense Superior Service Medal.

Order of Precedence: The Defense Meritorious Service Medal is worn after the Purple Heart and before the Meritorious Service Medal.

Devices: Additional awards of the Defense Meritorious Service Medal to the same individual are denoted by bronze (or silver) oak leaf clusters.

Designer: The Defense Meritorious Service Medal was designed and sculpted by Lewis J. King Jr. of the Army's Institute of Heraldry.

Description and Symbolism

Obverse

The Defense Meritorious Service Medal is a bronze medal that is 1½ inches in overall diameter and which consists of a circular wreath of laurel tied with a ribbon at its base and in the center. A pentagon shape slightly overlaps the wreath. In the center of the pentagon and standing on its base is an eagle with its wings displayed horizontally. The eagle is symbolic of the United States; the pentagon alludes to the Department of Defense — under whose authority the award is given — and the laurel wreath represents achievement.

Reverse

The reverse bears the inscription "Defense Meritorious Service" in raised letters stacked on three horizontal lines. Around the bottom appear the words "United States of America."

Ribbon

The ribbon consists of a broad white center stripe and three light blue stripes in the middle of the white field. The white stripe is bordered by ruby red and edged in white. The red and white colors are adapted from the ribbon of the Meritorious Service Medal, and the blue stripes represent the Department of Defense.

Historical Background

The first decoration established specifically for members of a joint service organization, as opposed to those assigned to one of the separate services, was the Joint Service Commendation Medal, which was established in 1963. The Joint Service Commendation Medal was followed in 1970 by the Defense Distinguished Service Medal and, in 1976, by the Defense Superior Service Medal. Thus, over time, the Department of Defense created a family of decorations for meritorious achievement that are comparable to those of the separate services. The Defense Department's decorations were created for military personnel assigned outside of their respective branches to joint staffs, de-

Defense MSM (obverse).

Defense MSM (reverse).

fense agencies, unified commands, or other Department of Defense organizations.

In an August 23, 1976, memorandum, Major General Adrian St. John, who was then serving as vice director of the joint staff of the Joints Chiefs of Staff, informed the secretary of defense that the Joint Chiefs had recommended the establishment of a Defense Department medal that was comparable to the Meritorious Service Medal "to complete the joint decorations inventory."[47]

Based on this recommendation the military departments were asked for their comments on the proposal. The replies were favorable, and the Defense Department requested on February 8, 1977, the Institute of Heraldry to prepare suggested designs for the new medal.[48] Shortly thereafter a proposed executive order was sent to the White House for approval and, on November 3, 1977, President Jimmy E. Carter signed Executive Order 12019, officially establishing the Defense Meritorious Service Medal.

Meanwhile, the Institute of Heraldry had prepared several designs for the medal, one of which was submitted to the Commission of Fine Arts for its consideration, and the Commission granted its full approval on November 22, 1977.

The first samples of the new medal were delivered to Assistant Secretary of Defense for Manpower, Reserve Affairs and Logistics John P. White on July 5, 1978. The contract to produce the medals was awarded to Lordship Products on February 21, 1979, calling for an initial order of 8,480 sets to be delivered by November 1979.

First Recipient

The first recipient of the Defense Meritorious Service Medal was Army Major Terrell G. Covington.

Selected Recipients (Chronological)

JAMES E. GILLILAND: JULY 1978–MAY 1981

Air Force Colonel Gilliland was awarded his Defense Meritorious Service Medal for his work with the North Atlantic Treaty Organization and Allied Command Europe. His citation is

> for meritorious service ... while serving as Branch Chief, Financial Services Branch, Budget and Finance Division, Supreme Headquarters Allied Powers Europe. During this period Colonel Gilliland was directly responsible for the preparation, coordination and presentation of SHAPE's 35-million dollar annual budget to the 14 nation North Atlantic Treaty Organization Military Budget Committee. His keen professional insight was key in the development of a detailed program for ensuring that NATO Military Budget Committee and NATO Infrastructure Committee requirements were met for 41 infrastructure projects managed by SHAPE. Colonel Gilliland's remarkable blend of responsible leadership, efficient management and sensitivity to the international environment enabled him to improve virtually every aspect of fiscal management at SHAPE.

TERRY D. OHLEMEIER: MAY 30, 1990–JULY 4, 1993

Air Force Lieutenant Colonel Ohlemeier was awarded his Defense Meritorious Service Medal for his service as Chief, Rotary Wing Operations Branch, Operations Directorate, Joint Special Operations Command. His citation says he

> distinguished himself by exceptionally meritorious service ... was deeply involved in the leadership of virtually every command training event, exercise, or contingency. He orchestrated the Joint Air Asset Allocation Program for all associated units. His continually successful efforts were indispensable to his command's readiness and improved the overall mission capability of the special operations community.

JASON U. QUESENBERRY: AUGUST 2, 2006–AUGUST 31, 2009

Air Force Senior Master Sergeant Quesenberry received the Defense Meritorious Service Medal for his service as Superintendent, Tactical Air Control Party, Aviation Tactics Evaluation Group, Joint Special Operations Command. According to his citation,

> Senior Master Sergeant Quesenberry's stalwart leadership, tireless dedication, and multifaceted

Joint Terminal Attack Controller expertise impacted all areas of fire support operations. His tireless devotion to duty proved vital during a time of unprecedented strain on Special Operations Forces directly contributing to transformational strides in capabilities across the Special Operations aviation spectrum.

THE MERITORIOUS SERVICE MEDAL

Overview

Establishing Authority and Effective Dates: The Meritorious Service Medal was established by Executive Order 11448 on January 16, 1969. It has been effective for service since that date.

Criteria: The Meritorious Service Medal may be awarded to members of the Armed Forces who distinguish themselves by outstanding noncombat achievement or by meritorious service to the United States that does not warrant the award of the Legion of Merit.

Order of Precedence: The Meritorious Service Medal is worn after the Defense Mer-

itorious Service Medal and before the Air Medal.

Devices: Additional awards are denoted by bronze (or silver) oak leaf clusters.

Designer: The Meritorious Service Medal was designed by Jay Morris and sculpted by Lewis J. King Jr., both of the Army's Institute of Heraldry.

Description and Symbolism

Obverse

The Meritorious Service Medal is a bronze medal that is 1½ inches in diameter overall and which consists of six rays issuing from the upper three points of a five-pointed star with beveled edges. The medal also contains two smaller stars defined by incised outlines. In front of the lower part of the medal there is an eagle with its wings displayed. It is standing on two upward curving branches of laurel tied with a ribbon.

The eagle, symbol of the United States, stands on laurel branches denoting achievement. The star is used to represent the military, and the rays emanating from the star reflect the constant efforts of individuals to

Left: MSM (obverse). *Right:* MSM (reverse).

achieve by providing excellent and meritorious service.

Reverse

The reverse of the medal is blank except for a circle consisting of the raised inscription "United States of America" at the top and "Meritorious Service" at the bottom. The two portions of the inscription are separated by bullets, and the space inside the circle is to be used for engraving the recipient's name.

Ribbon

The ribbon is ruby red with two white stripes just inside each edge. The ribbon's color and configuration echoes that of the Legion of Merit.

Historical Background

General Pershing's Initiative

As early as November 1918, General Pershing, who was then the commanding general of the American Expeditionary Forces, recommended to the War Department that it establish an "Order of Merit" to serve as a "new Government award to be employed as an acknowledgement of meritorious service deserving special recognition, which cannot be made by any of the rewards at present authorized."[49] The War Department was apparently confused as to exactly what Pershing wanted and disapproved his request. Pershing protested and asked the War Department to reconsider. On December 24, 1918, however, Secretary of War Newton Baker sent Pershing a cable informing him that

> Congress is being urged to establish many additional decorations for special services, for Selective Draft Boards, Emergency Fleet Workers, [and] Aircraft production civilian experts. As we already have several military decorations and are proposing [a] campaign badge, it is believed that creation of [an] Order of Merit would not be favorably received by Congress, though some sort of certificate issued by your authority would be a valued evidence of appreciation and there could be no objection to such a certificate. Both in

France and here the work done by thousands was devoted in spirit and invaluable in results; [and] that it deserves grateful recognition is evident, but my fear is that it is too widespread to permit of individual decorations and that those omitted would resent it.[50]

On February 11, 1919, the deputy chief of staff of the American Expeditionary Forces sent a memorandum to other staff members stating that General Pershing was, "desirous of issuing a Meritorious Service Medal, or a medal to be known by some other appropriate name, that may be presented for acts or services that are worthy of commendation but do not come within the requirements for the presentation of the Distinguished Service Medal or the Distinguished Service Cross." This memorandum noted that "the War Department has not authorized the presentation of such a medal, and it would therefore have to be presented for wear in the A.E.F. only." The respondents were asked to submit designs for the medal.[51] The assistant chiefs of staff who received the memorandum of February 11, 1919, responded by submitting several proposed designs.[52] However, because World War I had ended, the issue of new medals no longer seemed important. General Pershing's request was not acted on, even though he made a final appeal for an "Order of Merit" in May 1919.

Interwar Years

Between World War I and World War II, the Army briefly had a meritorious service medal when the Purple Heart was revived in 1932 as a "junior Distinguished Service Medal" that could be awarded in time of peace or war. This meant that military personnel who were serving with the Civilian Conservation Corps were eligible for the new medal for "outstanding distinguished service," but just one Purple Heart was awarded for peacetime merit before the War Department altered its regulations and restricted the Purple Heart to wartime service. As a result the Army again only had one decoration for peacetime meritorious service — the high-level Distinguished Service Medal.

World War II and Its Aftermath

During World War II, a substantial number of new decorations were approved to fill specific needs, and the idea of establishing a Meritorious Service Medal for military personnel was again considered. The end result, however, was the Legion of Merit, and although that award filled a very important role, it could not satisfy the entire range of meritorious service. In 1946, a joint Army-Navy board examined the issue yet again, and one of its recommendations was that the newly created Army Commendation Ribbon be redesigned as a medal and re-designated as the Meritorious Service Medal.[53] But no action was taken on this proposal.

In the mid–1950s the Air Force conducted a study of decorations and concluded that a meritorious service award was needed to bridge the tremendous gap between the Legion of Merit and the Air Force Commendation Medal. The study noted that in wartime, this gap was filled by the Bronze Star Medal but there was no peacetime decoration comparable to the Bronze Star. The Air Force specifically recommended that the Meritorious Service Medal be created and that it be used to recognize military members for "exceptionally meritorious performance of distinctive service of other than national or international significance." That proposal did not meet with success, and the push for a Meritorious Service Medal was again tabled.

The Vietnam War: The Proposal Revisited

At an Army, Navy and Air Force awards conference held in February 1968, the services again considered the need for a meritorious award to provide appropriate recognition for noncombat accomplishments. The driving force behind the idea was the Navy. Retired Vice Admiral William E. Gentner, who was then chief of the Navy Board of Decorations and Medals, argued that a Meritorious Service Medal would "do a great deal to establish a continuity in noncombat awards by maintaining the Legion of Merit in a selective category, and at the same time, keep the Service Commendation Medal in the area for which it was conceived."[54]

There was yet another reason supporting the creation of a Meritorious Service Medal. The Bronze Star Medal had been liberally awarded in Vietnam, especially for meritorious service, and this was seen as diluting the Bronze Star's value as a decoration for heroism. The idea of a Meritorious Service Medal that would be a noncombat decoration on a par with the Bronze Star Medal appealed to those who were concerned about the declining prestige of the Bronze Star.

A proposed executive order was prepared in April 1968 and forwarded for approval to the military departments, and an ad hoc committee was formed by the secretary of defense for Manpower and Reserve Affairs to select a name for the proposed medal. On November 8, 1968, the committee unanimously approved the name "Meritorious Service Medal."[55] As one of his last acts in office, President Lyndon B. Johnson signed Executive Order 11448 on January 16, 1969, creating the Meritorious Service Medal.

The Meritorious Service Medal is unusual in a key respect: it is one of only two decorations that cannot be given in a combat theater. This was done to preclude it from devaluing Bronze Star Medals awarded for meritorious achievement. Today, the Meritorious Service Medal is widely awarded in the Army and the Air Force to mid-grade officers and noncommissioned officers.

Selected Recipients (Chronological)

RALPH E. ADAMS: DECEMBER 16, 1967– JUNE 19, 1971

Air Force Lieutenant Colonel Adams received his Meritorious Service Medal for his service as a staff officer at Hickam Air Force Base, Hawaii. His citation states that he

> distinguished himself in the performance of outstanding service to the United States as an Air Operations Staff Officer, Aircrew Training and Support Operations Division, Directorate of Operations, Deputy Chief of Staff/Operations, Headquarters, Pacific Air Forces. During this period, Colonel Adams demonstrated an exceptional degree of initiative, technical competence, devotion to duty and mission orientation in accomplishing his assigned tasks as the Pacific Air Forces F-105 and F-102 Training and Standardization Officer. His relentless quest for perfection in the accomplishment of each assigned task contributed significantly to the enhancement of the command's mission in Southeast Asia and the readiness posture in the Western Pacific.[56]

ROBERT E. BLAKE: JULY 9, 1976–AUGUST 29, 1978

Air Force Colonel Blake was awarded his second Meritorious Service Medal for his performance at Luke Air Force Base, Arizona. According to his citation, he

> distinguished himself in the performance of outstanding service ... as Assistant Deputy Commander for Operations, F-4, and Deputy Commander for Operations, F4/F15, 58th Tactical Training Wing, Luke Air Force Base. During this period, Colonel Blake's effectiveness as a leader, manager, and instructor pilot resulted in outstanding aircrew performance, high esprit de corps, and exceptional mission accomplishment directly benefiting the tactical air forces.

JEFFREY B. FLOYD: MAY 30, 1982 TO MAY 30, 1985

While serving as an Air Force officer in Germany, Floyd was awarded his second Meritorious Service Medal for his service as Chief, Target Studies Branch, Targeting Division, Directorate of Intelligence Applications, Deputy Chief of Staff, Intelligence, Headquarters, United States Air Forces in Europe. His citation reads, in part:

> Major Floyd's outstanding professionalism, unsurpassed dedication to duty and unequalled

contributions in resolving the most complicated target intelligence problems have significantly enhanced the defense posture of the United States and the combat readiness of North Atlantic Treaty Organization military forces. His aggressive efforts in developing and integrating a wide variety of complex target initiatives dramatically improved the substance and timeliness of analytical and targeting support to theater war-fighting units.

Born in Mobile, Alabama, in June 1947, Jeffrey Burnside Floyd graduated from the University of Pittsburgh in 1968 and entered the Air Force in 1969. After training as a ground controlled intercept director, he served in Vietnam, where he was an instructor controller and senior director. In the mid–1970s, Floyd served at Udorn Royal Thai Air Force Base, Thailand, where he directed the production of target intelligence materials and provided direct targeting support for Air Force operations during the fall of Saigon, fall of Phnom Penh and the SS *Mayaguez* incident.

After service as the Chief of Conventional Targeting, Air Force Intelligence Service, Bolling Air Force Base, District of Columbia, then Major Floyd was reassigned to Germany, where he directed conventional targeting support for NATO planning and operations. In 1985, he became Chief of Intelligence, 12th Tactical Intelligence Squadron, which provided air intelligence support to 12th Air Force and the Army's XVIII Airborne Corps. Floyd retired from active duty in 1989.

THE PURPLE HEART

Overview

Establishing Authority and Effective Dates: The Badge of Military Merit established by George Washington on August 7, 1782, was revived as the Purple Heart by War Department General Orders No. 3 on February 22, 1932. Retroactive awards were permitted from the beginning, and Purple Hearts were awarded to Union veterans of the Civil

War, Indian Wars, Spanish-American War, Boxer Rebellion, Philippine Insurrection, and Punitive Expedition into Mexico. The bulk of the initial awards of the Purple Heart, however, went to soldiers who had been wounded in World War I.

Criteria: The Purple Heart may be awarded to any member of the Armed Forces of the United States who, while serving under competent authority in any capacity with one of the Armed Forces after April 5, 1917, was killed or wounded in any of the following circumstances:

1. in action against an enemy of the United States;
2. in action with an opposing armed force of a foreign country in which the Armed Forces of the United States are or have been engaged;
3. while serving with friendly foreign forces engaged in an armed conflict against an opposing armed force in which the United States is not a belligerent party;
4. as the result of an act of any such enemy or opposing armed force;
5. as the result of an act of any hostile foreign force;
6. as the result of friendly weapon fire while actively engaging the enemy;
7. as the indirect result of enemy action;
8. after March 28, 1973, as the result of an act of international terrorism or as the result of a peacekeeping mission outside the United States.

Order of Precedence: The Purple Heart is worn after the Bronze Star Medal and before the Defense Meritorious Service Medal.

Devices: Additional awards of the Purple Heart to the same individual are denoted by bronze or silver oak leaf clusters.

Designer: The overall design of the Purple Heart was specified by the War Department. The models for the medal were sculpted by John R. Sinnock of the Philadelphia Mint.

First Recipient: The first Purple Heart, with the Arabic number *1* stamped on its edge, was presented to Gen. Douglas MacArthur on July 21, 1931.

Description and Symbolism

Obverse

On a purple heart within a bronze-gilt border, a profile head in relief of George Washington in military uniform appears. Above the heart is the shield of Washington's coat of arms between two sprays of leaves in green enamel. Washington's profile was selected for use on the medal to commemorate his founding of the Badge of Military Merit.

Reverse

On the reverse of the Purple Heart there is a raised bronze heart with the inscription in relief "For Military Merit." The inscription was selected to provide a linkage with Washington's Badge of Military Merit.

Ribbon

The ribbon is purple and edged in white. The colors were selected because Washington's

Purple Heart (obverse with two oak leaf clusters).

original Badge of Military Merit was a cloth purple heart edged in white.

Historical Background

The Badge of Military Merit

The Purple Heart is the oldest American military decoration. It was originally established as the Badge of Military Merit by George Washington on August 7, 1782.[57] His orders of the day for that date announce the following:

> The General ever desirous to cherish a virtuous ambition in his soldiers, as well as to foster and encourage every species of Military Merit, directs that whenever any singularly meritorious action is performed, the author of it shall be permitted to wear on his facings, over his left breast, the figure of a heart in purple cloth, or silk, edged with narrow lace or binding. Not only instances of unusual gallantry, but also of extraordinary fidelity and essential service in any way shall meet with a due reward. Before this favor can be conferred on any man, the particular fact, or facts on which it is to be grounded, must be set forth to the commander-in-chief, accompanied with certificates from the commanding officers of the regiment and brigade to which the candidate for reward belonged, or other incontestable proofs, and upon granting it the name and regiment of the person with the action so certified are to be enrolled in the book of merit which will be kept at the orderly office. Men who have merited this last distinction to be suffered to pass all guard and sentinels which officers are permitted to do.[58] The road to glory in a patriot army and a free country is thus opened to all. This order is also to have retrospect to the earliest days of the war, and to be considered as a permanent one.

Recipients of the Original Badge of Military Merit (Purple Heart)

Since the "book of merit" mentioned in Washington's 1782 order has never been located, it is not known how many soldiers received the Badge of Military Merit. Only three awards are known to have been made, but it is entirely possible that others have been lost to history. It should be noted that the Badge of

Military Merit was not originally considered an award to be given for wounds suffered in combat, but rather as a high decoration for valor. In reality, the award that later became the Purple Heart was the forerunner of the Medal of Honor.

Elijah Churchill

The first known Badge of Military Merit went to Sergeant Elijah Churchill of the 2nd Regiment of Light Dragoons. He received his award for heroism in two raids behind British lines. The first raid was on November 23, 1780, and the second was on October 3, 1781. Both raids were planned and directed by Major Benjamin Tallmadge of the 2nd Continental Dragoons, who was the chief of General Washington's intelligence service.

William Brown

The second individual awarded the Badge of Military Merit was Sgt. William Brown of the 5th Regiment of the Connecticut Line. The citation for his decoration, which was awarded on April 24, 1783, states that "in the assault of the enemy's left redoubt at Yorktown, in Virginia, on the evening of October 14, 1781, Brown conducted a forlorn hope with great bravery, propriety and deliberate firmness."[59]

Daniel Bissell

Perhaps the most fascinating Badge of Military Merit award went to Sgt. Daniel Bissell, as it was based on his courage and intelligence after "deserting" from the Continental Army. Washington's General Orders, published on June 8, 1783, contain this citation for Bissell: "Serg. [sic] Bissell of the 2nd Connecticut Regiment having performed some important services within the immediate knowledge of the Commander-in-Chief, in which the fidelity, perseverance and good sense of the said Serg. Bissell were conspicuously manifested, it is, therefore ordered: That he be honored with the badge of merit; he will be called at headquarters on Tuesday next for the insignia and certificate to which he is hereby entitled."[60]

Revival of the Purple Heart

After the American Revolution the Badge of Military Merit fell into disuse, the Book of Merit was lost, and the "Purple Heart" medal was all but forgotten for almost 150 years. Then, immediately following World War I, General Pershing recommended the creation of an "Order of Merit" that could be awarded "for services which, while meritorious and worthy of recognition, were not of the importance necessary for the award of the distinguished service medal; and also for acts of gallantry in action which merited recognition but which were below the standard established for the award of the Distinguished Service Cross."[61] Pershing's recommendation was not acted upon, and when he complained, Pershing received a cable from Secretary of War informing him that Baker believed that Congress would not support the creation of the award Pershing sought, but that "some sort of certificate issued by your authority would be a valued evidence of appreciation and there could be no objection to such a certificate."[62]

In July 1921 Pershing, who was then the Army chief of staff, addressed a personal memorandum to his director of operations, in which Pershing pointed out the problems with the Army's system of awarding decorations. He ordered a study to consider providing a new decoration that could be awarded for gallantry in peacetime and during wartime that could also be awarded to civilians who were directly connected with the Army. The study ultimately resulted in the recommendation that a distinction be maintained between acts of outstanding service and acts of gallantry and that no single decoration be awarded for both purposes. The study group also recommended that legislation be sought that would substitute a "Military Cross" for the Silver Star and that a new decoration, the "Military Medal," also be established.

The legislative proposal was approved by Pershing on August 30, 1921. However, at a meeting of the Joint Chief's Advisory Council on Legislation held on October 19, 1921, the proposal was unanimously rejected because its members believed the introduction of such a bill would not result in its enactment but would only "open up old sores and provoke discussion and debate which would result in no good to the Army and more than likely, in actual harm."

The War Department continued to be frustrated by the narrow structure of its system of decorations and at its inability to secure legislation to resolve the problem. The issue was raised again in 1925, when the secretary of war sought the recommendations of the general staff concerning the possible reestablishment of George Washington's Badge of Military Merit. A number of comments were received relative to the proposal. For example, Col. John W. Wright of the Historical Section of the Army War College, made the following comments with respect to the proposed medal: "This should have been our first and highest decoration as it is older than the Constitution and founded by Washington; it should today be the Medal of Honor, but, unfortunately, it was neglected. The army disbanded, the men scattered over an immense territory, and all were tired of war; therefore it died.... Other decorations have been created and consecrated by blood. Our mission, clearly, is to revive it and respect the later decorations. However, if this decoration is recreated properly it will be unique and have a value all its own, assured by its history."[63]

Wright believed that the Army needed another decoration to complement the three then in existence — the Medal of Honor, the Distinguished Service Cross, and the Distinguished Service Medal. He particularly believed that a medal for distinguished service below that required for a Distinguished Service Medal was needed, particularly "where the man is in a position of responsibility; in other words, covering younger officers." Wright continued: "As the Purple Heart has its own history it will be a decoration that will have high standing. I would not call it a second D.S.M. (Distinguished Service Medal). It should stand alone as the decoration reserved for all officers and men, not being in positions of great responsibility, yet who perform services calling for recognition. It will be the decoration within the grasp of younger officers; afterwards they may also receive the D.S.M. but that could come only with high rank and very responsible duty."

Col. Robert E. Wyllie also agreed that the Distinguished Service Medal required a complementary, but subordinate, decoration to protect its status.[64] He also noted that, "a decoration is ... urgently needed to be awarded for deeds not warranting the award of any of the existing decorations. That means distinguished services in time of war or peace in other than positions of great responsibility and acts of valor performed which have no connection with hostile operations."[65]

John C. Fitzpatrick, assistant chief of the Manuscript Division of the Library of Congress, likewise concurred and felt the award should be given in peacetime, as well. He also wrote that "the design of the medal, if the decoration is revived, would need careful consideration... . I imagine that a heart in purple enamel with a green gold edge ... could be embossed on a circular medal."[66]

Based on this input the Army's general staff recommended to the secretary of war that the Badge of Military Merit be revived and conferred for exceptionally meritorious service not involving great responsibility; that it also be awarded for heroic acts not performed in actual conflict, and that it should be available in peacetime as well as during war only to members of the Army.

The issue of reviving the medal was given additional impetus in November 1925, when a well-known numismatist named of Carleton S. Gifford wrote to President Coolidge and recommended, among other things, that the president revive "General Washington's Badge of the Purple Heart which did not survive the Revolutionary War."[67] Gifford's letter was forwarded to the War Department, where, because of the ongoing interest in its subject, the letter was given serious consideration.

In December 1930 identical bills — HR 14570 and S 5207 — were introduced in both houses of Congress that proposed the establishment of a "Military Cross" to be subordinate to the Silver Star and a Military Medal. In response to this legislation, Secretary of War Patrick Hurley in early 1931 wrote nearly identical letters to members of the House military committee and Senate military. He informed the committee members that the War Department was "considering the continuance of General George Washington's Badge of Military Merit, for much the same purposes as are contemplated by the proposed legislation. This would be done in connection with the celebration in honor of the 200th anniversary of General Washington's birth. In view of these arrangements, which are considered as confidential for the present, the War Department does not recommend enactment [of the proposed legislation] at this time."

General MacArthur and the Revival of the Purple Heart

On April 8, 1931, Army Chief of Staff General Douglas MacArthur wrote to Charles Moore, the Chairman of the Commission of Fine Arts. MacArthur informed Moore that the Army's plan was to "revive" Washington's old Badge of Military Merit on February 22, 1932, the bicentennial of Washington's birthday. MacArthur went on to note that the project was to be kept confidential and pointed out that the re-established badge was to be awarded for "extraordinary fidelity or essential service" in war or peace. MacArthur further advised Moore that he wanted to retain the characteristics of the original award, which had been designed by Pierre Charles L'Enfant in accordance with Washington's personal instructions. At the same time, however, MacArthur wanted "to follow the modern design of decorations."

MacArthur included two proposed designs with his letter to Moore. Both drawings used the form of a heart and included Washington's coat of arms. MacArthur noted that the War Department preferred the design that also included a bust of Washington. MacArthur closed by stating that he would be grateful if "the subject can be given the earliest consideration of the Commission," and again stressed that in the interim the idea should be kept confidential.[68]

MacArthur's Recommendation Becomes a Medal

The Commission of Fine Arts turned General MacArthur's request over to A. A. Weinman, who was the sculptor member of the commission. Weinman, in turn, recommended selection of an obverse design with Washington's bust and a reverse design bearing the inscription "For Military Merit." Weinman made several other suggested changes to the design, which were passed on to MacArthur on April 18, 1931, along with a request for $1,500 to secure the services "of a competent medalist to prepare the models." As the chairman of the Commission of Fine Arts explained at that time:

> The execution of a medal is the production of sculpture in miniature, requiring skill and experience on the part of the artist. A satisfactory design on paper does not assure a satisfactory medal; and in view of the fact that his Badge of Merit is to be revived during the Bicentennial Celebration and to rank next to the Distinguished Service Medal and Distinguished Service Cross, the Commission of Fine Arts advises that at this stage the work should be placed in the hands of one of the leading medalists of the country. This can be done if the War Department will make $1,500 available for the production of models from which the medal will be cast. If this meets with your approval, the Commission suggests that Mr. Gaetano Cecere, Sculptor, 412 West 33rd Street, New York City, be commis-

sioned to execute the models. Mr. Cecere designed the Soldier's Medal for Valor.

MacArthur agreed with this recommendation and on April 24, 1931, the chairman of the Commission of Fine Arts wrote again to MacArthur to tell him that the commission was asking several medalists to submit sketches. The result was that Gaetano Cecere, Walker Hancock, and John Sinnock, the Chief Engraver at the Philadelphia Mint, were asked to submit designs, and told that the successful competitor would be paid $1,500 for the final finished model.

The three sculptors submitted designs based on the criteria provided by Weinman, who reviewed the designs they submitted. Weinman selected the sketch by Sinnock and made some minor suggestions for its improvement. On May 29, 1931, the commission notified MacArthur of Sinnock's selection. Sinnock then completed his plaster models, and these were sent to MacArthur for approval. MacArthur was pleased with them, and on September 22, 1931, he sent the models to the Commission of Fine Arts. Sinnock had actually submitted four similar plaster models, and Weinman selected the one with a somewhat flat relief. The commission concurred with Weinman's choice, and that model became the basis for the new Purple Heart.

On February 22, 1932, the War Department announced in General Orders No. 3 that it had revived the Purple Heart, and that it "is to be awarded to persons who, while serving in the Army of the United States perform any singular meritorious act of extraordinary fidelity or essential service."

Who Designed the Purple Heart?

After World War II, a controversy arose as to who had designed the Purple Heart medal. In reporting Sinnock's death in its May 26, 1947, issue, *Time* magazine credited Sinnock with designing the medal. The June 16,

1947, issue of the magazine, however, contained a letter from Elizabeth Will of the Institute of Heraldry in which she claimed to have designed the medal.

An investigation conducted by the Commission of Fine Arts concluded that Sinnock had designed the Purple Heart based on sketches sent to the commission by MacArthur. As it is likely that Will prepared these sketches for MacArthur based on specifications provided by him, this explains why she believed she was the designer of the new decoration. But MacArthur's specifications for the medal were based on the recommendation by John Fitzpatrick of the Library of Congress, who had suggested in 1925 that the medal be a heart in purple enamel with a green-gold edge. Consequently, when assigning credit for the design of the Purple Heart, it is best to say that credit belongs to several individuals, including L'Enfant and Washington who were responsible for the original purple-cloth heart-shaped Badge of Military Merit, Fitzpatrick, MacArthur, and Will, with Sinnock designing the final plaster model for the modern-day Purple Heart medal.

Evolution of the Purple Heart as a Decoration for Wounds

When the Purple Heart was revived in 1932, it was not established specifically as a decoration for wounds. However, the regulation implementing the Purple Heart states:

Purple Heart, to whom awarded: The Purple Heart, established by General George Washington in 1782, is awarded to persons who, while serving in the Army of the United States, perform any singularly meritorious act of extraordinary fidelity or essential service. (A wound, which necessitates treatment by a medical officer, and which is received in action with an enemy of the United States, or as a result of an act of such enemy, may, in the judgment of the commander authorized to make the award, be construed as resulting from a singularly meritorious act of essential service.)[69]

As a result of the last sentence in this provision, such a large number of Purple Hearts were issued based on injuries sustained in action that those awards virtually established the medal as decoration for wounded service members. Some months after World War II began, the Army changed its regulations so that the Purple Heart was authorized exclusively for individuals who received combat wounds. This occurred after the creation of the Legion of Merit gave the War Department a decoration for merit, which made it unnecessary to continue to award the Purple Heart for meritorious service.[70]

The Purple Heart Becomes a Navy, Marine Corps, and Coast Guard Award

When the War Department revived the Purple Heart as a medal in 1932, the Navy took the position that it was purely an Army decoration for soldiers and airmen. This meant that no sailors or Marines were eligible for the Purple Heart unless they had been wounded while serving with the American Expeditionary Force during World War I.

After World War II began, some sea service personnel serving with Army units were awarded Purple Hearts. This meant that some sailors and Marines were receiving the decoration for their combat-related wounds while others were not. This disparate recognition was bad for morale and explains why, on December 3, 1942, President Roosevelt signed Executive Order 9277, which made the Purple Heart available to members of the sea services while serving in their own branch.

Evolution of Award Criteria

On April 25, 1962, the Purple Heart's award criteria was again expanded so that the medal could be awarded to American soldiers, sailors, airmen, and Marines serving as advisors in South Vietnam. This expansion was deemed necessary because under the executive orders signed by Roosevelt in 1942 and Truman in 1952, the Purple Heart could not be awarded to individuals "who receive wounds or are killed while serving in an advisory capacity with, or while assisting in the operations of friendly foreign forces engaged in armed conflict to which the United States is not formally a party."[71]

The Army, Navy, and Air Force believed that the services and sacrifices of advisory personnel merited the Purple Heart, and President Kennedy agreed when he signed Executive Order 11016. As a result of Kennedy's order the Purple Heart could be awarded to individuals who were wounded or killed "while serving with friendly foreign forces" and "as a result of action by a hostile foreign force." The Air Force had requested this "hostile foreign force" language specifically so it would have the legal authority to award the Purple Heart to Air Force personnel who were shot down over the Barents Sea by Soviet MiG aircraft in 1960. But the Navy and the Army liked the additionally flexibility that the provision gave them, as well.[72]

The next major change to the Purple Heart's award criteria occurred on February 23, 1984, when President Ronald Reagan signed Executive Order 12464. The order permitted the Purple Heart to be awarded to individuals killed or wounded as a result of an international terrorist attack and was retroactive to March 28, 1973. This same executive order also allowed the Purple Heart to be awarded to members of the U.S. Armed Forces who were killed or wounded while serving as part of a peacekeeping mission outside of the United States.

As a result of Reagan's expanded Purple Heart criteria, soldiers and airmen have received the following Purple Hearts:

Terrorism[73]:

- Germany, September 15, 1981: Army General Frederick Kroesen was wounded when terrorists attempted to assassinate him by blowing up his car in Heidelberg; he was awarded the Purple Heart on March 26, 1984

- France, January 18, 1982: Army Lt. Col. Charles Ray was killed by a terrorist assassin in Paris on January 18, 1982; he was serving as an assistant Army attaché at the U.S. Defense Attaché Office in Paris when he was killed; the Army awarded Ray a posthumous Purple Heart on July 13, 1984

- Philippines, October 2, 2002: Army First Sergeant Mark W. Jackson was killed when a nail-laden bomb fastened to a motorcycle exploded outside a karaoke bar and restaurant in Zamboanga, Philippines; the Army awarded him a posthumous Purple Heart after the Philippine government determined that the al-Qaida-linked Abu Sayyaf terrorist group was responsible for the attack.

Peacekeeping[74]:

- Lebanon, September 25, 1982: Army Major Randall Carlson was killed when his jeep hit a landmine near Beirut, Lebanon; he was a member of the U.N. Truce Supervision Organization, a peacekeeping force, with a duty station in Israel; the Army awarded him a posthumous Purple Heart on September 18, 1984

- Lebanon, September 20, 1984: Army Chief Warrant Officer Two Kenneth Welch was killed in a terrorist attack on Beirut; he was awarded a posthumous Purple Heart on September 24, 1984.

Order of Precedence Change

Prior to 1986, the Purple Heart was worn after Army and Air Force Commendation and Achievement Medals. But, after Major General Aubrey S. Newman, a decorated World War II veteran (and recipient of the Purple Heart) argued in *Army* magazine that the Purple Heart's precedence should be elevated because it was a combat decoration and should outrank awards for commendation or achievement,[75] veterans groups took up Newman's suggestion and lobbied Congress for a change. At the urging of the Military Order of the Purple Heart and other constituents, Senator John Warner

(R-Va.) Warner introduced legislation in Congress to elevate the Purple Heart's status. After this legislation passed in 1986, "the Secretary of the military department concerned" was required to "accord the Purple Heart a position of precedence, in relation to other awards and decorations ... not lower than that immediately following the bronze star medal."[76] The result is that the Purple Heart today is worn after the Bronze Star Medal and before the Defense Meritorious Service Medal.

Fratricide

The next major change affecting the Purple Heart occurred in 1993, when Congress enacted a new law that gave the Army and Air Force a legislative basis for awarding the Purple Heart to the victims of fratricide and other friendly fire incidents.[77] As a general rule, friendly fire awards are given for death or injury occurring "while actively engaging the enemy" and when the projectile or agent causing the harm was released with the full intent of inflicting damage or destroying the enemy or its equipment. A self-inflicted wound would qualify, provided that the injury occurred during combat and did not involve gross negligence. For example, an airman who wounds himself or herself while firing a weapon with the intent of destroying the enemy is eligible for the Purple Heart.

Prisoners of War

In 1996, Congress again modified the award criteria for the Purple Heart when it passed a statute requiring the services to award the Purple Heart to soldiers, sailors, airmen, Marines, and Coast Guardsmen who were wounded by the enemy while being held as prisoners of war in World War II and Korea.[78]

No More Purple Hearts for Civilians

The last major change to the Army and Air Force's Purple Heart award authority occurred in 1997, when Congress passed legislation prohibiting the award of the Purple Heart to civilians. The Army had awarded a handful of Purple Hearts to civilians who were serving alongside soldiers in World War II and in Vietnam, and both the Army and the Air Force had awarded the Purple Heart to civilians injured in a terrorist attacks in Germany, Greece, Malta and Saudi Arabia in the 1980s and 1990s, but the loss of this authority was not greatly missed.[79]

Purple Hearts for Brain Injury

One recent development affecting eligibility for the Purple Heart must be mentioned: on April 25, 2011, the Defense Department adopted uniform criteria permitting the award of the Purple Heart to soldiers and airmen who sustain "mild traumatic brain injuries and concussive injuries" in combat. This development was based on the recognition that brain injuries caused by improvised explosive devices qualify as wounds, even though such brain injuries may be invisible.

While the Army and Navy apparently had been awarding the Purple Heart as early as 2008 to soldiers, sailors and Marines suffering from traumatic brain injury, they had their own standards for determining whether the severity of such wounds merited the Purple Heart. Concerned about this lack of uniformity, and the large number of the soldiers and Marines receiving organic brain injuries in Afghanistan and Iraq, the Army and the Marine Corps pushed for Defense Department guidance that would clearly state when the services were authorized to award the Purple Heart for concussive injuries. Consequently, when the Defense Department announced uniform criteria for the award of the Purple Heart in April 2011, this meant that the type and severity of a concussive injury qualifying for a Purple Heart is the same for soldiers and airmen — and sailors and Marines.

Awards are retroactive to September 11, 2001. On the issue of severity of a brain injury, the new guidance expressly states that a soldier or airman need not lose consciousness in order to qualify for the Purple Heart. On the contrary, if a "medical officer" or "medical professional" makes a "diagnosis" that an individual suffered a "concussive injury" and the "extent of the wound was such that it required treatment by a medical officer," this is sufficient for the award of the Purple Heart. Additionally, the new Defense Department guidance identifies types of qualifying "treatment," to include pain medication to treat the brain injury (headache), referral to a neurologist or neuropsychologist, and rehabilitation by an occupational therapist or physical therapist.[80]

It is too early to know the extent to which Purple Hearts will be awarded to soldiers for these concussion injuries, but the number of awards could be sizable given the wounds inflicted upon Army personnel by improvised explosive devices. The number of awards to airmen for such wounds, however, will certainly be fewer in number, given the smaller number of airmen in Afghanistan and Iraq.

A final note: the decision to award the Purple Heart for concussive injuries is very different from the 2009 decision not to award the decoration to troops suffering from post traumatic stress disorder or "PTSD." The latter is difficult to diagnose, has symptoms that often arise later in life, and is not necessarily linked to any specific battlefield event or direct or intentional action of an enemy. On the contrary, PTSD is a "secondary effect caused by witnessing or experiencing a traumatic event." Consequently, while the disorder is serious and affects "up to 20 percent of returning Iraq war veterans," the Defense Department decided to exclude those suffering from PTSD from receiving the Purple Heart.[81]

Selected Recipients (Chronological)

RODNEY C. COLE: JANUARY 3, 1945

Private First Class Cole was killed in action near Rarmont, Belgium by a gunshot wound to the neck. Cole was a combat infantryman in the 325th Glider Infantry Regiment, 82nd Airborne Division, and had been previously decorated with the Purple Heart for wounds received in combat.

Born in Wayland, Michigan in August 1921, Cole entered the Army in November 1942. While his remains were permanently interred in the Henri Chapelle American Cemetery and Memorial in Belgium in 1948, Cole's mother later received his posthumously awarded Purple Heart with oak leaf cluster.

MATTHEW B. RIDGWAY: MARCH 24, 1945

Major General Ridgway was wounded by an enemy hand grenade on March 24, 1945. At the time, he was commanding the XVIII Airborne Corps in the Wesel-Hamminkeln area of Germany.[82]

The son of a Regular Army colonel, Matthew Bunker Ridgway was born in March 1895 at Fort Monroe, Virginia. Like his father, who had graduated in 1883, Ridgway attended the U.S. Military Academy. When he graduated in 1917, Ridgway was commissioned in the infantry. He then served in a variety of assignments prior to World War II, including overseas duty in China, Nicaragua, and the Philippines.

Ridgway rose to prominence in World War II, when he organized and then commanded the 82d Airborne Division in Italy and France (he parachuted into Normandy on June 6, 1944). Then Major General Ridgway assumed command of XVIII Airborne Corps in August 1944 and led it during the Allied breakout from Normandy. At the end of the war, he was a three-star general and, for his heroism and service, had been awarded two Distinguished Service Crosses, the Distinguished Service Medal, three Silver Stars and the Bronze Star Medal.

During the Korean War, Ridgway again proved that he was an outstanding soldier. After Lieutenant General Walton Walker was killed in action, Ridgway took command of the badly demoralized Eighth Army. He turned the unit around and is credited with its success in 1951. President Harry S. Truman was sufficiently impressed with Ridgway that, when Truman relieved General Douglas MacArthur in April

Purple Heart (reverse). Officially engraved Purple Heart to Army Captain Harry A. Logsdon (wounded in action in France on September 14, 1918) along with his World War I Victory Medal and French Croix de Guerre.

1951, he appointed Ridgway as Far East Commander and Commander-in-Chief, United Nations Command. Ridgway later also served as Supreme Allied Commander, Europe.

Ridgway ended his career as Army Chief of Staff. He insisted that the Army focus on conventional forces rather than funding nuclear forces, and opposed the post–Korean War "New Look" national strategic direction (which relied heavily on strategic nuclear weapons) being pursued by Eisenhower. Ridgway retired as a four star general in 1955 after 38 years of service. When he died in 1993 at the age of 98, Ridgway was widely considered to be one of the greatest soldiers of the 20th century.[83]

GEORGE E. DAY: AUGUST 26, 1967, SEPTEMBER 1967, AND JULY 16–OCTOBER 14, 1969

Retired Air Force Colonel George Edward "Bud" Day was awarded four Purple Hearts. He is the most highly decorated living American, having been awarded nearly seventy military decorations and awards, including the Medal of Honor.

Day's first Purple Heart was for wounds received on August 26, 1967, when he was badly injured after ejecting from his F-100; his plane had been hit by a North Vietnamese 57-mm shell and Day bailed out before the plane could crash into the ground.

Taken prisoner by the enemy, Day managed to escape. Although he evaded the North Vietnamese for an incredible fourteen days, and actually walked back into South Vietnam, Day was shot and recaptured in mid–September; this wound at the hands of the enemy resulted in the award of a second Purple Heart.

Day spent the next sixty-seven months as a POW in Hanoi. Between July 16 and October 14, 1969, the North Vietnamese applied "maximum torture and punishment" to Day in order "to obtain a detailed confession of escape plans, policies, and orders of the American senior ranking officer in the camp." Day withstood this brutal abuse "and gave nothing of value to the Vietnamese although he sustained many injuries and open wounds to his body."[84] Day was awarded two more Purple Hearts for injuries received during this time as a POW.

Day retired from active duty in 1977 and lives today in Florida. He is a licensed attorney and has his own law firm.[85]

LEWIS L. O'HERN III: DECEMBER 30, 2010

Army First Lieutenant O'Hern was awarded the Purple Heart for wounds received

Purple Heart (reverse). Army Private Ernest Marino was wounded in action on December 7, 1941.

in action in Afghanistan on December 30, 2010. While on patrol as an infantry platoon leader in Kandahar province, O'Hern was seriously wounded by an improvised explosive device. He lost his right hand, his right leg below the knee, and his left leg above the knee.

Lewis Larkin O'Hern III entered the U.S. Military Academy at West Point in 2004 and was commissioned as an infantry second lieutenant when he graduated in 2008. He had completed the infantry officer basic course and airborne and Ranger school before deploying to Afghanistan.

JAMES DAVIS: APRIL 23, 2011

Air Force Technical Sergeant James "Jim" Davis was shot in the leg while on a mission in Afghanistan to recover the pilots of a downed Army helicopter; he was awarded the Purple Heart that same day by Air Force Brigadier General Darryl Roberson at the Craig Joint Theater Hospital.

On April 23, 2011, two HH-60 Pave Hawk helicopters assigned to the 83rd Expeditionary Rescue Squadron took off from Bagram Airfield. Their mission: proceed to a dangerous Afghan valley where an Army helicopter had crashed, leaving one Army aviator dead and another injured. When the Air Force pararescuemen arrived at the crash site, enemy forces began shooting at the helicopters and Technical Sergeant Davis, the flight engineer operating the hoist in one of the HH-60s, was hit by a bullet that came through the helicopter and hit him in the leg.

Davis' wound forced both Pave Hawk aircraft to return to Bagram so that Davis could get medical treatment. After getting a replacement flight engineer, the two Pave Hawks returned to rescue the downed Army aviator — and five Air Force pararescuemen who also had been left behind on the ground. After four attempts, and despite withering fire from Afghani insurgents, the rescue mission was accomplished — with all personnel safely returned to Bagram.[86]

Aerial Achievement Medal

Overview

Establishing Authority and Effective Dates: The Aerial Achievement Medal was established by Secretary of the Air Force Edward C. Aldridge, Jr., on February 3, 1988. It may be awarded for acts occurring after January 1, 1990.

Criteria: The Aerial Achievement Medal may be awarded to any person who, while serving in any capacity with the Air Force, distinguishes himself by "sustained meritorious service while participating in aerial flight." It may not be awarded for heroism, for service, or for "single event flights."[87]

Order of Precedence: The Aerial Achievement Medal is worn after the Air Medal and before the Joint Service Commendation Medal.

Designer: The Aerial Achievement Medal was designed by Air Force Technical Sergeant Gerald E. Woo.

Devices: Additional awards of the Aerial Achievement Medal are denoted by bronze (and silver) oak leaf clusters.

Description and Symbolism

Obverse

An American bald eagle (symbolizing the United States) with its wings displayed, is centered on a 1⅜ inch bronze disc. The eagle is facing to its right and the tips of its wings extend beyond the edge of the disc, so that the overall width of the medal is 1¾ inches. Above the eagle are thirteen five pointed stars (representing the thirteen original colonies). The stars on either end of this array and the star in the center are larger than the other ten.

Behind the eagle are two intersecting arcs (representing the flight paths of aircraft); these cross behind the eagle's head. The eagle clutches six lightning bolts (representing the Air Force) in its talons, and the bottom two lightning bolts extend beyond the rim of the medal.

Reverse

A raised plaque (to permit engraving of the recipient's name) is centered on the reverse of the Aerial Achievement Medal. Above the plaque are the words, "For Military" and below the plaque, the word, "Merit."

Ribbon

The ribbon consists of a wide center stripe of "Bird Blue," bordered on either side by a ⅛ inch stripe of "Golden Yellow." The ribbon is edged with a ⅛ inch stripe of "Flag Blue."[88]

Historical Background

The impetus for creating the Aerial Achievement Medal came from senior officers in the Air Force's Tactical Air Command, who complained in May 1987 that "too many Air Medals" were being awarded to aircraft "crew members who were not an integral part of the flight crew." Under award criteria for the Air Medal as it existed in the 1980s, the Air Force permitted the decoration to be awarded to *any* airman for *sustained* achievement in the air. In the view of these Tactical Air Command leaders, however, the Air Medal should be restricted to those personnel involved in the "flight or navigation of the aircraft." These officers insisted that they were "not attempting to change existing Air Medal criteria or preclude any crew member from receiving an Air Medal for a specific action, but only to limit the number of Air Medals given for sustained activity by providing an alternative and thereby preserving its [the Air Medal's] value."[89]

But these Tactical Air Command leaders were being disingenuous: in fact, they wanted a "junior" Air Medal that could be awarded to air crew personnel who were not pilots or navigators; the latter would continue to be awarded the Air Medal for sustained aerial achievement whereas the other men and women on the aircraft would get a medal with less prestige.

When the Tactical Air Command's recommendation was made public, there was considerable criticism. Military Airlift Command, Strategic Air Command, Electronic Security Command, and the National Guard Bureau did not support the proposal. In their view, the Air Medal was the most appropriate means to recognize all aircrew members, if for no other reason than all personnel serving on the same aircraft experience the same hazardous conditions while participating in an aerial flight.

But General Larry D. Welch, Chief of Staff of the Air Force, liked the idea of a new decoration and, on November 25, 1987, decided that the award of the Air Medal would now be restricted to "single acts of achievement while participating in aerial flight;" there would be no more Air Medals for sustained operational activities and flight.[90]

On February 3, 1988, Secretary of the Air Force Aldridge approved the creation of the Aerial Achievement Medal. Technical Sergeant Gerald E. Woo, a member of the 2146th Communications Group, Osan Air Base, Korea,

submitted a design for the medal. His design was accepted by the Air Force Chief of Staff and approved by the Commission of Fine Art in May 1988. A year later, prototypes of the new decoration had been produced and accepted.

First recipient

Captain Toby M. Kay was the first recipient of the Aerial Achievement Medal. His citation says he

distinguished himself by meritorious achievement while participating in sustained aerial flight as an F-15 Aircraft Commander and F-15 Flight Lead at Keflavik Naval Air Station, Iceland, from 25 July 1988 to 15 March 1990. During this period, Captain Kay displayed exceptional airmanship by intercepting, over the North Atlantic, twenty-one armed Soviet bomber aircraft attempting to penetrate the Icelandic Military Air Defense Identification Zone. Several of these intercepts were at night, at low altitude, and without the aid of other groundbased or airborne radar systems.

Left: Aerial Achievement Medal (obverse). *Right:* Aerial Achievement Medal (reverse).

Selected Recipients (Chronological)

CHRISTOPHER R. VALLE: DECEMBER 16, 1990–MAY 19, 1991

Captain Valle received his Aerial Achievement Medal for his "meritorious achievement" as a C-20A pilot with the 58th Military Airlift Squadron, Ramstein Air Base, Germany. His citation lauds his "airmanship and courage ... in the successful ... transporting of [Army] General [Norman] Schwarzkopf and his staff throughout the Southwest Asia theater of operations, under hazardous conditions."

WILLIAM F. ANDREWS: APRIL 5, 1998– MAY 11, 1998

Then Lieutenant Colonel Andrews was awarded the Aerial Achievement Medal for "meritorious achievement while participating in sustained aerial flight" while deployed to Shaikh Isa Air Base, Bahrain, as an F-16 pilot assigned to the 389th Fighter Squadron, 366th Operations Group, 366th Wing. His citation reads, in part:

> During this period of heightened tensions and open hostilities with Iraq, Colonel Andrews supported our vital national interests by demonstrating strategic force presence in the Southwest Asia region. He also maintained the highest state of combat readiness and forged important ties with our allies in the Middle East by conducting Dissimilar Air Combat Training with the United States Navy and the Air Forces of Bahrain, Kuwait, and the United Arab Emirates as part of Operation INITIAL LINK.

Andrews, a career Air Force officer, is best known for his exploits during the Persian Gulf War: he was awarded the Air Force Cross for his extraordinary heroism on the ground on February 27, 1991. On that date, Andrews was leading a flight of four F-16s when he was shot down by an Iraqi surface-to-air missile. He successfully ejected from his damaged fighter but was badly injured when he landed. Once on the ground, Andrews managed to establish radio contact with the remaining F-16s in his flight and warned them that the Iraqis were launching more surface-to-air missiles at them.

His fellow airmen dropped decoy flares, made hard turns, and eluded the climbing missiles. The Iraqis, who knew that warnings from the downed pilot had thwarted their attack, were furious. They fired at Andrews but, luckily for him, their shots missed. Andrews was taken prisoner and transported to Baghdad. He was released from captivity on March 4, 1991.[91]

JOINT SERVICE COMMENDATION MEDAL

Overview

Establishing Authority and Effective Date: The Joint Service Commendation Medal was established by Secretary of Defense Robert E. McNamara on June 25, 1963, for acts occurring after January 1, 1963.

Criteria: The Joint Service Commendation Medal is awarded in the name of the secretary of defense to members of the Armed Forces who, while assigned to a joint activity, distinguish themselves by outstanding achievement or meritorious service that does not justify award of the Defense Meritorious Service Medal. The decoration may be awarded with the bronze "V" device when the award is for acts of valor during participation in combat operations.

Order of Precedence: The Joint Service Commendation Medal is worn after the Air Medal and before the Commendation Medals of the separate services.

Devices: Additional awards of the Joint Service Commendation Medal to soldiers and airmen are reflected by bronze (or silver) oak leaf clusters. The "V" for valor device also is authorized.

Designer: Stafford F. Potter of the Army's Institute of Heraldry designed the medal.

Description and Symbolism

Obverse

The medal consists of four conjoined hexagons, two of which are displayed vertically and two of which are displayed horizontally. The hexagons are green enamel and edged in gold. The top hexagon is charged with thirteen gold five-pointed stars shown points up, and the lower hexagon has a gold stylized heraldic delineation. In the center of the conjoined hexagons is an eagle with its wings displayed horizontally and with a shield on its breast. The eagle is shown grasping three arrows in its talons. The conjoined hexagons are contained within a circular laurel wreath that is bound with gold bands. The areas between the gold band and the reentrant angles of the hexagons are pierced.

The conjoined hexagons represent the unity of the Armed Forces in providing for national defense. The eagle is taken from the seal of the Department of Defense and represents the authority under which the award is given. The thirteen stars allude to the thirteen colonies and, by extension, all fifty states; however, since the stars also represents the military, the configuration also represents the military tradition of the United States. The heraldic de-

lineation in the lower hexagon represents land, sea, and air, and the laurel wreath represents achievement.

Reverse

In the center of the back of the medallion there is a plaque for engraving the recipient's name. Above the plaque, on two lines, are the raised words "For Military." Below the plaque appears the word "Merit." There is also a laurel spray below the word "Merit." The inscription and laurel spray are taken from the Army Commendation Medal and the Navy Commendation Medal.

Ribbon

The ribbon consists of a center stripe of green bordered by stripes of white, green, white, and light blue. The green and white are adapted from the colors of the Army Commendation Medal and the Navy Commendation Medal, and the light blue represents the Department of Defense.

Left: Joint Service Commendation Medal (obverse). *Right:* Joint Service Commendation Medal (reverse).

Historical Background

Prior to 1963, the Department of Defense did not have any military decorations. Members of the armed forces assigned to the Office of the Secretary of Defense, the Organization of the Joint Chiefs of Staff, the defense agencies, unified commands, or joint forces normally received recognition from their own branch. Differences in award policies among the Army, Navy, Air Force, Marine Corps, and Coast Guard occasionally resulted in inequitable awards. Additionally, the lack of a Defense Department award meant that command officials in the so-called "purple suit" organizations were not able to provide direct recognition for outstanding service or meritorious achievement.

On March 26, 1963, General Maxwell D. Taylor, who was then the chairman of the Joint Chiefs of Staff, sent a memorandum to Secretary of Defense McNamara concerning "recognition of outstanding service with joint activities." Taylor wrote that "during recent years the establishment of unified and specified commands and other joint agencies has increased the number of personnel assigned to joint activities." He noted that several of the commanders of unified commands had expressed a need for some means by which they could recognize outstanding service or meritorious achievement by individuals assigned to the headquarters of those commands.

Taylor proposed establishing a "Joint Service Commendation Medal" as the solution to this problem. His memorandum also clearly identified the kinds of organizations that would be eligible to award the medal and was equally clear as to those which should not be. The latter category included such agencies as the Atomic Energy Commission, the Federal Aviation Administration, the National Aeronautics and Space Administration, the Selective Service System, the Central Intelligence Agency, and the State Department. As Taylor pointed out, "If we broadened the lease to include such agencies ... we would then have to include all agencies ... which have military personnel assigned outside their respective service." Taylor felt that such a broad eligibility for the award violated the intent of a Joint Service Commendation Medal, which he envisioned as being used only by joint or unified military organizations composed of members of the various branches of the military.

Taylor's recommendation was accepted, and the Joint Service Commendation Medal was established under the authority of the secretary of defense on June 25, 1963, as announced in Department of Defense Directive 1348.14.

Selected Recipients (Chronological)

Kenneth M. Taylor: August 17, 1961–June 1, 1965

Air Force Colonel Taylor received his Joint Service Commendation Medal for his "meritorious service" at Hamilton Air Force Base, California. According to his citation, he

> distinguished himself while serving as Deputy for Operations and Chief of Staff, Headquarters, 28th North American Air Defense Command Region. During this period, Colonel Taylor demonstrated outstanding leadership, resourcefulness and professional competence providing a major contribution in the forging of the 28th NORAD Region into a valuable deterrent for peace. His effort and guidance resulted in a mission-oriented region composed of Army, Navy, and Air Force component defense forces. Colonel Taylor established firm and amicable working relationships with the Commander, U.S. Naval Defense Forces, Eastern Pacific, and the resultant agreements provided U.S. Navy fighter aircraft augmentation as well as training support of the mission in the Region.

Kenneth Taylor had a remarkable career as a soldier and airman. Born in December 1919 in Oklahoma, he put on his first uniform as a soldier in the Oklahoma National Guard in 1936. In September 1940, he enlisted in the Army Air Corps Aviation Cadet Program and was commissioned as a second lieutenant and presented his pilot's wings in April 1941.

During the Japanese attack on Pearl Harbor, Taylor was assigned to Wheeler Army Airfield, Hawaii, and flew a P-40 Warhawk as part of the 47th Pursuit Squadron. He was credited with the destruction of two Japanese aircraft in aerial combat (and two probables) on December 7 and was awarded the Distinguished Service Cross for extraordinary heroism. Taylor subsequently flew combat missions in the Pacific (at Guadalcanal) and was credited with one more aircraft destroyed and one more probable. After being badly wounded, he returned to the United States to recuperate.

After World War II, Taylor served in a variety of increasingly important assignments, including overseas service in the Philippines and the United Kingdom. Taylor retired from the Air Force as a colonel in 1967 and joined the Alaska Air National Guard. He retired as an Assistant Adjutant General and brigadier general in 1971. Taylor died in 2006 and is interred in Arlington National Cemetery.[92]

CLARK P. CAMPBELL: MARCH 14, 1986– MAY 8, 1987

Army Lieutenant Colonel Campbell was awarded his Joint Service Commendation Medal for his service on the Joint Chiefs of Staff in the Pentagon. He

distinguished himself by exceptionally meritorious service from 14 March 1986 to 8 May 1987, while serving as Requirements and Development Programs Planner, Force Planning and Programming Division, Plans and Policy Directorate, Organization of the Joint Chiefs of Staff. Throughout this assignment, Colonel Campbell's superior technical knowledge of all Service weapons systems, how they are acquired, and their application in military planning and operations, combined with hard work, enlightened judgment and professional initiative provided unparalleled support to the Chairman, Joint Chiefs of Staff. His outstanding contributions in formulating joint requirements in the area of Follow-on Forces Attack have been the catalyst for improved cross–Service planning and saved

the Department of Defense millions of dollars in duplicative weapon systems. His forceful and dynamic ability to focus on the key points of complex issues and his flawless management of numerous joint actions has directly and positively influenced our future warfighting capability.

GUADALUPE SOROLA: AUGUST 1999– AUGUST 2001

Army Staff Sergeant Sorola was awarded the Joint Service Commendation Medal for his service with the National Security Agency. His citation says he

distinguished himself by meritorious service ... while serving within the Office of General Counsel, National Security Agency. Sergeant Sorola continually demonstrated outstanding professionalism and managerial expertise as the Legal Assistance Non-Commissioned Officer in Charge. For example, he prepared wills and legal documents for over 350 legal assistance clients and maintained and upgraded the office's legal automation software.... Additionally, he undertook the duties of Claims Non-Commissioned Officer in Charge, successfully processing Federal Tort Claims, Personnel Claims, and Rental Claims seeking, in total, over twelve million dollars.[93]

ARMY COMMENDATION MEDAL

Overview

Establishing Authority and Effective Dates: The Army Commendation Medal was initially established as the "Army Commendation Ribbon" on December 18, 1945. The award was renamed the "Commendation Ribbon" on July 6, 1948 and redesignated as the "Army Commendation Ribbon with Metal Pendant" on June 27, 1950. On March 31, 1960, it received its current name of "Army Commendation Medal." The decoration may be awarded to members of the armed forces for acts occurring after December 6, 1941; a member of the armed forces of a friendly foreign nation may be awarded the decoration for acts occurring after June 1, 1962.

Criteria: The Army Commendation Medal may be awarded to any member of the Armed Forces who, while serving in any capacity with the Army after December 6, 1941, distinguishes himself by heroism, meritorious achievement or meritorious service. The decoration may be awarded to any member of the Armed Forces of a friendly nation who, after June 1, 1962, distinguishes himself by heroism, meritorious achievement or meritorious service which has been of mutual benefit to a friendly nation and the United States. The Army Commendation Medal may not be awarded to general officers.[94]

For Acts of Heroism: The Army Commendation Medal may be awarded for an act or acts of combat valor (including aerial flight) which are of lesser degree than required for the Bronze Star Medal; awards of the medal for combat heroism are denoted by the "V" for valor device. The Army Commendation Medal may also be awarded for an act of non-combat valor which does not meet the requirements for an award of the Soldier's Medal.

For Meritorious Achievement or Service: To be awarded for meritorious achievement or service, the act or acts meriting the Army Commendation Medal must be outstanding and worthy of special recognition but not of the degree that would merit the Bronze Star Medal when combat is involved or the Meritorious Service Medal when no combat is involved.

Order of Precedence: The Army Commendation Medal is worn after the Joint Service Commendation Medal and before the Joint Service Achievement Medal.

Devices: Additional awards of the Army Commendation Medal to the same individual are denoted by bronze (or silver) oak leaf clusters. The "V" for valor device is authorized if the award is for combat heroism.

Designer: The Army Commendation Medal was designed and sculpted by Thomas Hudson Jones of the Army's Institute of Heraldry.

Description and Symbolism

Obverse

Centered on a 1⅜ inch bronze hexagon, one point up, is an American bald eagle with horizontally displayed wings. The eagle is grasping three crossed arrows in its talons and, on its breast, is bearing a shield paly of thirteen pieces and a chief.

The six-sided shape of the medal is intended to distinguish the Commendation Medal from all other decorations. The eagle is from the seal of the Department of Defense, and the shield on the eagle's breast is taken from the Great Seal of the United States.

Reverse

In the center of the reverse of the bronze hexagon, there is a plaque for engraving the recipient's name. Above the plaque, on two lines, the inscription "For Military" in raised letters appears. Below the plaque is the word "Merit," and under that, and in the bottom point of the medal, there is a spray of laurel that represents achievement.

Ribbon

The ribbon of the Army Commendation Medal measures 1⅜ inches in width and is composed of white stripes and myrtle green bands as follows: white (³⁄₃₂ inch), green (²⁵⁄₆₄ inch), white (¹⁄₃₂ inch), green (¹⁄₁₆ inch), white (¹⁄₃₂ inch), green (¹⁄₁₆ inch), white (¹⁄₃₂ inch), green (¹⁄₁₆ inch), white (¹⁄₃₂ inch), green (¹⁄₁₆ inch), white (¹⁄₃₂ inch), green (²⁵⁄₆₄ inch), and white (³⁄₃₂ inch).

Historical Background

Army Commendation Ribbon

The years immediately following World War II brought a revolutionary change in the structure of the U.S. armed forces. For the first time in its history, America abandoned the idea of a small peacetime Army and Navy in favor of a large standing force. The long-term occupation of Germany and Japan, and new al-

liances like the North Atlantic Treaty Organization, meant a new emphasis on peacetime
soldiering. Neither the War nor Navy Departments, however, had many awards to recognize
such service. Of course, the Army Distinguished Service Medal and Legion of Merit
were available, but the former could only be
awarded to those "in a duty of great responsibility" and the latter required "exceptional"
achievement or service.

Recognizing that there was a need for an
award or decoration to recognize meritorious
peacetime soldiering, the War Department decided to create the Army Commendation Ribbon in late 1945. War Department Circular
377, published on December 18, 1945, announced that the

> commendation ribbon may be awarded to mem-
> bers of the United States serving in any capacity
> with the Army for meritorious service rendered
> since 7 December 1941, not in sustained opera-
> tional activities against an enemy nor in direct
> support of such operation, i.e., in areas and at
> times when the Bronze Star Medal may not be
> awarded because of its operational character.[95]

This was a unique event for two reasons: never
before had the Army created a ribbon-only
award and never before had a military award
been established that specifically excluded
combat valor, or related military achievement
against an enemy, in its award criteria.

Circular 377 explained that the new ribbon could be awarded either for "specific accomplishments which are outstanding" or "periods of service ... not normally ... less than 6
months." Commanders were reminded that the
ribbon was not to be awarded for minor
services or good work generally. Rather the ribbon was for "achievement of distinction of the
same standard for which the Bronze Star
[Medal] is awarded in operations." Finally, Circular 377 advised that any person who had received a "letter of commendation" for meritorious achievement or service, signed by a major
general or higher, could apply for the new
Army Commendation Ribbon.[96]

In 1947, the Army published Memorandum No. 600-45-2, which amended the award
criteria for the Army Commendation Ribbon.
First, the ribbon could now be awarded to a
soldier whose act of non-combat valor, while
deserving of recognition, was not sufficiently
heroic to merit the award of the Soldier's
Medal. Second, the award of the ribbon to general officers was prohibited. This was another
first in Army history: the first time that officers
wearing stars were not permitted to receive a
military award.[97]

Three weeks later, when the Army
amended its regulation governing the award of
military decorations, yet another important
change occurred in the award criteria governing the Army Commendation Ribbon: the
Army removed the prohibition on awarding
the ribbon in connection with military operations; the ribbon could now be awarded "when
the operational requirements for the award of
the Bronze Star Medal or the Air Medal are not
fully met."[98] This was the beginning of the evolution of the decoration away from being the
strictly peacetime award originally contemplated.

Commendation Ribbon

In 1947, a new and separate Air Force was
born, and it and the old War and Navy Departments were "unified" in a new Department
of Defense. During this transition, the Army
Commendation Ribbon was renamed the
Commendation Ribbon to allow the new Air
Force to continue to award it.[99]

The "Metal Pendant" for the Commendation Ribbon

In 1949, the Army and the Air Force decided to add a "metal pendant" to their respective commendation ribbons. When the Army
officially announced this development in June
1950, it was another unique event in the history
of awards and decorations for soldiers: a unique
ribbon award had been transformed into a
medal. Any soldier (or airman) who had previously been awarded the Commendation Ribbon was now entitled to the new Commen-

dation Ribbon with Metal Pendant and thousands made application for the new ribbon with its unusual six-sided pendant.[100]

Army Commendation Medal

When the Air Force created its Air Force Commendation Medal in 1958, the Army decided to rename the "Commendation Ribbon with Metal Pendant" as the "Army Commendation Medal." This redesignation was announced in General Orders No. 10 on March 31, 1960.

In 1962, the award criteria for the Army Commendation Medal were amended to permit its award to foreign military personnel. The final major change to the decoration's award criteria occurred on February 29, 1964, when the Army authorized the wear of the "V" device. This was a fundamental shift in award criteria, as the Army Commendation Medal could now be awarded for combat heroism up to the level of the Bronze Star Medal with "V" device.

Since the creation of the Army Achievement Medal in 1981, the Army Commendation Medal, or "ARCOM" as it is called by soldiers, has achieved a measure of prestige. This is because those individuals whose achievement or service is insufficient for the ARCOM are awarded the Army Achievement Medal instead.

Selected Recipients (Chronological)

LEONARD L. LEWANE: SEPTEMBER 3, 1951–APRIL 1, 1952, MAY 7, 1952–APRIL 30, 1953, AUGUST 15, 1959–AUGUST 6, 1962

"Lee" Lewane was awarded two Commendation Ribbons with Metal Pendant and one Army Commendation Medal. His first decoration was for his "meritorious achievement" while commanding a reconnaissance platoon in Korea; his second award was for "meritorious service" in Korea.[101] Lewane's Army Commendation Medal was awarded for "meritorious service" as an assistant professor of military science. The citations for the first and third awards read, in part:

Army Commendation Medal (obverse).

First Lieutenant Leonard L. Lewane, 502d Reconnaissance Platoon, Eighth U.S. Army, is cited for meritorious service for the period 3 September 1951 to 9 March 1952 ... Lewane served as commanding officer ... upon assuming command of this unit he immediately established and

Army Commendation Medal (reverse).

put into effect a training program for all personnel of the unit and perfected plans for the defense of Army Headquarters (Advance). By his untiring efforts, initiative and outstanding devotion to duty he was able to overcome many problems facing him and in a short period of time the 502d Reconnaissance Platoon was a very efficient fighting unit, maintaining the highest standards. Army Headquarters (Advance) was provided with security of the highest degree, adding much to the safety, morale and efficiency of the personnel.[102] Major Lewane is cited for exceptionally meritorious service during the period 15 August 1959 to 6 August 1962 ... as Assistant Professor of Military Science ... Virginia Military Institute. He has devoted time in excess of that normally expected, voluntarily performing additional duties to produce outstanding results for the ROTC program and to enhance the close working relationship between the Army and VMI. On his own initiative, with vigor and enthusiasm, he undertook the task of training and participating in a Cadet Ranger Unit, a volunteer Tank Platoon of VMI cadets, a Cadet Combat Arms Unit, a Cadet Judo Team, a group known as the Civil War Roundtable, and writing for military publications. In addition he served as the Company Tactical Officer of a Cadet Company of the VMI Corps of Cadets in a most commendable manner contributing greatly in the military training of that unit in matters beyond those required subjects presented in the classroom.[103]

Leonard Lamarr "Lee" Lewane is a remarkable soldier by any measure. Born in New Jersey in 1928, he graduated from the Virginia Military Institute in 1950, and entered the Army as an armored cavalry second lieutenant. Lewane subsequently completed airborne and ranger training and served two combat tours in Korea as a tank platoon leader and company commander. From 1956 to 1958, he patrolled the West German-Czech border as the commander of armored cavalry companies in the 6th and 11th Armored Cavalry Regiments.

Lewane returned to VMI in 1959, serving as an assistant professor of military science until 1962. After finishing Command and General Staff College in 1963, he served briefly at U.S. Strike Command, MacDill Air Force Base, Florida.

In November 1965, now Lieutenant Colonel Lewane arrived in Saigon. Although he had been assigned to Military Assistance Command, Vietnam, Lewane immediately volunteered to command the 1st Squadron, 4th Cavalry Regiment, then a part of the 1st Infantry Division. In April 1966, Lewane's request was approved and he took command; he and his troopers would repeatedly distinguish themselves in combat.

On June 8, 1966, Troop A of Lewane's squadron moved north on Route 13, through an area held by the Viet Cong 9th Division. When the lead tank hit a command-detonated mine, it signaled a massive attack by three VC battalions from both sides of the road. Lewane's troop faced withering fire from recoilless rifles, mortars and automatic weapons.

According to an account by General William E. DuPuy, Troop A had run into the elite 272nd Regiment and was about to fight and win "an epic battle of the Vietnam war." Despite being outnumbered 9-to-1— Troop A had 135 soldiers and the VC unit was 1,200 strong—the troopers "immediately closed with the insurgent forces in a fierce assault."[104]

For the next six hours of the bloody battle that followed, Lewane was in his OH-13 Sioux helicopter, coordinating with commanders on the ground to bring in tactical airstrikes from Air Force F-4 Phantoms and F-100 Super Sabres. Despite the fragile nature of his helicopter, with its goldfish bowl, glassed-in cockpit, Lewane ignored the danger and twice directed his pilot to land inside the squadron's defensive perimeter. Lewane wanted to ensure that his troopers had sufficient ammunition — and he wanted to inspire them. That explains why he walked from vehicle to vehicle, making his presence known in the heat of the battle and to show his troopers that he was really with them in this fight.

According to DuPuy, then commanding the 1st Infantry Division, Lewane was a "striking commander" with his "close shaven head, open face, strong physique, flashing eyes, and energy oozing out of every pore." DuPuy continued: "Since the legendary Brevet Maj. Gen. Ranald S. Mackenzie who, as a colonel, led the regiment against the Apaches, Kiowas, Commanches, Arapahos and Cheyennes in the frontier wars, there had not been a more valiant and dashing leader of the 4th Cavalry — the best Regular Army cavalry regiment in the Indian campaigns." This was high praise, as generations of leaders had served in the 4th Cavalry in the years between Mackenzie and Lewane.

At the end of the battle on June 8, Air Force bombs, napalm and cluster bomblets combined with the firepower from Troop A to crush the Viet Cong. A total of 105 VC were killed and a large cache of weapons was seized, making the battle at Ap Tao O a decisive victory. Lewane, whose presence had been critical to success, was awarded the Silver Star.

Lewane was awarded a second Silver Star for his gallantry in action the following month, in what became known as the Battle of Minh Thanh Road. The citation for that decoration states that Lewane "was constantly exposed to intense insurgent fire [and] always appeared to be where the fighting was heaviest, inspiring his men by his calm demeanor and mastery of the situation."[105] As for the squadron, its extraordinary heroism as a unit in June and July 1966 resulted in the award of the U.S. Presidential Unit Citation in July 1967. It is a very high honor (requiring a level of unit heroism equivalent to the Distinguished Service Cross); only one other unit in the 1st Infantry Division received it during the Vietnam War.

After his service in Southeast Asia, Lewane continued to serve with great distinction. He commanded 1st Brigade, 1st Armored Division and served as chief of staff, U.S. Army Berlin. Lewane retired as a colonel in 1976 and now teaches American history at a community college in Virginia.

MAX L. PETTIJOHN: NOVEMBER 25, 1966

Major Pettijohn, an Air Force officer serving as a Forward Air Controller in Kontum Province, Vietnam, was awarded the Army Commendation Medal for heroism. His citation reads, in part:

> At approximately 1703 hours on 25 November 1966, an American-advised patrol surrounded by a superior Viet Cong requested assistance from Major Pettijohn. Major Pettijohn, piloting an L-19 aircraft, realizing the patrol's dire predicament, immediately requested air support. Before the arrival of tactical aircraft, he circled the besieged unit's position in an attempt to pinpoint their location and simultaneously locate the enemy positions. On each pass he received a heavy volume of fire from the enemy strongholds. Upon the arrival of the tactical aircraft, he directed a variety of ordnance be placed on selected targets around the encircled patrol. As darkness approached he marked the suspected enemy locations with his rockets, again purposely drawing a volley of ground fire in an attempt to locate enemy buildup positions. At approximately 2115 hours, the patrol broke out of the encirclement as Major Pettijohn continued to direct covering airstrikes on positions. Major Pettijohn continued to protect the patrol's withdrawal throughout the night allowing the unit to proceed without suffering casualties. Major Pettijohn's extremely accurate direction of tactical aircraft saved the patrol from complete annihilation and resulted in an estimated 34 Viet Cong killed.[106]

Given the heroism described in Pettijohn's lengthy citation, there must have been a very conservative awards policy in effect.

MARIA C. FLORES-SANZ: JULY 2, 2003

Specialist Flores-Sanz was awarded the Army Commendation Medal with "V" for valor device for her heroism in Iraq. On July 2, 2003, she was part of a three-vehicle convoy traveling from Baghdad International Airport to central Baghdad. The vehicles were attacked simultaneously by a rocket-propelled grenade shot from a rooftop and an improvised explosive device that was remotely detonated on the ground. As her citation explains, despite the "smoke and confusion," Flores-Sanz "drove the two passengers of her vehicle to safety and later returned to the attack site to help evacuate the wounded soldiers."[107]

MOHAMMAD FAZEE: AUGUST 27, 2010

Fazee, a major in the Afghan National Police, was awarded the Army Commendation Medal for his heroism during an ambush by insurgents. Fazee was leading a police convoy from Kandahar Province to Herat when his men were attacked by Taliban fighters. The police unit fought for an hour before air support arrived — and continued fighting for another hour before the enemy retreated. Although he was wounded in the attack, Fazee insisted he would continue to serve: "I want to stay in the ANP [Afghan National Police] ... I will serve as long as I have the capacity; as long as there is a single drop of blood in my body."[108]

Fazee was presented his Army Commendation Medal by Army Brigadier General Jefforey Smith, Assistant Commanding General, Afghan National Police Development, NATO Training Mission (Afghanistan), in a ceremony in Kabul on March 31, 2011.

AIR FORCE
COMMENDATION MEDAL

Overview

Establishing Authority and Effective Dates: The Air Force Commendation Medal was established on March 24, 1958.

Criteria: The Air Force Commendation Medal may be awarded to members of the U.S. Armed Forces and to foreign military personnel serving in any capacity with the Air Force who distinguish themselves by (1) "outstanding achievement or meritorious service," (2) acts of courage that do not meet the requirements for the award of the Airman's Medal, and (3) "sustained meritorious performance by [air] crew members." The Air Force Commendation Medal may not be awarded to general officers.[109]

Order of Precedence: The Air Force Commendation Medal is worn after the Joint Service Commendation Medal and before the Joint Service Achievement Medal.

Devices: Additional awards of the Air Force Commendation Medal to the same individual are reflected by bronze (or silver) oak leaf clusters. The "V" device is authorized for acts occurring after January 11, 1996, if the act or service being recognized occurs during a "contingency deployment operation" in an Area of Operation that has been "declared a hostile environment," and if the recipient was "exposed to personal hazards due to direct hostile action" during that contingency operation.[110]

Designer: Thomas Hudson Jones of the Institute of Heraldry designed the Air Force Commendation Medal. Jones also designed the Army Commendation Medal and a number of other U.S. decorations and medals.

Description and Symbolism

Obverse

Centered on a 1⅜ inch bronze hexagon, one point up, is the coat of arms of the U.S. Air Force. Above this coat of arms is an American bald eagle with displayed wings; behind the eagle is a cloud formation. The six-sided shape of the medal is in keeping with the commendation medals of the Army and the Navy, and is intended to distinguish it from all other decorations.

The Air Force coat of arms indicates that the medal is an Air Force decoration. The eagle "symbolizes the United States and its airpower," and the clouds behind the eagle "show the start of a new sky — The Department of the Air Force."[111]

Reverse

In the center of the back side of the medal there is a blank plaque for inscribing the recipient's name. Above the plaque, displayed in three lines, are the words "For Military Merit."

Air Force Commendation Medal (obverse).

Air Force Commendation Medal (reverse).

Ribbon

The ribbon is made of moiré silk and is predominantly yellow, with a stripe of Air Force blue in its center. This stripe is edged in yellow, which is followed on both sides by a pinstripe of Air Force blue. The outer edges of the ribbon also are edged in blue.

Historical Background

After its creation in 1947, the Air Force continued to award Army decorations to airmen, including the Army Commendation Ribbon. The Army not only approved of this practice, but encouraged it: in July 1948, for example, the Army dropped the word "Army" from "Army Commendation Ribbon" so that both the Army and the Air Force would be awarding a "Commendation Ribbon" to deserving soldiers and airmen.[112]

In 1949, the Army and the Air Force jointly decided to add a "metal pendant" to the Commendation Ribbon and, as a result, the Air Force awarded the "Commendation Medal with Metal Pendant" to airmen during the Korean War and the Cold War era that followed. By the late 1950s, however, as the Air Force developed its own identity, separate and apart from the Army, Air Force leaders wanted distinctive decorations and medals for airmen. Ultimately, this desire for Air Force decorations led to the creation of an Air Force Cross (replacing the Army's Distinguished Service Cross), Air Force Distinguished Service Medal (replacing the Army's Distinguished Service Medal), and Airman's Medal (replacing the Army Soldier's Medal). However, as these three decorations had been created by acts of Congress, new legislation was required before the Air Force had legal authority to substitute new Air Force awards for these existing Army medals.

This was not the case with the Commendation Ribbon with Medal Pendant: since its legal basis was an Army regulation promulgated in 1945, the Air Force retained the authority to make any changes to the decoration by regulation as well. The result was that, on March 24, 1958, Secretary of the Air Force James H. Douglas, Jr. established the Air Force Commendation Medal. Four days later, the Department of the Air Force announced the new medal in General Orders No. 16.

While the Army and the Navy had identical hexagon shaped metal pendants, and nearly identical ribbons for their respective commendation awards, the Air Force wanted its new decoration to have a clear link to airmen and airpower. Consequently, while it retained the six-sided shape of the other services commendations medals, the Air Force asked the Institute of Heraldry to design a new ribbon and metal pendant for the Air Force Commendation Medal. As a result, Thomas Hudson Jones proposed an obverse featuring the Air Force coat of arms and the American bald eagle. As for the ribbon, Jones used ultramarine blue and golden yellow, as these are the official Air Force colors.[113]

Unlike the Army Commendation Medal, which may be awarded to a soldier for combat heroism of a lesser degree than that required for the Bronze Star Medal with "V for valor" device, the Air Force Commendation Medal may not be awarded for combat valor. After January 11, 1996, however, the Air Force authorized airmen awarded the Air Force Commendation Medal to wear a "V" device on the decoration if the recipient was exposed to personal hazards due to direct hostile action during a contingency deployment operation. Consequently, the "V" on an Air Force Commendation Medal does not reflect individual combat heroism, but indicates that the recipient received the decoration for acts or services in a hostile area of operations. This explains why an Air Force Component Commander "may authorize the 'V' device when a single event, i.e., terrorist attack, isolated combat-type incident, etc., warrants the 'V' device distinction."[114]

Selected Recipients (Chronological)

George G. Clausen: June 3, 1963– July 20, 1966

Major Clausen received his Air Force Commendation Medal for his "distinguished" service as a tactical operations officer, Flight commander, and squadron operations officer in the 49th Tactical Fighter Wing. His citation reads, in part:

> During his tenure as Tactical Operations Officer, he revised the Wing scheduling programs between Tactical Operations, Maintenance Control and the Tactical Squadrons, thus insuring outstanding utilization of Wing resources during extreme adverse weather conditions and providing maximum flying capabilities of the F-105 weapons system. As a result of Major Clausen's superior bombing and gunnery scores, he was awarded the "Wing Nuclear Trophy" for the period January to June 1964 and January to June 1965. In addition to this he was awarded the "Wing Overall Weapons Championship Trophy." As Operations Officer he was instrumental in his squadron receiving the USAFE Flight Safety Award for two consecutive years. His outstanding abilities have contributed immeasurably to the operational capability and combat effectiveness of the 49th Tactical Fighter Wing.

Dennis L. Butler: June 5, 1965–September 9, 1966

Captain Butler was awarded the Air Force Commendation Medal for his "meritorious service" as Chief, Space Surveillance Analyst Branch, 1 Aerospace Control Squadron, Ent Air Force Base, Colorado. His citation reads, in part:

> His aggressive leadership in the design and operational testing of the Space Defense Center computer programs produced exceptional results. Captain Butler's actions were instrumental in identifying program discrepancies in the establishment of the new Space Defense Center in the Cheyenne Mountain Complex.

RONALD E. CATTON: FEBRUARY 25, 1967–OCTOBER 1, 1967

Major Catton received an Air Force Commendation Medal for a six-month tour as a Squadron Tactics Officer in Thailand. His citation says he

distinguished himself by meritorious service as Squadron Tactics Officer, 433rd Tactical Fighter Squadron, Ubon Royal Thai Air Force Base, Thailand from 25 February 1967 to 1 October 1967. During this period, Major Catton developed and implemented many vital changes to the air combat tactics employed by his squadron and the 8th Tactical Fighter Wing in Southeast Asia. Additionally, Major Catton provided briefings for the entire Wing on a recurring basis to insure thorough understanding by all aircrews. The energetic application of his knowledge has played a significant role in contributing to the success of the United States Air Force mission in Southeast Asia.

JEFFREY B. FLOYD: AUGUST 31, 1974– AUGUST 4, 1975

Captain Floyd was awarded his Air Force Commendation Medal for meritorious service at Udorn Royal Thai Air Force Base. His citation states he was

Officer in Charge, Targets Section, Exploitation Branch, 432nd Reconnaissance Technical Squadron ... from 31 August 1974 to 4 August 1975. During this period, his expertise in dealing with the imagery products of various tactical and strategic reconnaissance platforms contributed significantly to the accuracy and timely distribution of critical and sensitive target materials in support of the United States Support Activities Group.

JOINT SERVICE ACHIEVEMENT MEDAL

Overview

Establishing Authority and Effective Date: The Joint Service Achievement Medal was established by Secretary of Defense Caspar W. Weinberger on August 3, 1983. It has been in effect since that date.

Criteria: The Joint Service Achievement Medal is awarded in the name of the secretary of defense to members of the Armed Forces below the rank of colonel in the Army and Air Force who, while being assigned to a joint activity, distinguish themselves by outstanding achievement or meritorious service that would not warrant the award of the Joint Service Commendation Medal.

Order of Precedence: The Joint Service Achievement Medal is worn after the Army, Air Force and Navy and Marine Corps Commendation Medals and before all service Achievement Medals.

Devices: Additional awards of the Joint Service Achievement Medal to the same individual are denoted by bronze (or silver) oak leaf clusters.

Designer: The Joint Service Achievement Medal was designed by Jay Morris and sculpted by Donald Borja, both of the Army's Institute of Heraldry.

Description and Symbolism

Obverse

The decoration is a bronze medal that is 1.4375 inches in overall diameter, consisting of a star of twelve points. An eagle holding three arrows is superimposed in the center of the star. The shape of the medal was chosen to make it distinctive from all other decorations, and the eagle was taken from the Seal of the Secretary of Defense, under whose authority the medal is awarded.

Reverse

In the center of the reverse of the Joint Service Achievement Medal, there is a circle composed of the following inscription in raised letters: "Joint Service," which comprises the upper portion of the circle, and "Achievement Award," which comprises the lower portion of the circle. The space in the center of the circle is left blank for inscribing the recipient's name.

Ribbon

The ribbon of the medal consists of a center stripe of red that is flanked on either side by stripes of light blue, white, green, white, and blue.

Historical Background

On March 11, 1982, Lt. Gen. William J. Hilsman, director of the Defense Communication Agency, sent a memorandum on the subject of "joint awards" to Lt. Gen. R. Dean Tice, the deputy assistant secretary of defense for military personnel and force management, in which Hilsman recommended the establishment of an achievement medal to rank with the service achievement medals. Hilsman wanted a decoration that would complete the Department of Defense awards hierarchy and, thereby, provide a system of decorations for

meritorious achievement that was comparable to those of the separate military branches. The establishment of such a medal, Hilsman believed, would also protect the integrity of the more senior Joint Service Commendation Medal and would negate any connotation that being assigned to a joint activity would be likely to result in decreased opportunity for military members to earn recognition.

Hilsman's proposal was coordinated with the Army, Navy, and Air Force. Although there was generally strong support for the proposal, the services did comment that the proposed award was perhaps unnecessary because its stature was too low to play a valid role in the hierarchy of Defense Department awards. This was because the level of responsibility of military personnel assigned to Defense Department or joint billets is such that most individuals would be eligible for the either the Joint Service Commendation Medal or the Defense Meritorious Service Medal. It followed that the number of individuals who

Joint Service Achievement Medal (obverse).

Joint Service Achievement Medal (reverse).

would be eligible for an achievement-level award would be small and that those who were eligible could be adequately recognized by receiving the Achievement Medal of their respective services.

On August 30, 1982, Assistant Secretary of Defense Lawrence J. Korb sent a memorandum to the appropriate assistant secretaries of the Army, Navy, and Air Force informing them that, "after consideration of all comments, the development of a Defense Achievement Medal is not warranted." Korb went on to say that, "members assigned to organizations that qualify them for joint awards can be adequately recognized with Military Department awards and organizational certificates if the Joint Service Commendation Medal or higher awards is not warranted." Finally, Korb stated that "each department must develop a policy permitting recognition of their members jointly assigned and members from their sister services, if not currently established. This is to include individuals assigned to joint activities for which your department has been established as the executive agent."[115]

But the issue of a Defense Achievement Medal did not die. On the contrary, several months later, on March 10, 1983, Adm. Robert J. Long, who was the Navy's commander-in-Chief, Pacific, sent a message to Tice in which he asked that the matter of a Defense Achievement Medal reexamined.[116] On May 9, 1983, Tice sent a memorandum to the appropriate assistant secretaries of the Army, Navy, and Air Force, as well as to Director of the Joint Staff. Tice wrote that the Defense Department had previously "indicated that a Joint Service Achievement Medal was not warranted in response to a Defense Communications Agency memorandum." He went on to state that "we suggested several actions to you to make the utilization of service Achievement Medals feasible. This has not worked to the benefit of our jointly assigned people." As a result of these service shortcomings, Tice concluded that it was "time to develop a Joint Service Achievement Medal."[117]

Tice requested that each of the services furnish their recommendation by June 22, 1983. They did, and they concurred in the proposal. On July 7, 1983, an assistant general counsel for manpower and health affairs pointed out that since the proposed Joint Service Achievement Medal would rank as the least prestigious Department of Defense-sponsored medal for joint duty, it should most properly be established by a Department of Defense directive rather than by an executive order. Accordingly, on August 1, 1983, a memorandum was prepared for Secretary Weinberger recommending that he establish the Joint Service Achievement Medal. On August 3, 1983 Weinberger signed his approval to the memorandum, thus creating the decoration and establishing the earliest date of eligibility for its award.

On August 9, 1983, the Defense Department Comptroller was asked to provide approximately $15,000 for the development and procurement of the new medal. On the same day the Institute of Heraldry was tasked with preparing suggested designs. On December 7, 1983, a proposed Department of Defense directive establishing eligibility criteria and award procedures was forwarded to all concerned agencies and offices along with instructions to return comments by February 10, 1984. The directive was approved, and on March 29, 1984, it was published and disseminated. On January 31, 1984, the proposed design for the medal was approved by the Commission of Fine Arts.[118]

Recipient

THOMAS W. MCSHANE: JUNE 1993– JULY 1994

Army Lieutenant Colonel McShane was awarded the Joint Service Achievement Medal for his work as lawyer on the Joint Service Committee on Military Justice. According to his citation, he

distinguished himself by exceptionally meritorious service as Army Representative, Joint

Service Working Group, Joint Service Committee on Military Justice. Colonel McShane distinguished himself through his research, legal and practical analysis, and drafting and editing of proposed changes to military justice procedures. He contributed greatly to the development of substantive and technical amendments to the Uniform Code of Military Justice and changes to the *Manual for Courts-Martial, United States, 1984,* that will greatly enhance the quality and efficiency of the military justice system. Most notable was Colonel McShane's oversight of the editing and proofreading in the republication of the *Manual for Courts-Martial.* His endeavors resulted in a substantial increase in the quality of military law and efficiency of military criminal procedure.[119]

Army Achievement Medal

Overview

Establishing Authority and Effective Dates: Secretary of the Army John O. Marsh established the Army Achievement Medal on April 10, 1981. It may be awarded for achievement or service occurring after August 1, 1981.

Criteria: The Army Achievement Medal is awarded to any member of the Armed Forces of the United States, or to any member of the Armed Forces of a friendly foreign nation who, after August 1, 1981, distinguishes himself by meritorious service or achievement of a lesser degree than required for the award of the Army Commendation Medal. The Army Achievement Medal may not be awarded to general officers.

Order of Precedence: The Army Achievement Medal is worn after the Joint Service Achievement Medal and before the Prisoner of War Medal or Good Conduct Medal.

Devices: Additional awards of the Army Achievement Medal to the same individual are denoted by bronze (or silver) oak leaf clusters.

Designer: The medal was designed by Jay Morris and sculpted by Donald Borja, both employees of the Army's Institute of Heraldry.

Description and Symbolism

Obverse

The 1½ inch diameter medal is eight-sided and bronze in color. The obverse consists of the Department of the Army seal; this reflects the Army's heritage.

Reverse

At the top of the reverse are the words FOR MILITARY ACHIEVEMENT and two sprigs of laurel. The words reflect the purpose of the decoration; the sprigs are the traditional symbol of achievement.

Ribbon

The ribbon consists of green, white and ultramarine stripes.

Historical Background

Impetus for the Medal

While the Navy created an achievement medal in the 1960s, the Army did not begin thinking about an achievement medal for soldiers until after the Vietnam War, when the Army's Military Personnel Center began receiving a number of proposals for new awards. None of these suggestions came to fruition, however, because senior personnel specialists in the Army were generally opposed to adding yet another medal to the awards system. Even those who agreed that some new decoration was needed could not reach a consensus on the criteria for a new award, so nothing happened.

All this changed on August 28, 1980, when Lieutenant General Robert M. Elton, then the commander of the Military Personnel Center, sent a memorandum to General Edward C. Meyer, then Army Chief of Staff. As Elton saw the problem, what was 'missing' was an award for junior soldiers that could be liberally awarded to them. He wrote in his memo to Meyer that there was "a widespread perception that 'something' is needed — primarily *an award for junior soldiers*—and that recognition *is needed on a large scale.*"[120] (emphasis supplied).

Elton did not think that the solution was to increase the number of awards of existing decorations, like the Meritorious Service Medal or Army Commendation Medal, as that would depreciate their value. Rather, Elton proposed that the Army create an Army Achievement Medal that would recognize achievement that did not rise to the level required for an Army Commendation Medal.

Elton's recommendation was approved by General Meyer on April 10, 1981, and Secretary of the Army John O. Marsh established the new medal that same day.

Designing the Medal

As Dr. Charles P. McDowell notes in his excellent book *Military and Naval Decorations of the United States*, the Commission of Fine Arts approved the design on May 29, 1981—but it was not happy with it. As the Secretary of the Commission wrote: "After considerable discussion, the Commission members voted to approve the submission, although they did so with some reluctance. They do not feel that the design is particularly distinguished and hope that future medals will be of a higher caliber."[121]

Awarding the New Medal

Since General Elton had wanted a medal that would be an award for significant non-combat achievement, this meant that from the beginning the focus of the Army Achievement Medal was on achievement — not service. Although the Army subsequently published award criteria that in fact allowed the medal to be awarded for *both* achievement and service, the point is that the new Army Achievement Medal — as its name suggested — was not intended to be yet another service award. Interestingly, the new medal's restriction to peacetime acts meant that it was quite different from the Navy's Achievement Medal, which was for *both* combat and non-combat service or achievement.

When the medal was first established,

Left: Army Achievement Medal (obverse). *Right:* Army Achievement Medal (reverse).

most commanders understood that it should be used as an "impact" award — awarded quickly if not "on the spot." They also understood that the Army leadership had identified "staff sergeants and below, lieutenants, warrant officers 1 and chief warrant officers 2" as the preferred recipients of the medal.[122]

From the beginning, however, there were complaints that some commanders were too restrictive in making the award, while others were so liberal as to be ridiculous. But uniformity of result was difficult to achieve, especially after the award authority was delegated from colonel to lieutenant colonel. Moreover, what type of act merited recog-nition was very much a matter of individual opinion. For example, some battalion commanders in the mid–1980s awarded the Army Achievement Medal to any soldier who had a perfect score on the Army Physical Fitness Test. Others awarded the medal to soldiers who volunteered to coach in youth athletic leagues. Still others waited until the soldier was leaving the unit and then presented the medal to him or her as a service award.

Today, although the Army Achievement Medal is still awarded for achievement (for example, to an individual who wins a soldier of the quarter competition), the medal has gradually evolved into a service award for junior enlisted personnel. That is, whereas a Specialist (E-4) or Sergeant (E-5) would have received the Army Commendation Medal as an end of tour award in the late 1970s, he or she now receives the Army Achievement Medal; the Army Commendation Medal is reserved for higher ranking noncommissioned officers.

Finally, a small number of Army Achievement Medals are awarded as retirement awards, with most going to soldiers retiring in the rank/grade of Sergeant First Class (E-7), Staff Sergeant (E-6) and Sergeant (E-5).[123]

Selected Recipient

JAMES F. ADAMOUSKI: OCTOBER 1998

First Lieutenant Adamouski was awarded the Army Achievement Medal for his service with the 158th Aviation Regiment in Bosnia as part of Operation JOINT FORCE. His citation reads, in its entirety:

> For meritorious achievement while serving as the company operations officer during Task Force SIXSHOOTER's deployment to Bosnia in support of Operation Joint Forge. 1LT Adamouski's dedication to duty and selfless service are in keeping with the finest traditions of the military service and reflect great credit upon him, his unit and the United States Army.[124]

Born in Tampa, Florida in June 1973, James F. Adamouski was commissioned in the Army's Aviation Branch after graduating from the U.S. Military Academy in 1995. After he completed training as a rotary wing aviator at Fort Rucker, Alabama, Adamouski served in various assignments, including overseas duty in Germany, Hungary, Bosnia and Albania. He deployed with the 3rd Aviation Regiment, 3rd Infantry Division to Kuwait in March 2003. Captain Adamouski was killed in action on April 2, 2003. He is buried in Arlington National Cemetery.[125]

AIR FORCE ACHIEVEMENT MEDAL

Overview

Establishing Authority and Effective Dates: Secretary of the Air Force Hans M. Mark established the Air Force Achievement Medal on October 20, 1980; it may be awarded for achievement or service occurring after that date.

Criteria: The Air Force Achievement Medal may be awarded to member of the U.S. Armed Forces and to foreign military personnel who, while serving in any capacity with the Air Force, distinguish themselves by outstanding achievement or meritorious service that does not meet the requirements of the Air Force Commendation Medal.

Not more than one Air Force Achievement Medal may be awarded during a one-year period "except under extraordinary circumstances." The decoration also may not be awarded for aerial achievement or retirement. Finally, it may not be awarded to personnel above the rank of lieutenant colonel.[126]

Order of Precedence: The Air Force Achievement Medal is worn after the Joint Service Achievement Medal and before the Presidential Unit Citation.

Designer: Air Force Captain Robert C. Bonn designed the Air Force Achievement Medal, which was sculpted by Donald Borja of the Army's Institute of Heraldry.

Devices: Additional awards of the Air Force Achievement Medal to the same individual are reflected by bronze (or silver) oak leaf clusters. While the decoration may not be awarded for heroism, the "V" device may be worn on the Air Force Achievement Medal when the medal is awarded for acts or services occurring after January 11, 1996 and during a "contingency deployment operation" in a "hostile environment."

Description and Symbolism

Obverse

The medal is a silver colored disc and measures 1⅜ inches in diameter. The outer border consists of eleven cloud-like shapes; these are the sum of "4" and "7," the digits of the year in which the Air Force was established as an independent service. Centered on the medallion are thunderbolts and wings, which signify striking power through aerospace; this heraldic image was adapted from the Seal of the Air Force.

Reverse

On the reverse of the Air Force Achievement Medal is the circular inscription "Air Force Meritorious Achievement" in raised letrters; the center of the medal is blank to permit the engraving of the recipient's name.

Ribbon

The ribbon consists of three sets of four vertical stripes of ultramarine blue over a silver-gray background. The colors were chosen to give the medal a distinctive appearance; they have no symbolic meaning.[127]

Historical Background

In June 1978, Air Force Captain Robert C. Bonn, Jr. proposed that the Air Force create an achievement medal. According to Dr. Charles P. McDowell, Bonn had three reasons for making his proposal. First, young airmen coming into the Air Force after Vietnam had few opportunities to receive decorations, and an Air Force Achievement Medal would remedy this problem. Second, an achievement medal would raise the prestige of the Air Force Commendation Medal, and halt its ever more liberal award. Third, Bonn believed it was time for the Air Force to have an achievement medal like those that existed in the Navy, Marine Corps and Coast Guard (the Army had not yet created an achievement medal).

Bonn formally proposed that his Air Force Achievement Medal be awarded to enlisted airmen and officers below the rank of lieutenant colonel. He recommended that the medal be used exclusively for recognizing non-combat meritorious service "based on sustained performance, leadership, or for some specific achievement of a superlative nature."[128]

While Bonn's 1978 proposal was not accepted by the Air Force, it was resurrected two years later, when the Air Force conducted a wide-ranging analysis of its awards and decorations. That analysis concluded that Bonn was correct in believing that an achievement medal was need to reward enlisted personnel and junior officers, and that such a medal would restore the prestige of the Air Force Commendation Medal and other higher ranking decorations. Finally, the 1980 analysis determined that creating an Air Force Achievement Medal would increase morale and esprit de corps among airmen.

As a result, Secretary of the Air Force

Hans M. Mark established the Air Force Achievement Medal on October 20, 1980. In keeping with Captain Bonn's original concept, the new decoration could not be awarded for combat-related heroism or peacetime acts of courage. Rather, the medal was only for outstanding achievement or meritorious service. The Air Force also followed Bonn's recommendation that Air Force Achievement Medal not be permitted as a retirement award. But the Air Force departed from Bonn's proposal that the achievement medal be restricted to majors and below; Secretary Mark decided that the award could be made to lieutenant colonels and below. Finally, in establishing the new decoration, the Air Force announced only one Air Force Achievement Medal should be awarded to an individual in a 12-month period (absent extraordinary circumstances). This was because the promotion system for airmen assigns points

for decorations, and there was a concern that multiple awards of the new decoration could adversely affect the system.[129]

The design for the Air Force Achievement Medal originated with Captain Bonn, who had included a sketch of the medal in his original proposal. The Air Force accepted his drawing but, as Bonn had only proposed a design for the obverse of the medal, Donald Borja at the Institute of Heraldry completed the reverse. As for the ribbon, it was designed by Master Sergeant William B. Dowling and Mr. Ruben Cortinas, both assigned to the Air Force Military Personnel Center.[130]

The Air Force Achievement Medal has a unique place in Air Force history, as it is the first decoration for airmen that does not have its roots in an earlier Army award. It was, in fact, the first decoration created by the Air Force for airmen.

Left: Air Force Achievement Medal (obverse). **Right:** Air Force Achievement Medal (reverse).

First Recipient

Airman First Class Heidi M. Uttrich, then assigned to the 6570th Air Base Group, Brooks Air Force Base, Texas, was the first recipient of the Air Force Achievement Medal.

Selected Recipients (Chronological)

JOSEPH S. STANALAND: JANUARY 16, 1990– JANUARY 22, 1990

Senior Master Sergeant Stanaland was awarded his Air Force Achievement Medal for his "outstanding leadership skills and professional knowledge." According to his citation for the award, an F-16 aircraft "had crashed on the steep 40 degree snow covered 3200 foot slopes of Mount Susitna, Alaska." Stanahand, who was "inserted below the crash site due to extreme weather conditions, walked the steep slope and initially verified the crash location." He then "immediately began recovery operations to locate the wreckage through constant digging in probable sites in the hopes of locating the missing pilot." While the pilot apparently was not located, "the operation was accomplished superbly, despite possible injury, explosive detonations, avalanches, and treacherous winter mountain climbing."

BYRON D. GREENE: NOVEMBER 16, 2000–MARCH 25, 2001

Second Lieutenant Greene received his Air Force Achievement Medal for "outstanding achievement" while serving in a civil engineer squadron at Tyndall Air Force Base, Florida. His citation states that he

> distinguished himself ... while assigned to the Tyndall Air Force Base Gulf Coast Salute 2001 open house and air show. Working as the civil engineering liaison, Lieutenant Greene handled a myriad of requests including the contracting of latrines and airfield set up and cleanup actions. His negotiation of the latrine contract ultimately resulted in savings of 25 percent over initial estimates. He expertly coordinated between the base fire department and the airshow chairman to ensure static displays met fire safety standards. Additionally, he spearheaded the effort to supply electrical power to 50 thousand square feet of indoor static displays.

KIMBERLY A. SWEENEY: NOVEMBER 28, 2006

Senior Airman Sweeney was awarded her Air Force Achievement Medal, with "V" device, for her personal courage in El Fashir, Sudan. While the official award criteria for the Air Force Achievement Medal do not permit its award for either heroism or courage, the Air Force nonetheless awarded Sweeney the decoration with the following citation:

> The President of the United States of America takes pleasure in presenting the Air Force

Achievement Medal (Second Oak Leaf Cluster, with Valor) to Senior Airman Kimberly A. Sweeney, United States Air Force. Senior Airman Sweeney distinguished herself by an action of courage as HC-130P Loadmaster, 79th Expeditionary Rescue Squadron, 449th Air Expeditionary Group, Camp Lemonier, Djibouti. On 28 November 2006, while in support of Operation ENDURING FREEDOM-HORN OF AFRICA, she engaged in ground operations against an opposing armed force as a peacetime governmental detainee at El Fashir, Sudan. Airman Sweeney and her crew were forcibly detained by armed members of the Sudanese military. In the face of an overwhelming force, Airman Sweeney boldly refused to surrender herself despite threats of torture. She secured sensitive equipment and prepared classified material for destruction. Without hesitation, Airman Sweeney took up arms, positioned herself in harm's way, and denied an overwhelming force of over 150 troops the ability to control the aircraft. Airman Sweeney's actions ensured all 17 American detainees returned with honor. By her prompt action and humanitarian regard for her fellow Airmen, Airman Sweeney reflected great credit upon herself and the United States Air Force.

JAMES WOOLSEY: NOVEMBER 28, 2006

Captain Woolsey was the mission commander and pilot of the HC-130P aircraft in which Senior Airman Sweeney was serving as the loadmaster. His citation reads:

> The President of the United States of America takes pleasure in presenting the Air Force Achievement Medal with Valor to Captain James R. Woosley, United States Air Force. Captain Woosley distinguished himself by heroism as HC-130P Pilot while engaged in ground operations against an opposing armed force at El Fashir, Sudan, on 28 November 2006. On that date, while on an air-land mission, Captain Woosley and his crew were held at gunpoint and ordered to surrender by Sudanese military officials. Accused of espionage and encountering an overwhelming force, Captain Woosley fearlessly refused to surrender. Facing possible execution, he exited the aircraft unarmed and negotiated crew release for 4 hours allowing time for diplomatic intervention. During this time, as mission

commander, he was assaulted by 10 Sudanese soldiers yet remained steadfast. Hostilities escalated when soldiers were cleared to storm the aircraft. Surrounded and facing over 150 heavily armed troops, Captain Woosley again refused to yield and valiantly ordered his crew to man defensive firing positions. The aircraft defense lasted 2 hours until diplomatic channels prevailed. Captain Woosley's courageous actions resulted in the recovery of all assets and the honorable return of 17 detainees. By his heroic actions and unselfish dedication to duty, Captain Woosley has reflected great credit upon himself and the United States Air Force.[131]

The story behind the awards to Sweeney and Woolsey is remarkable. According to an account published in *Air Force Times* in 2009, an HC-130 aircraft piloted by Woolsey, with Sweeney and fifteen other Americans aboard, had flown to Sudan to pick up a U.S. military liaison. But Sudanese military personnel at the airfield where the Americans landed soon were convinced that the Americans were there to collect evidence of war crimes, and they surrounded the aircraft and refused to allow it to depart.

The Sudanese accused Woolsey and his fellow Americans of espionage and demanded to search the plane. When Woolsey refused, the Sudanese threatened to kill him. At one point, a Sudanese soldier grabbed Woolsey and another "slapped sunglasses off his head." When the Sudanese learned that there were two women aboard the HC-130, one soldier informed the Americans that the women "would be raped and sold once the crew was arrested."

After the plane had been on the ground over three hours, trucks with about 50 Sudanese soldiers drove up and these men, armed with AK-47s and rocket propelled grenades, took positions around the Americans. Ultimately, the standoff ended when a U.S. military liaison on the ground convinced the airfield commander, a Sudanese colonel, to allow Woolsey and the HC-130 to depart. A few minutes after 8:00 P.M., the Americans were in the air — and safe.[132]

Woolsey was subsequently recommended for the Bronze Star Medal with "V" device; Sweeney for the Air Force Commendation Medal with "V" device. Six other members of the crew also were recommended for either Bronze Star Medals with "V" device or Air Force Commendation Medals with "V" device. Three years later, however, on June 29, 2009, Lieutenant General Gary North, then the commander of Air Forces Central Comand, downgraded all eight awards to Air Force Achievement Medals with "V" device.

Appendices

Appendix A. Order of Precedence

	For Soldiers	**For Airmen**
First	Medal of Honor	Medal of Honor
Second	Distinguished Service Cross	Air Force Cross
Third	Defense Distinguished Service Medal	Defense Distinguished Service Medal
Fourth	Army Distinguished Service Medal	Air Force Distinguished Service Medal
Fifth	Silver Star	Silver Star
Sixth	Defense Superior Service Medal	Defense Superior Service Medal
Seventh	Legion of Merit	Legion of Merit
Eighth	Distinguished Flying Cross	Distinguished Flying Cross
Ninth	Soldier's Medal	Airman's Medal
Tenth	Bronze Star Medal	Bronze Star Medal
Eleventh	Purple Heart	Purple Heart
Twelfth	Defense Meritorious Service Medal	Defense Meritorious Service Medal
Thirteenth	Meritorious Service Medal	Meritorious Service Medal
Fourteenth	Air Medal	Air Medal
Fifteenth	(no equivalent medal)	Aerial Achievement Medal
Sixteenth	Joint Service Commendation Medal	Joint Service Commendation Medal
Seventeenth	Army Commendation Medal	Air Force Commendation Medal
Eighteenth	Joint Service Achievement Medal	Joint Service Achievement Medal
Nineteenth	Army Achievement Medal	Air Force Achievement Medal

Appendix B. Certificate of Merit

The Certificate of Merit — now obsolete — was available to recognize gallantry and distinguished service in the Army from 1846 until 1918.

Establishing Authority and Effective Dates: The Certificate of Merit was authorized by Congress on March 3, 1847. After the Mexican War (May 13, 1846, to May 30, 1848), awards of the Certificate ceased until the decoration was revived by the War Department in 1877 (retroactive to June 22, 1874). Awards of the Certificate of Merit continued until July 9, 1918, when Congress rescinded the statutory authority for the award.

Criteria: *For gallantry between May 13, 1846–May 30, 1848,* when "any private soldier shall ... distinguish himself" by gallantry in action, that soldier "may be granted a "certificate of merit" and "additional pay at the rate of two dollars per month."[1] The category "private soldier" included those men holding the rank of private as well as "artificiers, farriers, blacksmiths, and musicians who do duty in the ranks and in battle."[2] Non-commissioned officers were ineligible.

For gallantry between June 22, 1874–February 10, 1892, "any private soldier" who "shall have distinguished himself in the service" may be granted a certificate of merit, which "shall entitle him to additional pay, at the rate of two dollars a month."[3] Since "bravery and fidelity to duty are the characteristics of every soldier ... the certificate of merit will only be conferred for acts which distinguish a soldier above his comrades ... the soldier must be of good standing and of undoubted courage." Any recommendation for the award "must originate with an eyewitness, preferably the immediate commanding officer of the soldier."[4] Noncommissioned officers were ineligible for the Certificate of Merit.

For distinguished service between February 11, 1892 and July 9, 1918, "any enlisted man of the Army" who "shall have distinguished himself in the service" may be granted a Certificate of Merit "on the recommendation of the commanding officer of the regiment or chief of corps to which such man belongs."[5] Such distinguished service may occur during wartime or peacetime, and should be "of a valuable character to the United States as, for example, extraordinary exertion in the preservation of human life ... or public property ... or any hazardous service by which the Government is saved loss in men and materiel."[6] Non-commissioned officers were eligible for the Certificate of Merit after February 11, 1892.

Order of Precedence: The Certificate of Merit medal was worn after the Medal of Honor but before all campaign and service medals.

Devices: No devices were authorized.

Designer: Francis David Millet (1846–1912) designed the Certificate of Merit medal. Millet was an American painter and sculptor who served as a drummer boy and surgical assistant during the Civil War. Educated at Harvard and at Belgium's Royal Academy of Fine Arts, Millet designed the Certificate of Merit medal at the request of the War Department. He also designed the Civil War Campaign Medal. Millet was a passenger on the RMS *Titanic* and died when the ship sank on April 15, 1912.

Description and Symbolism

Obverse

A Roman war eagle, facing left and with its wings partly displayed, is centered on a bronze planchet 1¼ inches in diameter (the same diameter as U.S. campaign medal planchets). The eagle is surrounded by the inscription "Virtutis et Audaciae Monumentum et Praemium" ("Virtue and Audacity are Their Own Monument and Reward").

Reverse

Centered on the planchet are the words "For Merit," in two lines. These are surrounded by a wreath consisting of oak branches joined at the bottom by a bow. Circling the wreath at the top are the words "United States of America. Circling the wreath at the bottom of the planchet are thirteen stars — symbolizing the original thirteen colonies that joined together to become the United States.

Ribbon

The ribbon consists of two red stripes, three white stripes and two blue stripes. The two blue stripes are on the outer edges of the ribbon; the two red stripes are in the middle of the ribbon; the three white stripes separate the other colors. The colors are taken from the U.S. flag.

Historical Background

While the Mexican War did not officially begin until President James K. Polk signed a declaration of war with Mexico until May 13, 1846, U.S. and Mexican forces had already fought several engagements along the Rio Grande; the first major battle, in fact, had occurred at Palo Alto on May 8 when American troops under the command of Brigadier General Zachary Taylor defeated a much larger Mexican force.[7]

Left: **Certificate of Merit (obverse).** *Right:* **Certificate of Merit (reverse).**

As the war continued, and as thousands and thousands of Regular and volunteer troops fought in Mexico, Congress decided that enlisted men who were distinguishing themselves in combat should be recognized with both promotions and a "certificate of merit." As a result, Congress enacted legislation on March 3, 1847 providing that

> when any non-commissioned officer shall distinguish himself ... in the service, the President of the United States shall be ... authorized ... to attach him by brevet of the lowest grade of rank ... and when any private soldier shall ... distinguish himself in service, the President may ... grant him a certificate of merit, which shall entitle him to an additional pay at the rate of two dollars per month.

This meant that a sergeant who distinguished himself in battle was rewarded with a brevet promotion to second lieutenant. A private, however, was rewarded with a certificate and more money.

While the Mexican War ended on May 30, 1848, Certificates of Merit continued to be awarded until February 1851, when the War Department published its final list of recipients. A total of 539 soldiers received the Certificate of Merit, which was a parchment document measuring 9¾ inches by 15¾ inches. The top of the document contained the heading "Army of the United States," the image of an American eagle, and the words "Certificate of Merit." The text that followed identified the recipient and announced that he had "distinguished himself in the service of the United States" on a particular date, at a particular action or battle. The text concluded that, based on the recommendation of the commanding officer of his regiment, the soldier was being awarded the Certificate of Merit. The firm J.V.N. Troop, Washington, D.C., printed the certificates and the President and the Secretary of War signed each certificate.[8]

After the Mexican War ended, commanders continued to recommend enlisted men for the Certificate of Merit. But these recommendations — for combat gallantry during the Civil War and various military operations against Indians — were not acted upon because the War Department interpreted the March 7, 1847 statute as restricting the Certificate of Merit to the Mexican War.

In 1874, Congress pulled together all the various statutes governing the Army and reorganized and codified them as "Revised Statutes." When the War Department discovered that these Revised Statutes included the legislation creating the original Certificate of Merit in 1847, it was clear that Congress had — intentionally or unintentionally — now given the Army the authority to resurrect awards of the Certificate of Merit. Not until December 1877, however, did the Adjutant General issue General Orders No. 110, which announced the revival of the Certificate of Merit for enlisted personnel. Awards were made retroactive to June 2, 1874, the date the Revised Statutes had been enacted by Congress.

General Orders Number 2, published in January 1878, set out the criteria for the Certificate of Merit. Certificates would "only be issued for acts of extraordinary gallantry in the presence of the enemy" and each application had to "contain a full record of the specific case ... be forwarded through the regular channel, and be endorsed with an approval and recommendation in every office through which it passes ... especially that of the regimental commander."[9]

From 1878 through 1891, fifty-nine Certificates of Merit were awarded. Almost all were for gallantry in action against hostile Indians. One unusual exception was the block of eight Certificates awarded to African-American troopers in the 10th Cavalry and 24th Infantry Regiments. These soldiers received the award for their "gallant and meritorious conduct" in Arizona in 1889, when they were attacked by a band of robbers while escorting an Army paymaster named Wham. The robbers did not qualify as an "enemy" within the meaning of General Orders No. 2, but the Army wanted to recognize their heroism with Certificates of Merit — and it did.[10]

As Albert F. Gleim noted in his monograph on the Certificate of Merit, the Wham escort awards "signaled a shift in the application of the Certificate of Merit," and this change in policy was reflected in an Adjutant General circular published in February 1892.[11] That circular stated that while the Medal of Honor was restricted to acts of bravery in combat, the Certificate of Merit was for both distinguished wartime and peacetime service "of a valuable character to the United States." Consequently, any "extraordinary exertion in the preservation of human life or in the preservation of public property" might be recognized with the Certificate of Merit.[12]

During the Spanish-American War, the Army awarded about 200 certificates for military operations in Cuba, Puerto Rico, and the Philippines; these were announced in General Orders No. 15 on February 13, 1900. While the majority were for distinguished service in battle, other awards reflected the new non-combat character of the Certificate. For example, Corporal Thaddeus R. Hyatt, Company L, 19th Infantry, received a Certificate "for capturing two of the worst criminals in Puerto Rico" on November 8, 1898. Similarly, Private Louis A. Sillito, Co. C, 3rd Infantry, was awarded the Certificate of Merit "for volunteering to nurse and nursing yellow fever patients at Guantanamo Cuba, September 1, 1898."[13]

While soldiers liked the Certificate of Merit — and the additional monthly pay that accompanied it — the award had a major deficiency: there was no visible symbol to distinguish those who had received it. The War Department corrected this shortcoming on January 11, 1905, when it announced in General Orders No. 4 that a Certificate of Merit "badge" would be created for wear. The medal, designed by the celebrated painter and sculptor

Francis D. Millett, was produced by the U.S. Mint and the first medal was issued on December 30, 1907. Each medal was serial numbered on the bottom rim and have a "No." prefix before the number. As the medals were issued to active duty and retired Certificate of Merit holders, the Army Quartermaster Badge Office listed in a register the identity of each recipient, the medal No. number and the date of issuance.[14]

Between 1905 and 1918, most Certificate of Merit awards were for lifesaving acts.[15] Awards of the Certificate ended after Congress created high-level decorations for combat heroism (the Distinguished Service Cross) and meritorious service in a position of great responsibility (the Distinguished Service Medal), on July 9, 1918: the legislation creating these two new medals expressly stated that awards of the Certificate of Merit were to cease with the passage of the act.[16]

Since the 1918 legislation revoking the legal authority to award the Certificate of Merit also provided that the new Distinguished Service Medal could be issued to Certificate recipients, the War Department began issuing the Distinguished Service Medal to all Certificate holders who applied for the new decoration. But, as many recipients had been awarded the Certificate for combat gallantry, they naturally thought that the Distinguished Service Cross would be more appropriate — and chose not to apply for the Distinguished Service Medal. In 1934, Congress concurred with this sentiment and passed legislation permitting soldiers to receive the Distinguished Service Cross in lieu of their Certificates of Merit. Additionally, those who had previously been issued the Distinguished Service Medal could surrender it and be issued a Distinguished Service Cross.

By the time that the last Certificate of Merit was issued to Corporal Paul Scaletta in May 1918 (for rescuing soldiers in a dangerous surf at Ocean Beach, California), a total of 1,001 awards had made for gallantry in action and 205 for distinguished service other than combat — for a grand total of 1,206 Certificates.[17] The awards fall into the following categories:

Mexican War	539
Indian Wars	61
Spanish American War	203
Philippine Insurrection	175
Boxer Rebellion	21
Mexican Border	2
Lifesaving (water rescues)	133
Saving U.S. property (from fire)	23
Accidents and Natural Disasters	23
Law Enforcement	16
Health Services	10

First Recipient

WILLIAM B. BAKER: AUGUST 13, 1898

First Lieutenant William B. Baker received the first Certificate of Merit medal (No. 1) on December 30, 1907. Baker's award was for "distinguished service in action" on August 13, 1898, while he was serving as a corporal in the Astor Battery at Manila, Philippine Islands. Baker later was issued the Distinguished Service Medal in lieu of his Certificate of Merit medal.[18]

Selected Recipients (chronological)

GEORGE ARRINGTON: MAY 11, 1889

While Arrington's heroism occurred in 1889, he was in fact the last soldier to be awarded the Certificate of Merit medal. Arrington received his medal (No. 361) on May 1, 1919 for "gallant and meritorious conduct while serving with a detachment escorting Major Joseph W. Wham, Paymaster, U.S. Army, in an encounter with a band of robbers, by whom the party was attacked." Then Private Arrington was an African-American soldier assigned to Co. C, 24th Infantry Regiment. The moneys taken in the armed robbery, which occurred between Forts Grant and Thomas, Arizona, on May 11, 1889, were never recovered, and the robbers were never identified.[19]

GEORGE W. CARNER: SEPTEMBER 5, 1901

Carner, then serving as a Musician, Co. H, 4th Infantry, was awarded the Certificate of Merit "for assisting in saving his company commander and a private soldier from almost certain drowning in the Borac River, near Nasugbu, Philippine Islands."[20]

On the afternoon of September 5, 1901, during an operation in pursuit of insurgents, Private Alexander Hewison fell into the swift flowing Borac River. Hewison's company commander, 1st Lieutenant Louis Van Schiack, saw Hewison in the water and jumped into the river to rescue him.

Van Schiack was able to reach Hewison and keep him afloat, but the water was flowing so quickly and the river bank was so steep that Van Schiack was not able to do more than "hold the semi-conscious Hewison out of the water with one arm and cling to an overhanging bamboo branch with the other."[21]

Carner, who was a strong swimmer, now jumped into the water and attempted to rescue both Van Schiack and Hewison. The current was so swift, however, that Carner was helpless and the fast moving water "washed him back to the bank opposite Van Schiack and Hewison." Carner climbed out of the water and, aided by another soldier, found a long bamboo pole. Then, while his fellow soldier held Carner down over the perpendicular river bank, Carner managed to float the end of the bamboo pole to Van Schiack. Hewison was then passed along the pole and pulled ashore. Van Schiack subsequently recommended that Carner be awarded the Certificate of Merit because, as Van Schiack put it, he and Hewison would have drowned "had it not been for the courageous and persistent efforts of Carner."[22]

Born in Danbury, Connecticut in December 1880, Carner enlisted in the Army in June 1889. He served in Cuba and the Philippines with the 4th Infantry, and along the Mexican border while a member of the New York National Guard. During World War I, Carner was a lieutenant in the New York State Police.

In 1934, Carner was issued a Distinguished Service Medal in lieu of this Certificate of Merit medal but later that same year, he exchanged this decoration for the Distinguished Service Cross. Carner died at Long Beach, California, in May 1959.

ROY F. COX: FEBRUARY 28–29, 1908

Corporal Cox was awarded the Certificate of Merit medal "for highly meritorious services in voluntarily travelling about 30 miles during a severe blizzard, rescuing a civilian from freezing near Lake Minto, and dragging him by sled 65 miles to Fairbanks, Alaska. Cox was subsequently issued a Distinguished Service Medal in lieu of the Certificate of Merit medal.[23]

THOMAS JOHNSON: AUGUST 22, 1912

First Sergeant Johnson received his Certificate of Merit medal "for pursuing and disarming an enlisted man bent on murdering his first sergeant at Camp McGrath, Batangas, Philippine Islands." Johnson was subsequently issued a Distinguished Service Medal in lieu of his Certificate of Merit medal.[24]

Appendix C. Oak Leaf Cluster

In both the Army and the Air Force, second and subsequent awards of a decoration to the same recipient are reflected by affixing one or more bronze or silver oak leaf clusters to the medal's ribbon or ribbon bar. The story behind the use of this cluster — rather than the five-pointed gold star used in the Navy, Marine Corps and Coast Guard — is not well known.

When Congress created the Army's Medal of Honor in 1862, it did not provide a means for reflecting multiple awards of the new decoration — probably because the drafters of the legislation thought it unlikely that a soldier would receive more than one Medal of Honor. Consequently, those soldiers who "won" more than one medal — like Captain Thomas W. Custer, a double Medal of Honor recipient — were awarded two medals and wore both.

But this practice changed when President Wilson authorized the Army Distinguished Service Cross and Army Distinguished Service Medal on in January 1918. General Orders No. 6, which announced these two new awards on January 12, 1918, also provided that an individual who was awarded a second medal would reflect this second award with a "bronze oak leaf." The actual language is:

> No individual will be entitled to more than one Distinguished Service Cross or one Distinguished Service Medal, but each additional citation in War Department orders for conduct or service that would warrant the award of either of these decorations will entitle the person so cited to wear upon the ribbon of the decoration and upon the corresponding ribbon a *bronze oak leaf* of approved design, and the right to wear such oak leaf will be announced as part of the citation[1] [emphasis supplied].

Captain Aymar E. Embury (the principal designer of the Distinguished Service Cross) probably designed the first oak leaf insignia. But Embury's insignia in fact was more of an oak branch (rather than a leaf) as it consisted of a branch and three oak leaves spread apart in the shape of a three-pronged fork. It also was large — about one half inch in length.[2] At least 100 of these spread oak leaf devices were manufactured in April 1918 and as many as 33 of the new appurtenances were issued to men who received multiple awards of the Distinguished Service Cross in 1918 and 1919. Most of these recipients had been in the 94th Aero Squadron, with Captain Edward V. Rickenbacker receiving a Distinguished Service Cross with an unprecedented seven bronze oak leaves.[3]

In early 1919, however, the War Department decided that the Embury's spread oak leaf device should be replaced with an oak leaf *cluster* consisting of oak leaves and acorns. Herbert

Adams, the sculptor member of the Commission of Fine Arts, prepared the design (and sculpted the plaster model) for the new appurtenance — which was approved by Secretary of the Army Newton D. Baker on February 11, 1919. The U.S. Mint in Philadelphia produced samples of the clusters in bronze metal and the Army approved them for production on March 29, 1919.

This new oak leaf cluster, while very similar to that used by the Army and the Air Force today, was considerably larger, as it measured $^{15}/_{16}$ of an inch in length. Army Regulation 600–35, *Specifications for the Uniform*, described the device as follows: "A bronze twig of four oak leaves with three acorns on the stem, $^{15}/_{16}$ of an inch in length, to be worn on the ribbon suspending the medal." These large "thumb nail clusters" were used by the War Department from 1919 through 1933; multiple awards of the Distinguished Service Cross and Distinguished Service Medal made during this period used them.

Interestingly, at least one senior leader recognized that the large size of the oak leaf cluster might pose a problem. As Army Chief of Staff General Peyton C. March expressed it, while the device was "just the right size to go on the ribbon of the medals when only one is to go on ... to men who have been awarded two or more, it will be necessary to increase the length of the ribbon."[4] While March was not concerned about lengthening a medal's ribbon to accommodate the large oak leaf clusters — as this was not prohibited by regulation — in fact his observation was prescient. This is because, when the Army began issuing its new Purple Heart and Silver Star medal in 1932, it discovered that the size of the $^{15}/_{16}$ inch oak leaf cluster was a problem. More than a few soldiers who applied for these new decorations were entitled to wear two or more oak leaf clusters — which would not fit on the standard length of ribbon.

The result was that, on September 3, 1932, the War Department announced that the oak leaf cluster would be reduced in size from

¹⁵⁄₁₆ inches to ¹³⁄₃₂ of an inch. Army Regulation 600–35 was revised to state that the oak leaf cluster was a "bronze twig of 4 oak leaves with 3 acorns on the stem, ¹³⁄₃₂ of an inch in length, to be worn on the ribbon suspending the medal."[5] But, while the size of the oak leaf cluster was now officially reduced, the War Department continued to award the larger oak leaf cluster until at least March 1933 — probably to exhaust existing stocks of the appurtenance rather than discarding them.[6]

Two final events in the history of the oak leaf cluster occurred in March 1947. First, the Army announced for that "a silver Oak Leaf Cluster may be worn in lieu of five bronze Oak Leaf Clusters."[7] This meant, for example, that a bronze oak cluster would now be used to reflect the 2d through 5th awards and 7th through 10th awards. A silver oak leaf cluster would be used to denote the 6th and 11th awards. The creation of a silver oak leaf cluster was probably required because of the high number of Air Medals awarded by the Army Air Forces between 1942 and 1945. Ultimately, even *silver* oak leaves were insufficient, as the Army abandoned oak leaves for the Air Medal and replaced them with Arabic numerals during the Vietnam War.

The second change announced in March 1947 was that the oak leaf cluster would now come in two sizes: ¹³⁄₃₂ inches in length for the suspension ribbon and ⁵⁄₁₆ inches in length for the service ribbon bar. These different size oak leaf clusters continue exist today in both the Army and the Air Force, although soldiers and airmen usually ignore the different sizes when attaching the appurtenance to their suspension ribbon or service ribbon bar.[8]

Appendix D. "V" Device

The Army and the Air Force use the "V" device on a variety of individual decorations and medals; the Air Force also uses the device on unit and organization awards. Soldiers may wear the appurtenance on the Bronze Star Medal, Air Medal, Joint Service Commendation Medal and Army Commendation Medal. Airmen may wear the "V" device on the Distinguished Flying Cross, Bronze Star Medal, Air Force Commendation and Air Force Achievement Medal; they may not wear it on the Air Medal. But airmen are authorized to wear the "V" device on two ribbon-only awards: the Air Force Outstanding Unit Award and the Air Force Organizational Excellence Award.

The "V" device arose out of the desire to distinguish between Bronze Star Medals awarded for combat valor and those awarded for meritorious achievement or service in World War II. The decoration was created to reward either minor acts of heroism or meritorious service, a dual-role that was controversial from the beginning — because there was no way for people seeing the medal to know whether the recipient had received the decoration for heroism or service. This was an issue of particular

Oak Leaf Cluster and V Device (on Bronze Star Medal).

importance to those who were awarded the Bronze Star Medal for combat gallantry.

In January 1945 the Army Ground Forces commander, Lieutenant General Benjamin Lear, recommended that a bronze service star be attached to any Bronze Star Medal when it was awarded for heroism. The War Department Personnel Division (G-1), however, did not like this proposal. But in the absence of a better idea, the Army asked its theater commanders to give their views on the subject.

The American theater and Asiatic-Pacific theater commanders endorsed the idea of using a small bronze star. The commanders of the European–African–Middle Eastern Theater and China–Burma–India Theater, however, did not like the idea of an appurtenance to reflect heroism. Rather, they suggested that a soldier who received the Bronze Star Medal *for gallantry* should wear a Bronze Star Medal with *a different-colored ribbon*.[1]

While the Army was considering how to distinguish between Bronze Star Medals for achievement and for heroism, the Navy was asked for its views. The Navy did not offer an opinion on the subject but was somewhat opposed to anything that would set a precedent that could be applied to other decorations, such as Distinguished Flying Cross, which also served dual purposes.

The controversy was resolved on December 11, 1945 — months after fighting had ended — when the Army decided that a bronze, ¼-inch high block letter "V" be designated "as a device for wear on the ribbon of the Bronze Star Medal to denote an award for valor." Both the Army and Army Air Force called the device the "V for Valor," while the Navy named it the "Combat Distinguishing Device."

Army Use

Until the mid–1960s, a soldier was permitted to affix the "V" device only to the Bronze Star Medal. Then, in February 1964, the Army announced that the "V" could be attached to both the Air Medal and the Army Commendation Medal when those decorations were awarded for individual combat valor. Today, a soldier is authorized to wear the "V" for valor on the Bronze Star Medal, Air Medal and Army Commendation Medal; since the Defense Department also awards the "V" device when its Joint Service Commendation Medal is awarded for combat heroism, a soldier also is authorized to wear the appurtenance on that decoration.

Air Force Use

The use of the "V" in the Air Force evolved differently. From the late 1940s to the mid-1990s, airmen wore the "V" only with the Bronze Star Medal.[3] In January 1996, however, the Air Force announced that the "V" device could be worn by individual airmen on the Air Force Commendation Medal and Air Force Achievement Medal to "appropriately recognize noteworthy accomplishments of ... personnel placed in harm's way during contingency operations" after January 11, 1996.[2] This was an important development: while a "V" device on the Bronze Star Medal still signaled that decoration had been awarded for combat heroism, the same "V" on an Air Force Commendation Medal or Achievement Medal simply meant that the recipient was in harm's way during a deployment.

In June 2004, Air Force Secretary James Roche expanded the use of the "V" in the Air Force by authorizing its placement on the Distinguished Flying Cross — retroactive to September 18, 1947, when the Air Force was established. Finally, current Air Force regulations allow the use of the "V" as a unit and organization award. The appurtenance may be worn on the Air Force Outstanding Unit Award ribbon and the Air Force Organizational Excellence Award ribbon when those ribbons are awarded during contingency operations.

Notes

Chapter 1

1. Title 10, U.S.C., Section 3741, *Medal of Honor: Award.*

2. Army Regulation 600-8-22, *Military Awards*, December 11, 2006, paragraph 3-7(b).

3. Ibid., para 3-19r.

4. Ibid., para., 3-19t.

5. DoD Manual 1348.33-V1, *Manual of Military Decorations and Awards: General Information, Medal of Honor, and Defense/Joint Decorations and Awards*, November 23, 2010, 15-16.

6. Title 10, U.S.C., Section 3744(d)(1) and (2)

7. Richard Goldstein, "Roy P. Benavidez, Recipient of Medal of Honor, Dies at 63," *New York Times*, December 4, 1998, A22; Rudi Williams, "Medic Receives Long-Delayed Medal of Honor," Armed Forces Press Service, February 9, 2000; Mitchell Yockelson, "I Am Entitled to the Medal of Honor and I Want It: Theodore Roosevelt's Quest for Glory," *Prologue* (Spring 1998): 6-15.

8. Charles P. McDowell, *Military and Naval Decorations of the United States* (Springfield, VA: Quest, 1984), 28.

9. John E. Strandberg and Roger J. Bender, *The Call of Duty: Military Awards and Decorations of the United States*, 2d ed. (San Jose, CA: R. James Bender, 2004), 15-54.

10. Ibid., 44.

11. Sundry Civil Appropriations Act, 37th Congress, 2d Session, March 3, 1863, Sec. 6.

12. McDowell, *Military and Naval Decorations*, 19.

13. Ibid., 29.

14. The forerunner of today's Legion of Valor of the United States, Inc. Chartered by Act of Congress in 1955, membership in the Legion of Valor is open to Medal of Honor, Distinguished Service Cross, Navy Cross and Air Force Cross recipients. See www.legionofvalor.com (accessed February 13, 2011).

15. McDowell, *Military and Naval Decorations*, 29.

16. Public Law 109-364, Sec. 555 (flag); Title 38, U.S.C., Sec. 560 (pension); Dept. of Defense Regulation 4515.13-R (air travel).

17. See for example, Medal of Honor to Pvt. John Mentor, Apr. 6, 1865 ("Capture of flag"); Simmons, April 6, 1865 ("Capture of flag").

18. William Manchester, *American Caesar* (New York: Dell, 1978), 316.

19. Stanley Weintraub, *15 Stars: Eisenhower, MacArthur, Marshall* (New York: Simon and Schuster, 2007), 58.

20. Ibid.

21. L. K. Hennighausen, Memo to Commanding General, U.S. Forces European Theater, August 3, 1945, subj: Recommendation for Award of the Medal of Honor; William R. Farquhar, 9th Indorsement, subj: Chilson, Llewellyn M., Recommendation for award of the Medal of Honor, May 17, 1946.

22. Report of Decorations Board, Washington, D.C., 28 August 1946.

23. For more on the story behind the failure to award a Medal of Honor to Chilson, see Fred L. Borch and Robert F. Dorr, "Above, Beyond and Forgotten," *World War II* (April 2006), 26-33.

24. Eric R. Caubarreaux , *The Decorations and Awards of Audie L. Murphy and Alvin C. York*, 2d ed. (Privately published, 2010), 11-12.

25. For more on the Andrews Raid, see Craig Angle, *The Great Locomotive Chase: More on the Andrews Raid and the First Medal of Honor* (Rouzerville, PA: C. Angle, 1992). A 1956 Walt Disney Productions movie, "The Great Locomotive Chase" (starring Fess Parker and Slim Pickens), also recounts the story.

26. U.S. Army Adjutant General, *American Decorations 1862-1926*, Vol. I (Washington, D.C.: Government Printing Office, 1927), 24.

27. Ibid., 16.

28. Ibid., 119.

29. For best modern treatment of Wood's life, see Jack McCallum, *Leonard Wood: Rough Rider, Surgeon, Architect of American Imperialism* (New York: New York University Press, 2006).

30. *American Decorations*, 35.

31. Thomas Bruscino, "Introduction," in Frederick Funston, *Memories of Two Wars: Cuban and Philippine Experiences* (Lincoln: University of Nebraska Press, 2009), vi.

32. *General Orders* (no number), War Department, March 11, 1902; *American Decorations*, 108; Fred L. Borch, *For Military Merit* (Annapolis, MD: Naval Institute, 2010), 35-36.

33. *General Orders No. 59*, War Department, 1919; *American Decorations*, 121.

34. Taylor V. Beattie with Ronald Bowman, "In Search of York: Man, Myth and Legend," *Army History* (Summer/Fall 2000): 1-14.

35. Fred L. Borch and Robert F. Dorr, "Blinded WWII Airman Picked Up Burning Bomb to Save B-29 Crew," *Air Force Times*, July 7, 2008, 31.

36. http://www.arlingtoncemetery.net/lafunk.htm (accessed February 5, 2011); Fred L. Borch and Robert F. Dorr, "Leadership, Bravery Netted Funk 7 Awards," *Army Times*, November 13, 2006, 48.

37. Ibid.

38. *General Orders No. 75*, War Department, September 5, 1945.

39. Forrest Bryant Johnson, *Phantom Warrior* (New York: Berkeley, 2007), 103.

40. Ibid., 269-70.

41. "Highly Decorated Veteran of Three Wars," *Los Angeles Times*, October 25, 2008, B5.

42. *General Orders No. 16*, War Department, February 8, 1946.

43. Larry Smith, *Beyond Glory* (New York: W.W. Norton, 2003), 143-57.

44. Franklin D. Miller with Elwood

J.C. Kureth, *Reflections of a Warrior* (Novato, CA: Presidio, 1991), 44.

45. *General Orders No. 35*, Department of the Army, July 16, 1971.

46. On July 12, 2011, Sergeant First Class Leroy Petry became the second living recipient of the Medal of Honor since the Vietnam War. Jason Ukman, "Sgt. 1st Class Leroy Petry awarded Medal of Honor," *Washington Post*, July 12, 2011, A3.

47. http://www.army.mil/medalofhonor/giunta/citation.html (accessed July 10, 2011).

48. Medal of Honor (Air Force), Title 10, United States Code, Section 8741.

49. Air Force Instruction 36–2803, *Air Force Awards and Decorations Program*, June 15, 2001, paragraph 2.5.

50. Letter, Col. John E. Horne, USAF Personnel Services Division, to Lt. Col. J. T. French, Army Quartermaster General Heraldic Officer (QMGHO), subj: Establishment of Distinctive Air Force Decorations, February 9, 1961.

51. Ibid.

52. Letter, Col. John E. Horne, USAF Personnel Services Division, to Lt. Col. Whiting, QMGHO, subj: Designs for New Air Force Medal of Honor, September 14, 1961.

53. Ltr, Lt. Col. J.T. French, QMGHO to Chief of Staff, U.S. Air Force, subj: 1st Ind., Designs for New Air Force Medal of Honor, November 28, 1961.

54. Ibid.

55. Ibid. The "U.S. ten-cent coin" referenced in this letter is the so-called Mercury dime, which featured the profile of Mercury on its obverse. While this dime had been replaced in 1946 by a new ten-cent coin honoring Franklin D. Roosevelt, both coins were still in circulation in the early 1960s, and those individuals involved in the design process mistakenly believed it was Liberty's profile on this dime.

56. Memo from Elizabeth Will, chief, Heraldic Specialist Office, for commanding officer, Institute of Heraldry, subj: Air Force Medal of Honor, May 4, 1962.

57. Ibid.

58. Ltr, David E. Finley, chairman, Commission of Fine Arts, to Col. Harry D. Temple, commanding officer, Institute of Heraldry, September 25, 1962.

59. Memo from Benjamin W. Fridge, special assistant for manpower, Personnel and Reserve Forces, Department of the Air Force, to Eugene M. Zuckert, Secretary of the Air Force, May 1, 1963.

60. "Medal of Honor Design," *Army-Navy-Air Force Journal*, November 9, 1963.

61. U.S. Congress, Senate, Committee on Veterans' Affairs, *Vietnam Era Medal of Honor Recipients, 1964–1972* (Washington, DC: Government Printing Office, 1973), 50–51.

62. http://www.airforcehistory.hq.af.mil/PopTopics/MOH.htm (accessed February 13, 2011). For more on Medal of Honor airmen, see Barrett Tillman, *Above and Beyond: The Aviation Medals of Honor* (Washington: Smithsonian Institution, 2002).

63. Fred L. Borch, "Tribute: Richard Etchberger," *Vietnam* (February 2011): 58–59.

64. http://www.af.mil/information/heritage/person.asp?dec=&pid=123006519 (accessed February 13, 2011); *Vietnam Era Medal of Honor Recipients 1964–1972*, 90–91.

65. Stuart I. Rochester and Frederick Kiley, *Honor Bound* (Annapolis, MD: Naval Institute, 1999), 289–91.

66. John L. Frisbee, "Lance Sijan's Incredible Journey," *Air Force Magazine* (December 1986): 12–13.

67. For a complete list of pre–World War I awards of the Distinguished Service Cross, see C. Douglas Sterner, ed., *Citations for Awards of the Distinguished Service Cross, For Actions Prior to World War I* (2006), http://www.homeofheroes.com/members/books/dsc/01_-DSC-PreWWI.doc (accessed January 29, 2011).

68. Title 10, United States Code, Section 3742; Army Regulation 600–8-22, para. 3–8.

69. Memo, from Brigadier General Lytle Brown, director, War Plans Division, for the Chief of Staff, subj: Distinguished Service Medal and Distinguished Service Cross, May 4, 1918.

70. Memo, from John R. Sinnock, Engraving Department, to Mr. Dressel, *National Geographic Magazine*, subj: Insignia and Decorations, January 17, 1946, 2.

71. http://www/tioh.hqda.pentagon.mil/Awards/distinguished_srv_cross.aspx (accessed February 5, 2011).

72. McDowell, *Military and Naval Decorations*, 49.

73. Public Law 193, 65th Congress, July 9, 1918.

74. McDowell, *Military and Naval Decorations*, 50.

75. Ibid., 51.

76. Thomas J. Nier, ed., "The First 100 DSC Awards (of the 1st Design)—Known Issue Roster," *Gleim Medal Letters* (Glassboro, NJ: Orders and Medals Society of America, 1998), 46.

77. Public Law 88–77, Congress 1963.

78. *General Orders No. 120*, War Department, 1918.

79. Douglas Waller, *A Question of Loyalty: Gen. Billy Mitchell and the Court-Martial That Gripped the Nation* (New York: HarperCollins, 2004), 20.

80. Ibid., 324, 331.

81. *General Orders No. 121*, War Department, 1918; *General Orders No. 32*, War Department, 1919; *American Decorations*, 523.

82. Edward V. Rickenbacker, *Rickenbacker, An Autobiography* (New York: Prentice Hall, 1967).

83. Robert F. Dorr, "WWI Ace Rickenbacker Was a Man of Many Skills," *Air Force Times*, May 23, 2005, 27.

84. http://www.mainememory.net/bin/Features?fn=119&fmt=list&n=1&supst=Exhibits&mr=all (accessed February 5, 2011); "The Distinguished Service Cross and Silver Citation Star to Women in World War I," *The Planchet Newsletter* (Winter 2010): 1.

85. *General Orders No. 37*, War Department, March 11, 1919; *American Decorations*, 211.

86. *General Orders No. 114*, Headquarters, Fifth Army, 1944.

87. *General Orders No. 127*, Eighth U.S. Army (Korea), October 20, 1950.

88. William T. Bower, William M. Hammond, and George L. MacGarrigle, *Black Soldier, White Army: The 24th Infantry Regiment in Korea* (Washington, DC: Government Printing Office, 1996), 132–33.

89. *General Orders No. 13*, War Department, 1919; *American Decorations*, 380.

90. *General Orders No. 5*, Headquarters, Southwest Pacific Area, 1943.

91. For more on Kenney, see Thomas E. Griffith, Jr., *MacArthur's Airman: General George C. Kenney and the War in the Southwest Pacific* (Lawrence: University Press of Kansas, 1998).

92. Memo from Maj. Gen. William Lassiter, commanding general, 32d Division to Adjutant General, American Expeditionary Force, subj: Recommendation of award of Distinguished Service Cross to Private 1st Class Leonard St. James, Company I, 125th Infantry, March 12, 1919; War Department, *Decorations 1862–1927*, 540.

93. *Order No. 16.103*, *"D,"* General Headquarters, French Armies of the East, April 16, 1919.

94. *General Orders No. 108*, War Department, 1919; Dennis Gordon, *Quartered in Hell: The Story of the American North Russia Expeditionary Force 1918–1919* (Missoula, MT: Doughboy Historical Society, 1982), 312.

95. *General Orders No. 44*, War Department, May 13, 1946.

96. Janie Blankenship, "Limping Lady Aids French Underground in World War II," *VFW Magazine* (March 2009): 22–23; Elizabeth McIntosh, *Sisterhood of Spies: The Women of the OSS* (Annapolis, MD: Naval Institute,

1998), 113–128; https://www.cia.gov/li-brary/center-for-the-study-of-intelligence/csi-publications/books-and-monographs/oss/art05.htm (accessed February 5, 2011).

97. *General Orders No. 1096*, Headquarters, U.S. Army, Vietnam, March 31, 1969.

98. John C. Bahnsen with Wess Roberts, *American Warrior* (New York: Citadel, 2007), xviii.

99. Neil Sheehan, *A Bright and Shining Lie: John Paul Vann and America in Vietnam* (New York: Random House, 1988); www.arlington-cemetery.net/jpvann.htm (accessed July 10, 2011).

100. http://northshorejournal.org-/master-sgt-brendan-oconnor-us-army-special-forces (accessed February 6, 2011).

101. The two recipients of the Air Force Cross for heroism not involving direct combat were Captains Tilford W. Harp and Dennis W. Traynor.

102. Fred L. Borch, "A History of the Air Force Cross," *Journal of the Orders and Medals Society of America* (March-April 2004): 2–14.

103. The two recipients were First Lieutenant Urban Drew and Lieutenant Colonel William J. Sloan. Borch and Floyd, *The Air Force Cross*, 1–3.

104. Ibid., 4–5.

105. Rochester and Kiley, *Honor Bound*, 133.

106. Ibid., 162.

107. Ibid., 312.

108. Robinson Risner, *The Passing of the Night: My Seven Years as a Prisoner of the North Vietnamese* (New York: Random House, 1973).

109. Borch and Floyd, *The Air Force Cross*, 45; *United States v. Fleener*, Court-Martial 20704, *Court-Martial Reports* 43: 981 (Air Force Court of Military Review 1971); findings and sentence affirmed *Court-Martial Reports* 44: 228 (Court of Military Appeals).

110. Borch and Floyd, *Air Force Cross*, 66–67; Rochester and Kiley, *Honor Bound*, 403–06.

111. Borch and Floyd, *Air Force Cross*, 56–57.

112. Information paper, "Chief Master Sergeant Duane D. Hackney, USAF, Flint Michigan," Michigan's Own Military and Space Museum, Frankenmuth, Mich, n.d. (2011).

113. Borch and Floyd, *Air Force Cross*, 79.

114. "This Week in History," *Air Force Times*, December 27, 2010, 23.

115. For more on Olds' colorful career as an airman, see Robin Olds with Christina Olds and Ed Rasimus, *Fighter Pilot: The Memoirs of Legendary Ace Robin Olds* (New York: St. Martin's, 2010).

116. Borch and Floyd, *Air Force Cross*, 82.

117. Michael Hoffman, "Air Force Cross Awarded 40 Years Late," *Air Force Times*, March 29, 2008, 3; Eric Durr, "Chief Receives Air Force Cross 40 Years After Mission," *Air Force Print News Today*, April 10, 2008, http://www.af.mil/news/story_print.asp ?id=123093805 (accessed February 13, 2011).

118. Borch and Floyd, *Air Force Cross*, 60, 104–05.

119. Borch and Floyd, 120–22. For the story of the events of October 3–4, 1993, see Mark Bowdon, *Black Hawk Down: A Study of Modern War* (New York: Atlantic Monthly, 1999).

120. Borch and Floyd, *Air Force Cross*, 123–126. For more on Chapman and Cunningham, see Michael Hirsh, *None Braver: U.S. Air Force Pararescue-men in the War on Terrorism* (New York: New American Library, 2003), 218–274.

121. Army Regulation 600–8-22, *Military Awards*, December 11, 2006, paragraph 3–10; Air Force Instruction 36–3803, *Air Force Awards and Decorations Program*, June 15, 2001, Table 2.1.

122. *General Orders No. 6*, War Department, January 12, 1918, sec. 5.

123. Memorandum from Brigadier General Campbell King, assistant chief of staff, G-1, to the chief of staff, subj.: The Order of Military Merit, June 12, 1925, 7.

124. Letter, Adjutant General to Quartermaster General, Subj.: Silver Star, July 19, 1932.

125. Frederic L. Borch and William R. Westlake, *The Silver Star: A History of America's Third Highest Award for Combat Valor* (Tempe, AZ: Borch and Westlake, 2001), 7.

126. http://www.arlingtoncemetery.net/jlhines.htm (accessed January 30, 2011).

127. *General Orders No. 14*, 4th Armored Division, January 27, 1945. For the details of Abrams role in the relief of Bastogne, see *Thunderbolt: From the Battle of the Bulge to Vietnam and Beyond: Creighton Abrams and the Army of His Times* (New York: Simon and Schuster, 1992), 74–81.

128. Sorley, *Thunderbolt*, 95–96.

129. *General Orders No. 28*, 1st Infantry Division, June 28, 1943.

130. *General Orders No. 2*, 1st Infantry Division, January 2, 1945.

131. *General Orders No. 130*, 1st Infantry Division, November 26, 1944.

132. *General Orders No. 131*, 1st Infantry Division, November 27, 1944.

133. *General Orders No. 137*, 1st Infantry Division, December 4, 1944.

134. http://www.arlingtoncemetery.net/gmgraham.htm (accessed February 20, 2011). For more on Graham, see his autobiography *Down for Double: Anecdotes of a Fighter Pilot* (Richmond, VA: Brandylane, 1996).

135. *General Orders No. 7*, U.S. Military Mission to Moscow (Moscow, U.S.S.R.), June 15, 1944.

136. *General Orders No. 68*, 24th Infantry Division, 1945.

137. *Follow Me: The Human Element in Leadership* (Novato, CA: Presidio Press, 1981); *What Are General's Made Of?* (Novato, CA: Presidio, 1987); *Follow Me II: More on the Human Element in Leadership* (Novato, CA: Presidio, 1996).

138. "Aubrey S. Newman, 90, Colonel Famed for 'Follow Me!' Battle Cry, *New York Times*, January 21, 1994, A22.

139. *General Orders No. 345*, 3rd Infantry Division, September 25, 1945.

140. *General Orders No. 575*, 2nd Infantry Division, 1951.

141. *General Orders No. 153*, 25th Infantry Division, February 21, 1951.

142. *General Orders No. 138*, 25th Infantry Division, February 19, 1951.

143. *General Orders No. 48*, I Corps, March 23, 1951.

144. *General Orders No. 208*, 25th Infantry Division, April 13, 1951.

145. *General Orders No. 510*, 25th Infantry Division, September 2, 1951.

146. *General Orders No. 8*, 25th Infantry Division, January 9, 1952.

147. For the story behind Hackworth's record eight Purple Hearts, see Fred L. Borch, *For Military Merit*, 299–301.

148. *General Orders No. 40*, Department of the Army, December 9, 1965.

149. Silver Star certificate and citation, Major Lawrence R. Friedman, Department of the Air Force, January 8, 1968.

150. *General Orders No. 3645*, U.S. Army Vietnam, June 11, 1966.

151. *General Orders No. 5321*, U.S. Army Vietnam, August 12, 1966.

152. *General Orders No. 3290*, 9th Infantry Division, March 18, 1969.

153. *General Orders No. 4192*, 9th Infantry Division, April 8, 1969.

154. *General Orders No. 4498*, 9th Infantry Division, April 14, 1969.

155. *General Orders No. 5933*, 9th Infantry Division, May 24, 1969.

156. *General Orders No. 6340*, 9th Infantry Division, June 4, 1969.

157. *General Orders No. 4590*, Headquarters, U.S. Army Vietnam, July 12, 1966.

158. *General Orders No. 10*, Department of the Army, April 20, 1984

159. Fred L. Borch and William R. Westlake, *The Silver Star: A History of America's Third Highest Award for Combat Valor* (Tempe, AZ: Borch and Westlake, 2001), 235–236.

160. Ibid., 236.

161. Sara Wood, "Woman Soldier Receives Silver Star for Valor in Iraq," *American Forces Information Service News Articles*, June 16, 2005; Steve Fainaru, "Silver Star Shines for Squad of MPs," *Washington Post*, June 26, 2005, A1.

Chapter 2

1. Title 10, United States Code, Section 3750.

2. AR 600–8-22, paragraph 3–13.

3. *General Orders No. 17*, War Department, Sec. XX, June 25, 1924.

4. Public Law 446, 69th Congress, Sess. I, Chapter 721 (1926).

5. Army Regulation 35–2340, *Finance Dept.: Pay of Enlisted Men, Rates of Pay*, October 2, 1923, para 1.

6. Title 10, United States Code, sec. 3991, Computation of retired pay, para. (a)(2).

7. Frederic L. Borch and William R. Westlake, *The Soldier's Medal: A History of the U.S. Army's Highest Award for Non-Combat Valor* (Tempe, AZ: Borch and Westlake, 1994), 2.

8. War Department Circular 79/1937, Section IV; Change 2, Army Regulation 600–45, *Personnel: Decorations*, August 10, 1938, paragraph 17.f.(4).

9. Army Regulation 600–8-22, *Military Awards*, December 11, 2006, para. 3–13b.

10. For more on these lifesaving awards, see McDowell, *Military and Naval Decorations of the United States*, 145–153.

11. *General Orders No. 19*, War Department, December 12, 1927.

12. Ibid.

13. Ibid.

14. Ibid.

15. *General Orders No. 15*, Headquarters, U.S. Army Forces in the Middle East, Cairo, Egypt, September 13, 1942, para. III.

16. Borch and Westlake, *The Soldier's Medal*, 251.

17. *General Orders No. 17*, War Department, Feb. 6, 1947, para. VII.

18. *General Orders No. 113*, Headquarters, 1st Logistical Command, May 22, 1966.

19. *General Orders No. 9285*, Americal Division (Chu Lai, Vietnam, December 3, 1968).

20. For more on Powell's military career, see Colin Powell with Joseph Persico, *My American Journey* (New York: Random House, 1995).

21. General Orders No. 1388, Headquarters, U.S. Army Vietnam/MACV Support Command, June 21, 1972.

22. Citation, Department of the Army, Soldier's Medal, First Lieutenant Damian T. Horne, March 5, 2007.

23. *General Orders No. 26*, Department of the Army, June 10, 1989.

24. *General Orders No. 14*, Department of the Army, April 11, 1997, para. III; "Soldiers Get Medals for Stopping Sniper," *Charlotte (N.C.) Observer*, December 12, 1995, A7.

25. Borch, *For Military Merit*, 87; "Breaking Through the Brass Ceiling," *USAA Magazine* (August/September 2002), 14–15; "Minefield Rescuers," *Army Times*, October 12, 2001, 55.

26. Title 10, United States Code, Section 8750, Airman's Medal: award; limitations, para. (a)(1).

27. Air Force Instruction 36–2803, *The Air Force Awards and Decorations Program*, June 15, 2001, Chapter 2, note 10.

28. Air Force Airman's Medal, Army Institute of Heraldry Description Sheet, n.d., 1.

29. *General Orders No. 5*, Department of the Air Force, March 2, 1953 (Masterson); *General Orders No. 8*, Department of the Air Force, March 12, 1952 (Macy).

30. Memorandum from Lt. Col. James S. Cook, Jr., Chief Heraldic Branch, to Chief, Awards Branch, Department of the Air Force, subj: Proposed Air Force Decorations, June 25, 1958.

31. Ltr, Lt. Col. Ross E. Norton, Chief, Awards Branch, Dept. of the Air Force to Chief, Heraldic Branch, Office of the Army Quartermaster General, subj: Design for Airman's Medal, June 22, 1960; Ltr, Col. John E. Horne, Personnel Services Division to Director of Operations, Office of the Quartermaster General, Department of the Army, subj: Establishment of Distinctive Air Force Decorations, February 9, 1961.

32. Patricia Sullivan, "Air Force Staff Sergeant Moses E. Willoughby, 72; Rescued Six Men," *Washington Post*, September 28, 2008, C7.

33. *Special Order G-2*, Headquarters, Pacific Air Forces, January 5, 1970.

34. Phyllis Duff, "Khobar Towers," June 26, 2006, http://usmilitary.about .com/od/terrorism/a/khobar.htm.

35. "Sergeant Honored for Lifesaving Action," *Air Force Times*, November 2, 2009, 3.

Chapter 3

1. Executive Order 4601, *Distinguished Flying Cross*, March 1, 1927, para. 8; amended by Executive Order 10189, *Distinguished Flying Cross*, December 6, 1950, 15 *Federal Register* 8710.

2. AR 600–8-22, *Military Awards*, December 11, 2006, para. 3–12.

3. Air Force Instruction 36–2803, *Air Force Awards and Decorations Program*, June 15, 2001, Chapter 2, note 9.

4. Fred L. Borch and Charles P. McDowell, *Sea Service Medals* (Annapolis, MD: Naval Institute, 2009), 37.

5. Ibid.

6. Letter from Maj. S. W. Fitzgerald (recorder) to the Commission of Fine Arts, September 20, 1926, National Archives Record Group 66, Entry 17.

7. Letter from Charles Moore, chairman of the Commission of Fine Arts, to the assistant secretary of war and the assistant secretary of the Navy, January 24, 1929, National Archives Record Group 66, Entry 17.

8. Letter from Charles Moore, chairman of the Commission of Fine Arts, to Senator Hiram Bingham, December 1, 1928, National Archives Record Group 66, Entry 17.

9. "Distinguished Flying Cross," National Archives Record Group 330, Entry 125, Box 1515.

10. Arthur E. DuBois, "Heraldry, Flag and Insignia Work of the Office of The Quartermaster General," *The Quartermaster Review* (May-June 1928), 1.

11. *General Orders No. 7*, War Department, 1929.

12. *General Orders No. 16*, War Department, 1929; War Department, *American Decorations*, Supplement I (Washington, D.C.: Government Printing Office, 1937), 66.

13. *General Orders No. 4*, War Department, 1933.

14. Amelia Earhart, *20 Hrs., 40 Min.: Our Flight in the Friendship*, (Washington, D.C.: National Geographic, 2003); Donald M. Goldstein and Katherine V. Dillon, *A Life of the Aviation Legend* (Dulles, VA: Potomac, 2007).

15. http://www.combatleadership.com/Heroes_Results.asp?MedalID=3152 (accessed January 23, 2011).

16. http://www.combatleadership.com/Heroes_Results.asp?MedalID=3148 (accessed January 23, 2011).

17. Jeffrey B. Floyd, "Colonel James M. Gillespie and the Flight of the Robert E. Lee: The First United States Air Force Distinguished Flying Cross," *Journal of the Orders and Medals Society of America* (January-February 2011): 35–41, 35.

18. Ibid, 40–41.

19. *General Orders No. 25*, Department of the Air Force, June 18, 1948, para. II

20. Charles E. Yeager, with Leo Janus, *Yeager: An Autobiography* (New York: Bantam), 1995; http://www.chuckyeager.com (accessed January 23, 2011).

21. *General Orders No. 6464*, U.S. Army Vietnam, November 23, 1966.

22. *General Orders No. 451*, II Field Force, February 17, 1969.

23. *General Orders No. 1119*, II Field Force, May 7, 1969.

24. Frederic L. Borch and Jeffrey B. Floyd, *The Air Force Cross: A History of Extraordinary Heroism* (Tempe, AZ: Borch and Westlake, 2004), 44.

25. http://www.veterantributes.org/TributeDetail.asp?ID=421 (accessed January 23, 2011).

26. http://www.combatleadership.com/Heroes_Results.asp?MedalID=3159 (accessed January 22, 2011).

27. http://www.combatleadership.com/Heroes_Results.asp?MedalID=405 (accessed January 22, 2011).

28. http://www.combatleadership.com/Heroes_Results.asp?MedalID=1411 (accessed January 22, 2011).

29. Jill Laster, "Pilot Honored for Organizing Afghanistan Airstrikes," *Air Force Times*, February 14, 2011, 19.

30. http://militarytimes.com/blogs/afteraction/2010/04/23/former-air-force-goalie-earns-distinguished-flying-cross/ (accessed February 13, 2011).

31. Memorandum, Col. Russell P. Reeder to the Commanding General, Army Ground Forces, subj.: Medal for Ground Troops, June 28, 1943, reprinted in Fred L. Borch, *The Bronze Star Medal* Orders and Medals Society Monograph (Bennington, VT: Merriam, 1994), 8–9.

32. Russell P. Reeder, *Born at Reveille* (New York: Duell, Sloan and Pearce, 1966), 218.

33. Borch, *Bronze Star*, 14.

34. Letter from Gen. George C. Marshall to Thomas W. Martin, House of Representatives, April 10, 1944.

35. H. Lobdell, "Bronze Star," *Soldiers Magazine* (October 1986), 20.

36. Ibid.

37. Borch, *Bronze Star*, 64.

38. Army Regulation 600–8–22, *Military Awards*, December 11, 2006, para. 3–14d(2) and (3).

39. Army Regulation 660–45, *Decorations*, Change 11, May 19, 1947, para. 16e.

40. Fred L. Borch, "Purple Hearts for Meritorious Achievement or Service: Army and Air Forces Awards in World War II," *Journal of the Orders and Medals Society of America* (November-December 2000), 3–15.

41. Eric R. Caubarreaux, *The Decorations and Awards of Audie L. Murphy and Alvin C. York*, 2d ed. (privately published, 2010).

42. *General Orders No. 84*, Headquarters, 3rd Infantry Division, March 4, 1945.

43. Letter Orders, Headquarters, Dept. of the Army, Office of the Adjutant General, December 11, 1954.

44. *General Orders No. 7*, Department of the Army (Washington, D.C.), January 23, 1948, para. V.

45. *General Orders No. 50*, 101st Airborne Division, May 8, 1945, para. I

46. *General Orders No. 107*, Department of the Army, December 14, 1971, para. IX.

47. Borch, *Bronze Star*, 43

48. Hal G. Moore and Joseph L. Galloway, *We Were Soldiers Once ... and Young* (New York: Random House, 1992).

49. http://www.weweresoldiers.net/joes-story.htm (accessed January 22, 2011).

50. Galloway's Bronze Star Medal with "V" was approved by Robert M. Walker, acting secretary of the Army. BG Earl M. Simms, the adjutant general, signed Galloway's award document on January 8, 1998.

51. *General Orders No. 38*, Department of the Army, September 18, 1967, para. VIII.

52. *General Orders No. 1819*, II Field Force, December 4, 1968.

53. *General Orders No. 1820*, II Field Force, December 4, 1968.

54. *General Orders No. 3429*, II Field Force, October 28, 1969.

55. *Permanent Order 195–25*, Department of the Army, December 23, 1993.

56. *Permanent Orders 148–1*, Department of the Army, September 19, 1994.

57. Mark Bowden, *Black Hawk Down: A Story of Modern War* (New York: Atlantic Monthly, 1999).

58. AR 600–8–22, paragraph 3–16.

59. Ibid., paragraph 13–6f.

60. Air Force Instruction 36–2803, Table 2.1, paragraph 16.

61. Ibid., Attachment 3, para. 3A8.

62. Walker Hancock, *A Sculptor's Fortunes* (Gloucester, MA: Cape Ann Historical Association, 1997); Hubert R. Herring, "Walker Hancock, 97, Sculptor On War and Religious Themes," *New York Times*, January 2, 1999, A22.

63. https://www.hrc.army.mil/site/active/tagd/awards/STATS/Historical_Stats.htm#ERA1900 (accessed January 22, 2011).

64. http://www.arlingtoncemetery.net/wjmaddox.htm (accessed January 29, 2011). Maddox also was awarded four Silver Stars, five Legions of Merit and eight Distinguished Flying Crosses.

65. Philip J. Conran, air medal (first oak leaf cluster), approved by Gen. George S. Brown, commander, Seventh Air Force, May 27, 1969.

66. *General Orders No. 598*, Headquarters, 1st Aviation Brigade (Vietnam), January 27, 1973.

67. Leo Shane III, "The Pedals Were Gone, and So Were My Legs," *Stars and Stripes*, June 14, 2005, 1; Ed O'Keefe, "She Is the Face of the New Generation," *Washington Post*, November 11, 2009, A5.

Chapter 4

1. Memorandum, Colonel James L. Cannell to Brigadier General Leo E. Benade, deputy secretary of defense, March 17, 1970.

2. Memorandum for Record, Institute of Heraldry, subj.: "Decorations for Distinguished Service (if Higher Precedence Than Current Distinguished Service Medals), to be Awarded by Secretary of Defense," March 29, 1970.

3. Memorandum for Record, Colonel Thomas P. Harrison, subj.: "Defense Distinguished Service Medal," June 22, 1970.

4. For more on Powell, see Colin L. Powell with Joseph Persico, *My American Journey*, (New York: Random House, 1995).

5. Title 10, United States Code, Section 3743.

6. Army Regulation 600–8–22, *Military Awards*, December 11, 2006, para. 3–9; http://www.tioh.hqda.pentagon.mil/Awards/distinguished_srv_medal.aspx (accessed February 13, 2011).

7. While the Certificate of Merit medal was technically still available, it had already fallen into disuse. See Appendix B.

8. War Department, *Annual Reports, 1918*, The Adjutant General (Washington, DC: Government Printing Office, 1919), 200.

9. *Medals of Honor, Distinguished Service Crosses, and Distinguished Services Medals,* Chapter 43, 65th Congress, July 9, 1918.

10. Sherwin T. McDowell, "Allen W. Gullion, Major General, U.S.A. Retired," *The Judge Advocate Journal* (March 1945), 43.

11. *General Orders No. 72*, War Department, 1920; *Army Decorations*, 712.

12. *General Orders No. 9*, War Department, 1923.

13. Ltr, Maj. Gen. C. R. Reynolds to 1st Lt. Carrie L. Howard, Army Nurse Corps, retired, December 21, 1935; Robert F. Dorr and Fred L. Borch, "Nurse Corps Expanded Rapidly During World War I," *Army Times*, November 7, 2005.

14. *General Orders No. 10*, War Department, February 24, 1942, Section IX.

15. For more on Lockard, see Gor-

don S. Prange, *At Dawn We Slept: The Untold Story of Pearl Harbor* (New York: McGraw-Hill, 1981), 499–501.

16. *General Orders No. 59*, War Department, November 4, 1942, Section VIII.

17. Duane P. Schultz, *Hero of Bataan: The Story of General Jonathan Wainwright* (New York: St. Martin's, 1981), 151–152.

18. *General Orders No. 88*, War Department, October 17, 1945.

19. *General Orders No. 22*, Department of the Army, 1951.

20. Program, Review in Honor of General John W. Vessey, Jr., vice chief of staff, U.S. Army, Fort Myer, Va., June 17, 1982.

21. Executive Order No. 11085, *The Presidential Medal of Freedom*, February 22, 1963, Sec. 2(a).

22. Title 10, United States Code, Section 8743.

23. Air Force Personnel Center, Fact Sheet: Air Force Distinguished Service Medal, www.afpc.randolph.af.mil/library/factsheets/factsheet_print.asp?fsID=7730&page=1 (accessed March 13, 2011).

24. *Special Order GB-1156*, Department of the Air Force, October 29, 1974.

25. Letter, Deputy Secretary of Defense William Clements to William K. Brehm, assistant secretary of defense (manpower and reserve affairs), September 23, 1975.

26. Memorandum for Record, Colonel Paul E. Raabe, Office of Assistant Secretary of Defense (Manpower and Reserve Affairs, Military Personnel Policy), subj.: Meeting with Admiral Carr, 1530–1600 hours, 6 Oct 75, on New Defense Medal," October 6, 1975.

27. Memorandum from Deputy Secretary of Defense William Clements, Subj.: "Defense Superior Service Medal," March 12, 1976.

28. Robert F. Dorr, "Stovall Flew Perilous Combat Rescue Missions in Vietnam," *Air Force Times*, March 1, 2004, 18.

29. Borch and Floyd, *Air Force Cross*, 100–103.

30. http://www.pownetwork.org/bios/r/r090.htm (accessed May 23, 2011).

31. http://www.veterantributes.org/TributeDetail.asp?ID=1362 (accessed May 23, 2011).

32. Joint Staff Permanent Order J-1SO-0218–02, Washington, D.C., July 1, 2001.

33. Joint Staff Permanent Order J-1SO-0116–06, Washington, D.C., May 24, 2006.

34. Joint Staff Permanent Orders J-1SO-0227–07, Washington, D.C., 28 December 2007.

35. Borch and McDowell, *Sea Service Medals*, 77.

36. Ibid.

37. Ibid.

38. Letter from Gilmore D. Clarke, chairman of the Commission of Fine Arts, to Maj. John K. Cunningham, Personnel Division G-1, War Department General Staff, subj.: "The Legion of Merit Medal," August 3, 1942.

39. Fred L. Borch and Charles P. McDowell, "A History of the Legion of Merit," *Journal of the Orders and Medals Society of America* 59 (March-April 2008): 5–29, 21.

40. *General Orders No. 30*, Headquarters, Army Ground Forces, Washington, D.C., May 22, 1946, para. 2.

41. Ely J. Kahn, *The Army Life* (New York: Simon and Schuster, 1942); *G.I. Jungle: An American Soldier in Australia and New Zealand* (New York: Simon and Schuster, 1943); *Fighting Divisions: Histories of Each U.S. Combat Division in World War II* (Washington, D.C.: Infantry Journal, 1945).

42. The award Culin's Legion of Merit was announced in General Orders No. 89, Headquarters, U.S. Army European Theater of Operations, 1944.

43. Biography, Chief Master Sergeant of the Air Force Paul Wesley Airey, http://www.af.mil/information/bios/bio_print.asp?bioID=4488&page=1 (accessed July 2, 2011).

44. Sam LeGrone, "AF Legend Airey Dies at 85," *Air Force Times*, March 23, 2009, 22.

45. *General Orders No. 766*, Headquarters, U.S. Army, Europe and Seventh Army, November 20, 1969, section II.

46. John K. Singlaub, *Hazardous Duty: An American Soldier in the Twentieth Century* (New York: Summit, 1991).

47. Memorandum, Major General Adrian St. John for Secretary of Defense (JCSM-298–77), subj.: "Establishment of a Defense Meritorious Service Award," August 23, 1976.

48. Memorandum for Director, Institute of Heraldry, subj.: "Establishing the Defense Meritorious Service Medal," February 8, 1977.

49. Letter from Gen. John J. Pershing to the chief of staff, through the adjutant general, December 15, 1918.

50. Cable No. 2343-R from Secretary of War Newton D. Baker to General Pershing, December 24, 1918. The certificate suggested by Baker was in fact created and was known as the "Meritorious Service Citation Certificate." When the Purple Heart medal was created in 1932, holders of the Meritorious Service Citation Certificate could petition the War Department for

the award of a Purple Heart for meritorious service (hereinafter cited as Cable 2343-R).

51. Memorandum from the deputy chief of staff, American Expeditionary Force (AEF), to the assistant chiefs of staff (G-1, G-2, and G-3), Subj.: "Medal for Meritorious Service," February 11, 1919.

52. See, e.g., Memorandum from Brig. Gen. Avery D. Andrews, assistant chief of staff, G-1, AEF, to the deputy chief of staff, dated February 21, 1919. Andrews stated that "the attached design of a 'Medal for Meritorious Service' is submitted for consideration. The ribbon as shown on the design was about three-quarters of an inch longer than was desired."

53. Joint Board to Study Matters of Decorations and Medals, *War Department Proposals on Awards and Decorations*, May 10, 1946, National Archives Record Group 330, Entry 125, Box 1509.

54. Memorandum from Vice Admiral (Ret.) William E. Gentner, subj.: "Establishing Meritorious Service Medal," February 22, 1968.

55. Memorandum for Record, Committee on Awards, Department of Defense Manpower and Reserve Affairs, November 8, 1968.

56. *Special Orders No. 177*, Headquarters, Pacific Air Forces, Hickam Air Force Base, Hawaii, July 20, 1971.

57. For a comprehensive examination of the Purple Heart, see Fred L. Borch and F. C. Brown, *The Purple Heart: A History of America's Oldest Military Decoration* (Tempe, AZ: Borch and Westlake, 1994) hereinafter cited as Borch and Brown, *Purple Heart*; see also, Fred L. Borch, *For Military Merit: Recipients of the Purple Heart* (Annapolis, MD: Naval Institute Press, 2010).

58. Borch, *For Military Merit*, 2.

59. For more detail on this Purple Heart to Brown, see Borch, *For Military Merit*, 18.

60. For more detail on this Purple Heart to Bissell, see ibid., 17.

61. Order of Merit, Adjutant General file 220.52, November 27, 1918.

62. Cable 2343-R.

63. See Memorandum from Brig. Gen. Campbell King, assistant chief of staff, G-1, for the chief of staff, subj.: The Order of Military Merit," June 12, 1925, National Archives Record Group 407, Central Decimal Files 1917–1925, 201.519–210.52, Box 362.

64. Col. Robert E. Wyllie was the former chief of the Heraldic Branch of the Quartermaster Corps and the author of *Orders, Decorations and Insignia, Military and Civil* (New York: G.P. Putnam's Sons, 1921).

65. Letter from Col. Wyllie to Capt. G.M. Chandler, April 21, 1925.

66. Letter from John C. Fitzpatrick, assistant chief, Manuscript Division, Library of Congress, to Captain Chandler, April 21, 1925.

67. Letter from Carleton S. Gifford to President Calvin Coolidge, November 18, 1925.

68. Records of the commission's participation in the development of the Purple Heart may be found in National Archives Record Group 66, Commission of Fine Arts, Entry 4, files pertaining to the Badge of Military Merit and the Purple Heart. Additional information may be found in Record Group 407, Adjutant General's Office, Decimal File 210.52, 1917–1939.

69. *War Department Circular No. 6*, February 22, 1932, paragraph 11 1/2.

70. See Change 4, Army Regulation 600–45, September 4, 1942, for details on restricting the award of the Purple Heart to those who are wounded in action by an enemy of the United States. However, a few of the Purple Hearts awarded for meritorious service between December 7, 1941 and September 1942 were allowed to stand.

71. Letter, Secretary of the Army Elvis J. Stahr, Jr., to D. Bell, director, Bureau of the Budget, subj.: "Executive Order 11016," April 24, 1962.

72. Borch and Brown, *Purple Heart*, 131–135.

73. For a fuller list of Purple Hearts awarded for wounds received in "international terrorist attacks," see Borch and Brown, *Purple Heart*, 211–218; see also, Borch, *For Military Merit*, 75–81.

74. For a fuller list of Purple Hearts awarded for wounds received in "peacekeeping operations," see Borch and Brown, *Purple Heart*, 200–203; see also, Borch, *For Military Merit*, 77–80.

75. Aubrey S. Newman, "Purple Heart Should Rank Higher Up," *Army* (February 1984), 69.

76. Title 10, United States Code, sec. 1127, *Precedence of the Award of the Purple Heart*.

77. Public Law 103–160, U.S. Code 57, Title 10, sec. 1129 (1993).

78. Public Law 104–106, U.S. Code 57, Title 10, sec. 1130 (1996).

79. Public Law 105–85, U.S. Code 57, Title 10, sec. 1131 (1997). The Defense of Freedom medal (created on September 27, 2001) is now the civilian equivalent of the Purple Heart; it is awarded to both Department of Defense (DoD) civilian employees and non–DoD employees (such as contractors) who are injured or killed in the line of duty. "Defense of Freedom Medal Unveiled," U.S. Department of Defense News Release No. 463–01, September 27, 2001, http://www.de-fense.gov/releases/release.aspx?releaseid=3068 (accessed June 26, 2011).

80. Army Human Resources Command, Fort Knox, Kentucky, MilPer Message 11–125, *Awarding the Purple Heart*, April 29, 2011; Jim Tice, "Purple Hearts OK'd for concussions," *Army Times*, May 16, 2011, 17.

81. William H. McMichael, "Pentagon: No Purple Hearts for PTSD," *Army Times*, January 19, 2009, 21; "PTSD and the Purple Heart," *New York Times*, January 12, 2009, A3.

82. *General Orders No. 25*, Headquarters, XVIII Airborne Corps, April 2, 1945.

83. Obituary, "Mathew Bunker Ridgway," *Assembly*, March 1994, 148; Matthew B. Ridgway, *Soldier: The Memoirs of Matthew B. Ridgway* (New York: Harper and Brothers, 1956).

84. Stuart I. Rochester and Frederick T. Kiley, *Honor Bound: American Prisoners of War in Southeast Asia (1961–1973)* (Annapolis, MD: Naval Institute, 1999), 311.

85. Borch, *For Military Merit*, 156–158.

86. Markeshia Ricks, "We Were '100 Percent Committed' to Rescue," *Army Times*, May 23, 2011, 24.

87. Air Force Instruction 36–2803, June 15, 2001, Table 2.1., paragraph 17.

88. http://www.afpc.af.mil/library/factsheets/factsheet.asp?id=7770 (accessed July 2, 2011).

89. Charles P. McDowell, "Aerial Achievement Medal," n.d., 2.

90. Ibid., 3.

91. Borch and Floyd, *Air Force Cross*, 117–18.

92. http://www.veterantributes.org/TributeDetail.asp?ID=1089 (accessed July 2, 2011).

93. *General Order No. D7–827–01*, National Security Agency/Central Security Service, Fort George Meade, Maryland, August 13, 2001.

94. Department of the Army, Army Regulation 600–8–22, *Military Awards*, December 11, 2006, para. 3–17.

95. War Department, Circular 377, *Army Commendation Ribbon*, December 18, 1945.

96. Ibid., para. 5b.

97. War Department, Memorandum No. 600–45–2, *Policy on Decorations for Peacetime Services*, October 7, 1947.

98. Department of the Army, *Army Regulation 600–45, Decorations*, Change 13, November 4, 1947.

99. Department of the Army, Army Regulation 600–45, *Decorations*, Change 14, July 6, 1948.

100. Fred L. Borch, "For Military Merit: A History of the Army Commendation Medal," *Journal of the Orders and Medals Society of America* 46 (June 1995): 13.

101. *General Orders No. 104*, Headquarters, Far East Command, Section II, October 19, 1953.

102. *General Orders No. 289*, Headquarters, Eighth U.S. Army Korea, Section III, June 5, 1952.

103. *General Orders No. 61*, Headquarters, XXI U.S. Army Corps, Indiantown Gap, Annville, Pennsylvania, Section II, August 31, 1962.

104. Fred L. Borch and Robert F. Dorr, "Cavalry Commander Lee Lewane Inspired His Men with His Daring Actions in the Midst of Fierce Combat," *Vietnam* (October 2008): 21.

105. Ibid., 22.

106. *General Orders No. 26*, Department of the Army, para. XIII, June 18, 1968.

107. Fred L. Borch, "The History of an Appurtenance: The "V for Valor" and "Combat Distinguishing Device," *Journal of the Orders and Medals Society of America* 58 (January-February 2007): 9.

108. http://ntm-a.com/wordpress2/?p=935 (accessed July 2, 2011).

109. Department of the Air Force, Air Force Instruction 36–2803, *Air Force Awards and Decorations Program*, June 15, 2001, Table 2–1, paragraphs 18 and 19.

110. Ibid., Table 2.1, paragraph 22.

111. http://www.lackland.af.mil/shared/media/document/AFD-070324–002.pdf (accessed July 2, 2011).

112. Army Regulation 600–45, *Decorations*, Change 14, paragraph 17.1, July 6, 1948.

113. http://www.lackland.af.mil/shared/media/document/AFD-070324–002.pdf (accessed July 2, 2011).

114. Air Force Instruction 36–2803, *Air Force Awards and Decorations Program*, Table 2.1, paragraph 22.

115. Memorandum from the assistant secretary of defense, manpower, reserve affairs and logistics (M&RAL) to the assistant secretaries of the Army for M&RAL, Navy for M&RAL, and Air Force for M&RAL, Subj.: "Proposal to Develop Defense Achievement Medal," August 30, 1982.

116. CINCPAC Message, date time group 1019247 Mar 83, to OASD MRA&L, subj.: "Military Departments Achievement Medals."

117. Memorandum from Lt. Gen. R. Dean Tice, deputy assistant secretary of defense for M&RAL, military personnel and force management, to the assistant secretaries of the Army for M&RAL, Navy M&RAL, Air Force M&RAL, and to the director of the Joint Staff, subj.: "Development of a Joint Service Achievement Medal," May 9, 1983.

118. Department of Defense Direc-

tive Number 1318.28, Subj.: "Joint Service Achievement Medal," March 29, 1984.

119. Office of the Secretary of Defense, Military Personnel Awards Memorandum 94–199, Joint Service Achievement Medal, August 29, 1994.

120. Harrison Lobdell, "Army Achievement Medal," *Soldiers* (May 1986), 17.

121. McDowell, *Military and Naval Decorations*, 218.

122. Lobdell, "Army Achievement Medal," 17.

123. Fred L. Borch, "For Military Achievement: A History of the Army Achievement Medal," *Journal of the Orders and Medals Society of America* 58 (November-December 2007): 3–10.

124. *Permanent Orders No. 98–245–025*, Headquarters, 6–6 Cavalry, October 5, 1998.

125. http://www.veterantributes. org/TributeDetail.asp?ID=796 (July 2, 2011).

126. Air Force Instruction 36–2803, Table 2.1., paragraph 20.

127. McDowell, *Military and Naval Decorations*, 214.

128. Ibid., 211.

129. Ibid., 212.

130. Ibid., 214.

131. http://militarytimes.com-/citations-medals-awards/recipient. php?recipientid=50634 (accessed July 2, 2011).

132. Michael Hoffman, "Trapped in Sudan: 11 Airmen in an HC-130 'Taxi' Run. 150 Sudanese Soldiers with Weapons. It added Up to Trouble," *Air Force Times*, October 28, 2009, 1.

Appendix B

1. *An Act making Provision for an additional Number of general Officers, and for other purposes*, March 3, 1847, sec. 17, U.S. Statutes, 29th Congress, Sess. II, Ch. 61.

2. *General Orders No. 4*, War Department, January 24, 1849, para. 3.

3. *Revised Statutes*, June 22, 1874, sec. 1216, 1285.

4. *General Orders No. 110*, War Department, December 6, 1877; War Department, *Regulations for the Army of the United States, 1889*, Article XXVI, paras. 176, 177.

5. *An act to amend sections 1216 and 1285 of the Revised Statutes relative to certificates of merit to enlisted men of the Army*, March 9, 1891, Chap. 22, U.S. Statutes, 51st Congress, Sess. II; War Dept., *Regulations for the Army of the United States, 1908*, para. 181.

6. Adjutant General, War Department, Circular No. 2, *Medals of Honor and Certificates of Merit*, February 11, 1892, para. 10; Albert F. Gleim, *The Certificate of Merit: U.S. Army Distinguished Service Awards 1847–1918* (Arlington, VA: privately published, 1979), 2.

7. Stephen A. Carney, *Guns Along the Rio Grande: Palo Alto and Resaca de la Palma*. U.S. Army Campaigns of the Mexican War (Washington, D.C.: Government Printing Office, 2005), 15–22.

8. Gleim, *Certificate of Merit*, 5.

9. *General Orders No. 2*, War Department, January 8, 1878.

10. Gleim, *Certificate of Merit*, 2.

11. Ibid.

12. Adjutant General, War Department, *Circular No. 2*, February 11, 1892, para. X.

13. *American Decorations*, 843.

14. Gleim, *Certificate of Merit*, 73–75 (complete list of recipients).

15. Ibid., 3.

16. An Act Making appropriations for the support of the Army for the fiscal year ending June 30, 1919, para. 1.

17. Gleim, *Certificate of Merit*, 4.

18. U.S. Army Adjutant General, *American Decorations 1862–1926*. (Washington, D.C.: Government Printing Office, 1927), 835.

19. Gleim, *Certificate of Merit*, 44.

20. Ibid., 28.

21. Ibid.

22. Ibid.

23. *American Decorations*, 836.

24. Ibid., 839.

Appendix C

1. *General Orders No. 6*, War Department, January 12, 1918, para. 5.

2. Albert F. Gleim, "Oak Leaves and Oak Leaf Clusters," *New Medal Letter 18*, November 15, 1984.

3. Todd Wheatley, "The Oak Leaf Cluster," *The Medal Collector* 43 (July 1992), 6, 17.

4. Wheatley, 8.

5. Army Regulation 600–45, Change 2, August 22, 1933, para. 26.

6. For example, the War Department issued a Purple Heart with large oak leaf cluster to Joseph Sink on March 25, 1933. Fred Borch, *For Military Merit*, 45.

7. AR 600–45, *Decorations*, Change 11, May 19, 1947, para. 18(a).

8. Army Regulation 600–8–22, *Military Awards*, December 11, 2006, para. 6–3; Air Force Instruction 36–2803, *Air Force Awards and Decorations Program*, June 15, 2001, para. A.3.3. Note finally that a third —and even smaller-size oak leaf cluster —-is used by soldiers and airmen on miniature medals.

Appendix D

1. Fred L. Borch, "The History of an Appurtance: The "V for Valor" and "Combat Distinguishing Device," *Journal of the Orders and Medals Society of America* (January-February 2007): 2.

2. Note that the Air Force does permit the Air Medal to be awarded for individual combat heroism, yet does not allow the "V" to be worn on the decoration.

3. AFI 36–2803, Attachment 3, para. A3.8

Bibliography

Official Documents

D'Acosta, Uriel P. "The Necessity for a Separate United States Air Force Decorations System," *Staff Study* (unpublished). Maxwell Air Force Base, AL: Air Command and Staff College, 1948.

U.S. Air Force Instruction 36–2803, *Air Force Awards and Decorations Program*. Washington, DC: August 15, 1994.

_____. *Air Force Awards and Decorations Program*. Washington, DC: June 15, 2001.

U.S. Air Force Regulation No. 30–14, *Decorations*. Washington, DC: August 22, 1950.

U.S. Air Force Regulation 900–48, *Awards, Ceremonies, and Honors: Individual and Unit Awards and Decorations*. Washington, DC: March 15, 1989.

U.S. Army Air Forces Regulation No. 35–7, *Decorations and Awards*. Washington, DC: April 10, 1946.

_____. July 17, 1946.

U.S. Army Regulation 600–8–22, *Military Awards*. Washington, DC: February 25, 1995.

_____. December 11, 2006.

U.S. Army Regulation 600–45, *Award and Supply of Decorations for Individuals*. Washington, DC:

_____. August 8, 1932.

_____. *Decorations*. Washington, DC: September 22, 1943.

_____. *Decorations*. Washington, DC: June 27, 1950.

U.S. Army Regulation 672–5–1, *Decorations, Certificates and Letters for Service: Decorations and Awards*. Washington, DC: July 20, 1956.

_____. *Awards: Decorations, Awards and Honors*. Washington, DC: May 3, 1961.

_____. *Military Awards*. Washington, DC: June 3, 1974.

_____. *Military Awards*. Washington, DC: April 12, 1984.

_____. *Military Awards*. Washington, DC: October 1, 1990.

U.S. Congress. Senate. Committee on Veterans Affairs. *Vietnam Era Medal of Honor Recipients, 1964–1972*. 93rd Cong., 1st sess. Washington, DC: Government Printing Office, 1973.

_____. *State Summary of War Casualties*. Washington, DC: Government Printing Office, 1946.

U.S. Department of Defense. Manual 1348.33-M, *Manual of Military Decorations and Awards*, September 1996.

U.S. Forces, European Theater. *Report of the General Board on Awards and Decorations in a Theater of Operations*, G-1 Section, Study No. 10, 1946.

Vietnam Veterans Memorial Fund. *Vietnam Veterans Memorial Directory of Names*. Washington, DC: Vietnam Veterans Memorial Fund, 1983.

War Department, Office of The Adjutant General. *American Decorations 1862–1926*. Washington, DC: Government Printing Office, 1927.

Books

Apgar, George H. *Awards of the U.S. Army Distinguished Service Medal 1942 to 1969*. Fort Myer, VA: Privately published, 1995.

Berger, Carl, ed. *The United States Air Force in Southeast Asia, 1961–1973: An Illustrated Account*. Washington, DC: Office of Air Force History, 1984.

Borch, Frederic L. *The Bronze Star*. Orders and Medals Society of America Monograph. Bennington, VT: Merriam, 1994.

_____. *For Military Merit: Recipients of the Purple Heart*. Annapolis, MD: Naval Institute, 2010.

_____, and Charles P. McDowell. *Sea Service Medals*. Annapolis, MD: Naval Institute, 2009.

_____, and F. C. Brown. *The Purple Heart: A History of America's Oldest Military Decoration*. Tempe, AZ: Borch and Westlake, 1994.

_____, and Jeffrey B. Floyd. *The Air Force Cross: A History of Extraordinary Heroism*. Tempe, AZ: Borch and Westlake, 2004.

_____, and William R. Westlake. *The Silver Star: A History of America's Third Highest Award for Combat Valor*. Tempe, AZ: Borch and Westlake, 2001.

Bowdon, Mark. *Black Hawk Down: A Study of Modern War*. New York: Atlantic Monthly, 1999.

Coyne, James P. *Airpower in the Gulf*. Arlington, VA: Air Force Association, 1992.

Day, George E. *Return with Honor*. Mesa, AZ: Champlin Museum, 1989.

Dramesi, John A. *Code of Honor*. New York: Norton, 1975.

Gleim, Albert F. *Army Silver Star Awards for World War II*, Parts I — III. Fort Myer, VA: Privately published, 1991.

_____. *U.S. Army and U.S. Air Force Silver Star Awards for the Korean War*. Fort Myer, VA: Privately published, 1996.

_____. *U.S. Army Awards of the Legion of Merit for World War II*. Fort Myer, VA: Privately published, 1993.

Gordon, Dennis. *Quartered in Hell: The Story of the American North Russia Expeditionary Force 1918–1919*. Missoula, MT: Doughboy Historical Society, 1982.

Grosvenor, Gilbert. *Insignia and Decorations of the U.S. Armed Forces*. Washington, DC: National Geographic Society, 1943

_____. *Insignia and Decorations of the U.S. Armed Forces*. Washington, DC: National Geographic Society, December 1, 1944.

Hirsh, Michael. *None Braver: U.S. Air Force Pararescuemen in the War on Terrorism*. New York: New American Library, 2003.

Lowry, Timothy S. *And Brave Men Too*. New York: Crown, 1985.

McDowell, Charles P., ed. *Index to Recipients of the Distinguished Service Cross*. Madison, VA: Foxfall, 2005.

_____. *Military and Naval Decorations of the United States*. Springfield, VA: Quest, 1984.

Moore, Robin. *The Green Berets*. New York: Crown Publishers, 1965.

National Jewish Welfare Board. *American Jews in World War II*. Vols. I and II. New York: National Jewish Welfare Board, 1947.

Murphy, Edward F. *Heroes of World War II*. Novato, CA: Presidio Press, 1990, 365 pp., illus.

_____. *Korean War Heroes*. Novato, CA: Presidio Press, 1992, 304 pp.

_____. *Vietnam Medal of Honor Heroes*. New York: Ballantine Books, 1987.

Nier, Thomas J., ed. *The Gleim Medal Letters 1971–1997*. San Ramon, CA: Order and Medals Society of America, 1998.

Patrick, James W. *Wood and Canvas Heroes: Awards of the Distinguished Flying Cross and Other Airmen Stories, 1927 to December 1941*. Fullerton, CA: James W. Patrick, 2002.

Risner, Robinson. *The Passing of the Night: My Seven Years as a Prisoner of War of the North Vietnamese*. New York: Random House, 1973.

Rochester, Stuart I., and Frederick Kiley. *Honor Bound*. Annapolis, MD: Naval Institute, 1999.

Ross, Donald K., and Helen Ross. *0755: The Heroes of Pearl Harbor*. Port Orchard, WA: Rokalu, 1988.

Sapienza, Madeline, ed. *Peacetime Awards of the Purple Heart in the Post-Vietnam Period*. Washington, DC: Staff Support Branch, U.S. Army Center of Military History, 1987.

Stevens, Paul D., ed. *The Medal of Honor: The Names, the Deeds*, rev. ed. Forest Ranch, CA: Sharps and Dunnigan, 1990.

Strandberg, John E., and Roger James Bender. *The Call of Duty: Military Awards and Decorations of the United States of America*. San Jose, CA: R. J. Bender, 2004.

Tillman, Barrett. *Above and Beyond: The Aviation Medals of Honor*. Washington: Smithsonian Institution, 2002.

Wiegand, Brandon T. *Index of Known Office of Strategic Services Decoration Recipients in World War II*. Brackenridge, PA: D-Day Militaria, 2002.

Williams, Dion. *Army and Navy Uniform and Insignia*. New York: Stoke, 1918.

Wylie, Robert E. *Orders, Decorations and Insignia, Military and Civil*. New York: G.P. Putnams's Sons, 1921.

Articles

Borch, Frederic L. "For Military Merit: A History of the Army Commendation Medal." *Journal of the Orders and Medals Society of America* 46 (June 1995): 5–22.

_____. "The History of an Appurtenance: The 'V' for Valor." *Journal of the Orders and Medal Society of America* 52 (July–August 2001): 3–20.

_____. "A History of the Air Force Cross." *Journal of the Orders and Medals Society of America* 53 (March–April 2004): 2–14.

_____., and Charles P. McDowell. "For Exceptionally Meritorious Conduct in the Performance of Outstanding Services and Achievements: A History of the Legion of Merit." *Journal of the Orders and Medals Society of America* 59 (March–April 2008): 3–25.

DuBois, Arthur E. "Heraldry, Flag and Insignia Work of the Office of The Quartermaster General. *The Quartermaster Review* (May-June 1928): 1–7.

_____. "The Heraldry of Heroism." *National Geographic Magazine* (October 1943): 409–444.

Fegan, J. C. "The Purple Heart Badge and the Order of Military Merit." *Marine Corps Gazette* 2 (August 1932): 39–44.

Floyd, Jeffrey B. "The Development of the First Unique United States Air Force Decorations." *The Medal Collector* 34 (March 1983): 2–9.

McDowell, Charles P. "The Meritorious Service Medal." *The Medal Collector* 20 (July 1969): 14–16.

_____, ed. *Planchet Press Newsletter*. Madison, VA: Planchet Research Group. Published quarterly since 1999, the *Planchet Press Newsletter* contains a wealth of material on U.S. military and civilian decorations and medals

Wheatley, Todd. "The Oak Leaf Cluster." *Journal of the Orders and Medals Society of America* 43 (July 1992): 5–18.

Wylie, Robert E. "The Romance of Heraldry." *National Geographic Magazine* 34 (December 1919): 463–526.

Index

Numbers in **_bold italics_** indicate pages with photographs.

Abrams, Creighton W. 57
Adamouski, James F. 166
Adams, Herbert 177
Adams, Ralph E. 134–135
Aerial Achievement Medal 147–149; citations 148–149; criteria 147; description and symbolism 147; designer 147; devices for additional awards 147; establishment 147; first recipient 148; historical background 147–148; order of precedence 147, 171; recipients 148–149
aerial heroism 28–29, 36–37, 39, 45–53, 58, 62–63, 65–66, 85–90, 99, 146
Afghanistan (Operation *Enduring Freedom*), medals for 41–42, 52–53, 90, 146
Air Force Achievement Medal 166–170; citations 168–170; criteria 166–167; description and symbolism 167; designer 167; devices for additional awards 167; establishment 166; first recipient 168; historical background 167–168; order of precedence 167, 171; recipients 168–170
Air Force Commendation Medal 158–161; citations 160–161; criteria 158; description and symbolism 158–159; designer 158; devices for additional awards 158; establishment 158; historical background 159–160; order of precedence 158, 171; recipients 160–161; relationship to Army Commendation Medal 159–160
Air Force Cross 42–53; citations 45–53; criteria 42; description and symbolism 43–45; designer 42–44; devices for additional awards 42; establishment 42; historical background 43–45; number awarded, order of precedence 42, 171; recipients 120, 149; relationship to Airman's Medal 42; relationship to Distinguished Service Cross 42–43
Air Force Distinguished Service Medal 112–118; citations 114–118; criteria 112; description and sym-

bolism 113; designer 113; devices for additional awards 113; establishment 112; first recipient 114–115; historical background 113–114; order of precedence 112–113, 171; recipients 114–118
Air Force Instruction 36–2803, *Air Force Awards and Decorations Program* 23
Air Force Medal of Honor 22–30; citations 27–30; criteria 22; description and symbolism 23–24; designer 23; establishment 22; first recipient 27; historical background 24–26; nomination and award process 22–23; number awarded 27; order of precedence 171; recipients 27–30; relationship to Army Medal of Honor 22, 24–25
Air Medal 96–99; citations 99; criteria 96; description and symbolism 97–98; designer 97; devices for additional awards 97; establishment 96; historical background 98–99; numbers awarded 99; order of precedence 97, 171; recipients 99; relationship to Aerial Achievement Medal 147–148; relationship to Bronze Star Medal 97; relationship to Distinguished Flying Cross 96
Airey, Paul W. **_128_**–129
Airman's Medal 74–79; citations 77–79; criteria 74; description and symbolism 75; designer 74–75; devices for additional awards 74; establishment 74; historical background 76–77; order of precedence 74, 171; recipients 77–79; relationship to Air Force Distinguished Service Medal 76–77; relationship to Soldier's Medal 74–75
Aldridge, Edward C., Jr. 147–148
Aldrin, Edwin E. (Buzz), Jr. 114–115
Allied decorations 32
Alston, Frank H., Jr. 113–114
Anderson, Rudolf 44–45
Andrews, William F. 149
Andrews raid 13

Army Achievement Medal 164–166; citations 166; criteria 164; description and symbolism 164; designer 167; devices for additional awards 164; establishment 164; historical background 164–166; order of precedence 164, 171; recipients 166; relationship to Army Commendation Medal 165
Army Commendation Medal 152–158; citations 155–158; criteria 153; description and symbolism 153; designer 153; devices for additional awards 153; establishment 152; historical background 153–155; metal pendant 154–155; order of precedence 153, 171; recipients 155–158; relationship to Commendation Ribbon 154; relationship to Bronze Star Medal 153; relationship to Soldier's Medal 153
Army Distinguished Service Cross 30–42; citations 34–42; criteria 30; description and symbolism 31–32; designers 30; devices for additional awards 30; establishment 30; historical background 32–33; order of precedence 30, 171; recipients 34–42; relationship to Air Force Cross 42; relationship to Certificate of Merit 30
Army Distinguished Service Medal 105–112; citations 107–112; criteria 105; description and symbolism 105–106; designer 105; devices for additional awards 105; establishment 105; first recipient 106; historical background 106; order of precedence 105, 171; recipients 107–112
Army Medal of Honor 5–22; citations 13–22; comparing recipients 11–12; criteria 5; description and symbolism 7–9; designer 7; establishment 5; historical background 9–11; nomination and award process 5–7; order of precedence 5, 175; recipients 13–22; special entitlements 11; types 9
Army Regulation 600–8–22, *Military Awards* 71

Army Regulation 600–45, *Personnel: Award and Supply of Decorations for Individuals* 70–71
Arrington, George 175
Arthur, Bertrand and Berringer 7

Babylift, Operation 51
Back, George I. 109–110
Badge of Military Merit 137–138; citations 137–138; criteria 137; designer 139; establishment 137–138; medals based on 124, 137; recipients 137–138; relationship to Legion of Merit 124; relationship to Medal of Honor 137; revival of as Purple Heart 138–144; *see also* Purple Heart
Badger, Stephen M. 74
Bahnsen, John L., Jr. 38–40, *39*, 62–63, 88–89, 95–96
Bailey, Banks and Biddle 53, 91, 127
Baker, Newton D. 32–33, 106, 133, 177
Baker, William B. 175
Barcase, Gregor 72
Bartlett, Paul W. 33
Barton, Leonard L. 72
Bates, Thomas W. 60–61
Belcher, Harry 94
Benevidez, Roy 7
Benken, Eric W. 117
Bennett, Steven 27
Bingham, Hiram, III 70, 82–84
Bissell, Daniel 137–138
Blake, Robert E. 135
Blinkinsop, Sonny P. 65
Bonn, Robert C. 167
Book of Merit 137
Borja, Donald 161, 164, 167
Bradley, Omar 127
British medals *see* Military Cross, Military Medal
Bronze Star Medal 90–96; citations 93–96; criteria 90; designer 91; devices 91; establishment 90; historical background 91–93; order of precedence 90–91, 171; recipients 93–96; relationship to Air Medal 91–92; relationship to Combat Infantryman Badge 93; relationship to Combat Medical Badge 93; relationship to Distinguished Unit Citation (Philippines) 93; relationship to Purple Heart 93; with "V" device 92–93, 178–179
Brown, William 137
Burger, John 77
Burnett, Cleophas C. 71
Burns, John F. 71
Butler, Dennis L. 160

Campbell, Clark P. 152
Carlson, Randall 142
Carner, George W. 176
Carney, William H. 13
Carter, Jimmy E. 131
Catton, Ronald E. 161
Cecere, Gaetano 30, 68, 70, 105, 140
Certificate of Merit (obsolete) 171–

176; citations 175–176; criteria 171–172; designer 172; establishment 171; first recipient 175; historical background 172–175; numbers awarded 175; order of precedence 172; recipients 175–176; relationship to Army Distinguished Service Cross and Army Distinguished Service Medal 30, 175
Champeny, Arthur S. 36
Chapman, John A. 52–53
Chilson, Llewellyn M. 12
Chipman, Dana K. 121–122
Churchill, Elijah 137
Civilian Conservation Corps 133
Clarke, Gilmore D. 126
Clausen, George C. 160
Clements, William 119–120
Clouse, James J. 77–78
Cole, Rodney C. 144
Combat Infantryman Badge (Army) 93
Combat Medic Badge (Army) 93
Commission of Fine Arts *see* Fine Arts, Commission of
Congo, medals for 61
Conran, Philip J. 77–78, 99
Coolidge, Calvin 70, 80, 83
Corley, John T. 57–58, 60, 110–111
Cortinas, Ruben 171
Covington, Terrell G. 131
Cox, Aulbert D. 37
Cox, Eleanor 42–44
Cox, Roy F. 176
Croix de Guerre (French) 32
Crowder, Enoch H. 107, 124
Cuba, medals for 44, 56
Cuban Missile Crisis 44
Culin, Curtis G., III 128
Cunningham, Jason D. 52–53
Custer, Thomas W. 13, 177
cyberwarfare 3–4

Davis, James 146
Day, George E. 27, 116–117, 145–146
Defense Distinguished Service Medal 100–105; citation 103–105; criteria 100–101; description and symbolism 101; designer 101; devices for additional awards 101; establishment 100; historical background 101–103; order of precedence 101, 171
Defense Meritorious Service Medal 129–132; citations 131–132; criteria 129; description and symbolism 130; designer 129; devices for additional awards 129; establishment 129; first recipient 131; historical background 130–131; manufacture 131; order of precedence 129, 171
Defense Superior Service Medal 118–122; citations 120–122; criteria 118; description and symbolism 118–119; designer 118; devices for additional awards 118; establishment 118; first recipient 120; historical background 119–120; order of precedence 118, 171

Dethlefsen, Merlyn 27
Distinguished Flying Cross 80–90; citations 85; criteria 80–81; description and symbolism 81; designers 81; devices 81; establishment 80; first recipients 85; historical background 82–85; numbers awarded 83–85; order of precedence 81, 171; relationship to Air Medal 84–85; relationship to Soldier's Medal 70, 83
Distinguished Service Cross *see* Army Distinguished Service Cross
Distinguished Service Medal *see* Air Force Distinguished Service Medal; Army Distinguished Service Medal
Distinguished Unit Citation *see* Presidential Unit Citation
Distinguished Warfare Medal 3–4
Donovan, William J. 38
Doolittle, James H. 85–86
Douglas, James H., Jr. 160
Dove, Aaron 90
Dowling, William B. 168
drones *see* unmanned aerial vehicles
DuBois, Arthur E. 81
Duckworth, L. Tammy 99
DuPuy, William E. 156–157

Earhart, Amelia M. 86
Edgington, David M. 117–118
Eisenhower, Dwight D. 125, 127
Elton, Robert M. 164–165
Embury, Aymar E. 32–33, 105, 177
Erwin, Henry E., Sr. 15–16
Etchberger, Richard L. 23, 27–28

Fazee, Mohammad 158
Ferguson, Charles M. 120
Fine Arts, Commission of 26, 44, 70, 76–77, 83–84, 92, 103, 114, 126–127, 131, 139–141, 148, 163, 165, 177
Finley, David E. 26
Firse, John A. 89
Fisher, Bernard F. 27
Fitzpatrick, John C. 139, 141
Fleener, Delbert W. 46–47
Fleming, James P. 27
Flores-Sanz, Maria C. 157–158
Floyd, Jeffrey B. 135, 161
Flynn, George T. 73
Ford, Gerald R. 120
foreign decorations 32
fratricide 136, 143
French, J.T. 24–25
French medals *see* Croix de Guerre, Legion of Honor
Freund, Rudolf 53, 91
Friedman, Lawrence E. 63
friendly fire incidents 136, 143
Funk, Leonard A., Jr. 16–17
Funston, Frederick 13–14

Gabreski, Francis S. "Gabby" 85
Gabreski, Terry L. *116*
Galloway, Joseph L. 94–95
Gentner, William E. 134

Gifford, Carlton S. 139
Gillespie, George L. 11
Gillespie, James M. 87
Gilliland, James E. 131
Giunta, Salvatore A. *21–22*
Graham, Gordon H. 58
Grand Army of the Republic 11
Greene, Byron D. 172
Greene, John N. 33
Grenada (Operation *Urgent Fury*), medals for 65
Ground Medal 92; *see also* Bronze Star Medal
Guarino, Lawrence N. 114, 116
Guerrero, Alfredo R. 78–79
Gullion, Allen W. 107

Hackney, Duane D. 48
Hackworth, David H. 55, 60–61, 63–64
Hagel, Charles T. "Chuck" 4
Hains, John T., Jr. *54*
Hall, Virginia 37–38
Halyburton, Edgar M. 107
Hancock, Walker 140
Harlan, Chris 79
Harp, Tilford W. 51
Heard, Robert T. 124–127
Heraldry, Institute of 23, 76, 84, 101–103, 113–114, 131, 141, 149, 153, 158, 160, 163–164, 167–168
Hester, Leigh A. 66–*67*
Hilsman, William J. 162
Hines, John L. 56
Hoffman, Martin 119
Hoover, Herbert 80
Horne, Damian T. 73
Horne, John E. 24–25
Howard, Carrie L. 107
Howard, Malcolm J. 1, 64–65
Hurley, Patrick J. 55, 139

IED (improvised explosive device) attacks 104, 143–144
Institute of Heraldry *see* Heraldry, Institute of
Iraq (Operation *Iraqi Freedom*), medals for 67, 99, 157–158

Jabara, James *44*
Jackson, Joe M. 27
Jackson, Mark W. 142
Jeffrey, Jane 35–36
Johnson, Lyndon B. 134
Johnson, Nels C. 103
Johnson, Thomas 176
Joint Distinguished Service Medal 102–103; *see also* Defense Distinguished Service Medal
Joint Service Achievement Medal 161–164; citations 163–164; criteria 161; description and symbolism 161–162; designer 161–162; devices for additional awards 161; establishment 161; historical background 162–163; order of precedence 161, 171
Joint Service Commendation Medal 149–152; citations 151–152; criteria

149; description and symbolism 149–150; designer 149; devices for additional awards 149; establishment 149; historical background 151–152; order of precedence 149, 171

Jones, Evan *66*
Jones, John G. 120
Jones, Thomas Hudson 42, 44, 74–75, 114, 158
Jones, William A., III 27

Kahn, Ely J. 127–128
Kasler, James H. 47–48
Kavlick, Adam B. 66
Kay, Toby M. 148
Kelly, Roger D. 102
Kennedy, John F. 26, 44–45, 142
Kenney, George C. 36–37
Kerr, Terry K. 90
King, Lewis J. 23, 26, 101, 118, 129, 132
Korb, Lawrence J. 163
Korean War, medals for 19–20, 36, 49–50, 59–61
Kreutzer, William J. 74
Kroesen, Frederick 142

Laird, Melvin 102
Lane, Katherine W. 123, 126
Leak, Terral *78*
Legion of Honor (French), 123–124
Legion of Merit 122–129; citations 127–129; criteria 122–123; description and symbolism 123–124; designers 123; devices for additional awards 123; establishment 122; historical background 124–127; manufacture 127; number awarded 127; order of precedence 123, 171; refusal to award 119; relationship to Purple Heart 124
LeMay, Curtis E. *38*
L'Enfant, Pierre Charles 139
Leontiev, Grigori F. 58
Levitow, John L. 27–*29*
Lewane, Leonard L. 155–157
Lewis, Matthew 74
Liberty, statue 25–26
Lincoln, Abraham 10
Lindbergh, Charles A. 83–84
Lockard, Joseph L. 108
Lofaro, Guy A. 74
Logsdon, Harry A. 145
Lordship Products 131
Lubas, Joseph 87

MacArthur, Douglas 12, 136, 139–140, 144
Macy, Peter T. 76
Marino, Ernest *146*
Mark, Hans M. 166, 168
Marsh, John O. 164
Marshall, George C. 12, 92, 125
Martin, James P. 72
Masterson, Fred A. 76
McInerney, James E., Jr. 88
McKemey, Thomas E. 72–73
McKinney, John R. 17–18

McNair, Leslie 92
McNamara, Robert E. 149
McShane, Thomas W. 163–164
Medal for Merit 125
Medal of Freedom *see* Presidential Medal of Freedom
Medal of Honor *see* Air Force Medal of Honor; Army Medal of Honor
Medallic Art Company 44, 68
Merit, Certificate of *see* Certificate of Merit (obsolete)
Meritorious Service Medal 132–135; citations 134–135; criteria 132; description and symbolism 132–133; designer 132; devices for additional awards 132; establishment 132; historical background 132–134; order of precedence 132, 171; relationship to Bronze Star Medal 134; relationship to Legion of Merit 134
Meyer, Edward C. 164
Military Cross (British) 32
Military Medal (British) 32
Miller, Franklin 20–21
Miller, William E. *9*
Miller, Robert J. 22
Millet, Lewis L. 19–20
Minerva 7, 25
Mitchell, William F. "Billy" 34, 83
Monti, Jared C. 22
Moore, Charles 84, 139
Morris, Jay 132, 161, 164
Morrow, Dwight W. 83
Moseley, T. Michael 104–105, *117*
Moyer, Donald R. *18*
Murphy, Audie L. 12–13, 93–94

Nett, Robert B. 18–19
Newman, Aubrey S. 59, 142–143
Nixon, Richard M. 21, 100
North, Gary 170
Norton, William N. 33

Oak Leaf Cluster 176–178; criteria 177; description 177; designer 177; establishment 177; historical background 177–178
O'Connor, Brendan W. 41–*42*
O'Grady, Joe M. 95
O'Hern, Lewis L., III 146
Ohlemeier, Terry D. 131
Olds, Robin 48–*49*
order of precedence table 171
Orloff, Mildred 101, 118

Panetta, Leon D. 3
Pankey, Russell G. 25–26
Paquet, Anthony 7
Parr, Ralph S. 49–50
Parrott, Jacob 13
Patton, George S. 57, 125
Pauly, Richard L. 90
peacekeeping, medals for 142
Pershing, John J. 32–35, 106, 124, 133, 138
Pettijohn, Max L. 157
Philippines, medals for 56
Pickering, Abner 57
Pierce, Clinton A. 108–109

Pitsenbarger, William H. 23, 27
Pittinger, William 8
Polidor, Michael 90
Porter, Horace 11
post-traumatic stress disorder 144
Potter, Stafford F. 149
Pour le Mérite (Prussian) 124
Powell, Colin L. 73, 103–104
Presidential Medal of Freedom 41, 112
Presidential Unit Citation 93, 157
prisoners of war, medals for 143
Purple Heart 135–146; citations 137; civilian recipients 143; criteria 136; description and symbolism 136–137; designers 135, 140–141; devices for additional awards 136; establishment 135; first recipient 136; historical background 137–144; MacArthur's role 139–140; order of precedence 136, 171; prisoners of war 143; recipients 144–146; relationship to Bronze Star Medal 93, 143; relationship to Medal of Honor 138; wounds 141, 143–144

Quesenberry, Jason U. 131–132

Rascon, Alfred V. 7
Rattan, Donald V. 61
Ray, Charles 142
Ray, Leslie M. 94
Reagan, Ronald 65, 142
Reeder, Russell P., Jr. 90–91
Reeder, William S. 121
Rhynér, Zachary 52
Richardson, Dennis M. 50–51
Rickenbacker, Edward V. 34–35
Ridgway, Matthew B. 144–145
Risner, Robinson 45–46
Ritland, Osmond J. 114–115
Roberts, Christine 74
Roberts, Gordon R. 20
Roosevelt, Franklin D.: Air Medal awards 96; Bronze Star Medal awards 92; Legion of Merit awards 125; Purple Heart awards 141
Roosevelt, Theodore 7
Ryan, Timothy J. 96

St. James, Leonard C. 37
St. John, Adrian 131
Saudi Arabia, medals for 78
Schultz, Adolph H. 59
Schussel, Christian 7
Schwartz, Norman A. 66
Schweickert, Jerome G. 86
Sijan, Lance P. 27, 29–30
Silver Star 53–67; citations 56–67, 157; criteria 53; description and symbolism 53–54; designer 53; devices for additional awards 53; establishment 53; first recipient 55; historical background 54–56; most awarded 55; order of precedence 53, 171; relationship to Silver Star Citation 53–55
Silver Star Citation 53–55; relationship to Silver Star 53–55
Singlaub, John K. 129
Sinnock, John R. 136, 140–141
Smith, Andre 32–33
Smith, Donavan F. 114
Smith, Lynn D. 111
Soldier's Medal 68–74; citations 71–74; criteria 68; description and symbolism 68–69; designer 68; devices for additional awards 68; establishment 68; historical background 69–71; order of precedence 68, 171; relationship to Air Medal 68, 76–77; relationship to Distinguished Flying Cross 68
Somalia (Operation Restore Hope), medals for 51–52
Sorola, Guadalupe 152
Stanaland, Joseph S. 168–169
Stanton, Edwin 10
Staples, Frank O. 69
Stimson, Henry L. 92
Stovall, Dale E. 120–121
Sudan, medals for 169–170
Sweeney, Kimberly A. 169

Tallmadge, Benjamin 137
Taylor, Kenneth M. 151–152
Taylor, Maxwell D. 151
terrorism, awards for 78, 142
Thorsness, Leo K. 27
Tice, R. Dean 162–163
Titus, Calvin P. 14–15
Traynor, Dennis W., III 51
Treasury Life Saving Medal 71
Trujillo, Stephen 65
Truman, Harry S. 80, 141, 144

Ulio, James A. 92
U.S. Defense Department awards 100–105, 118–122, 129–132, 149–152, 161–164; Defense Distinguished Service Medal 100–105; Defense Meritorious Service Medal 129–132; Defense Superior Service Medal 118–122; Joint Service Achievement Medal 161–164; Joint Service Commendation Medal 149–152
U.S. Mint (Philadelphia) 33, 70, 136, 140, 175, 177

unmanned aerial vehicles 3–4
Uttrich, Heidi M. 168

V device: Air Force use 81, 158, 167, 169–170, 179; Army use 41, 155, 179; description and symbolism 178–179; establishment 178–179; historical background 178–179; relationship to Army Commendation Medal 155; relationship to Bronze Star Medal 91; relationship to Distinguished Flying Cross 81, 179; relationship to Joint Service Commendation Medal 149
Valle, Christopher R. 149
Vann, John P. 40–41
Velez, James R. 73
Vessey, John W., Jr. 111–112
Victory Medal, 55
Vietnam War, medals for 20–21, 27–30, 39–41, 45–51, 62–65, 72, 88–89, 94–96, 99, 156–157

Walsh, Patrick 33
Warner, John 142–143
Washington, George 124, 137–138
Weinberger, Caspar W. 161, 163
Weinman, A.A. 140
Welch, Kenneth 142
Welch, Larry D. 148
Welles, Gideon 7
Westmoreland, William C. 57
Wheeler, Earle G. 103
White, James R. 94
White, John P. 131
Whitehead, John B. 99
Wilbanks, Hilliard A. 27
Wilkinson, Timothy A. 51–52
Will, Elizabeth 81, 140–141
Willoughby, Moses E. 77
Wilson, Henry 10
Wilson, James K. 72
Wilson, Woodrow 32–33, 106
Winters, Richard D. 94
Woo, Gerald E. 147
Wood, Leonard 13
Woolsey, James R. 169–170
World War I, medals for 15, 33–37
World War II, medals for 15–19, 36–38, 54, 57–59, 93–94
Wright, John W. 138–139
Wright, Orville 85
Wright, Wilbur 85
Wyllie, Robert E. 139

Yeager, Charles E. 87–88
York, Alvin C. 15
Young, Gerald O. 27
Yuss, Ronald B. 89